WES  Y COLLEGE

D0397584

Selective Nontreatment of Handicapped Newborns

Selective Nontreatment of Handicapped Newborns:
MORAL DILEMMAS IN NEONATAL MEDICINE

Robert F. Weir

New York   Oxford
OXFORD UNIVERSITY PRESS
1984

Library of Congress Cataloging in Publication Data

Weir, Robert F.
  Selective nontreatment of handicapped newborns.

  Includes index.
  1. Neonatal intensive care—Moral and ethical aspects.
2. Infants (Newborn)—Legal status, laws, etc.
3. Infanticide.   4. Medical ethics.   I. Title.   II. Title:
Handicapped newborns. [DNLM: 1. Abnormalities.
2. Emergency medical services.   3. Ethics, Medical.
4. Handicapped.   5. Infant, Newborn.   QS 675 W425s]
RJ253.5.W44   1984   174'.24   83-19376
ISBN 0-19-503396-5

Some of the material in Chapter 5 has previously appeared as "The Government and Selective Nontreatment of Handicapped Infants," *The New England Journal of Medicine* 309 (September 15, 1983): 661–663. The material is reprinted with the permission of *The New England Journal of Medicine*.

Printing (last digit):   9 8 7 6 5 4 3 2 1

Printed in the United States of America

For Frank and Erlene Weir

Preface

Selective nontreatment of handicapped newborns is one of the more complex issues in biomedical ethics. Part of the complexity of the issue lies in the dilemmatic alternatives available to decision makers in such cases: to prolong an anomalous neonate's life often means the unavoidable continuation of severe handicaps that few adults would choose for a child to endure, but in some instances the only way of avoiding such a handicapped life is to withhold treatment in the hope that the defective child will soon die. Is severely handicapped life always to be chosen for the child instead of death? Or is severely handicapped life sometimes correctly judged to be a fate worse than death for the child in question?

Another part of the complexity of selective nontreatment has to do with the number of persons in different professional areas who have wrestled with the issue—and arrived at different conclusions. Neonatologists and other pediatric specialists, philosophers, religious ethicists, scholars in legal medicine and other attorneys, economists, psychologists, specialists in health policy, social workers, and politicians have discovered numerous differences among themselves whenever they have addressed the issue of selective nontreatment. Differences across professional lines are not surprising, but the differences of opinion on selective nontreatment among specialists in the same professional area surely damages any stereotyped views suggesting that all pediatricians (or attorneys or ethicists) are alike.

Still another part of the complexity of selective nontreatment, at least for me as an author, lies in the publicity recently surrounding cases. There had been enough cases and debate about selective nontreatment prior to 1982 to convince me that a book-length analysis of the issue might be helpful, especially if it addressed the medical, legal, and ethical aspects of the issue. Yet I did not know that "Infant Doe" would be born in Bloomington, Indiana, several weeks after I submitted a prospectus to Oxford University Press for this book. Since the storm of publicity surrounding that case in April 1982, part of my efforts as a researcher has been to keep up with current events: subsequent cases have received more publicity than they would have prior to "Infant Doe," an incumbent president has written on the subject of selective nontreatment, the Reagan administration has become involved in several cases through the Departments of Health and Human Services and of Justice, a Handicapped Infants Protection Act has been introduced in the Congress, television's "60 Minutes" has discussed two cases on one of its programs, the President's Commission for the Study of Ethical Problems in Medicine and Biomedical and Behavioral Research has addressed the issue, one state has passed a law and others are considering laws governing the medical treatment of handicapped infants, and the U.S. government and several professional medical associations have been involved in ongoing litigation concerning selective nontreatment of anomalous newborns in the nation's hospitals.

Of course I cannot know what developments will occur in the medical, legal, ethical, and political debates about selective nontreatment after these words are written. By the time this book is published, the legal situation may be substantially different from the way it is now. What will not be different, I am reasonably sure, will be the debates among pediatricians, ethicists, other reflective persons, and advocacy groups about the appropriate courses of action to take with birth-defective newborns— whatever the law says about the matter. It is my hope that in the midst of these frequently heated debates, this book may provide some light.

Acknowledgments

Most authors incur debts of gratitude in writing books. I am surely no exception. In writing this book I have been helped by numerous persons and organizations.

The National Endowment for the Humanities has helped me at several stages along the way. Having discussed selective nontreatment for years in my biomedical ethics classes, I began the task of seriously wrestling with this moral problem while participating in an NEH summer seminar at Indiana University in 1978. Directed by David H. Smith, the seminar provided me an opportunity to do research on the birth defects sometimes encountered in genetic counseling. The following summer I was awarded an NEH postdoctoral fellowship in clinical medical ethics at the University of Tennessee Health Sciences Center in Memphis. Under the auspices of the Human Values and Ethics Program, I learned invaluable lessons while working with Robert Summitt, Sid Wilroy, and other members of the genetic counseling center. I also received numerous insights into the clinical realities of neonatal medicine by participating in rounds with Sheldon Korones at the newborn center. In the summer of 1981, I again participated in an NEH summer seminar. This seminar, under the direction of James F. Childress at the University of Virginia, provided me an opportunity to begin analyzing medical and legal perspectives on the issue of selective nontreatment.

Librarians at three institutions have helped me gather the research materials for the book. Karen Morris, Claudette Hagle, and several other librarians at Oklahoma State University have been consistently helpful in ordering materials for me. Cecily Orr at the Kennedy Institute of Ethics and Carol Dillingham at the Oklahoma City University School of Law have helped me locate medical and legal resources at crucial points along the way.

Other persons have responded to my written inquiries with helpful suggestions, advice, information, articles, and, in a few instances, un-published materials. Among physicians, Norman Fost, John Freeman, David McLone, and Jeffrey Pomerance were particularly helpful. Sena-tor David Boren, Representative Wes Watkins, and their staffs provided me with government documents. Among ethicists, John Fletcher, Edward Langerak, Richard McCormick, Richard O'Neil, Carson Strong, Robert Veatch, and Virginia Warren were most cordial and prompt in respond-ing to my requests for assistance.

In terms of the material presented in the book, I am indebted to several individuals who spent considerable time reading chapters and providing me with criticisms and observations. Jim Childress read an early draft of Chapter 3, suggested ways of improving it, and made overtures to two publishers on my behalf. Gordon Avery read Chapters 2 and 8, George Annas read Chapters 4 and 5, and both of them suggested ways to strengthen these chapters on the medical and legal aspects of selective nontreatment. The most extensive reading was done by Richard Egger-man, Richard O'Neil, and Robert Radford; their detailed criticisms and suggestions on all the chapters undoubtedly improved the final product. At Oxford University Press, Jeff House made helpful editorial sug-gestions at several points. To all of these readers, my sincere thanks.

Three persons helped in the typing of the manuscript. Rosemary Gates, Betty Miller, and Barbara Converse were all exceptionally attentive to details and patient with me in turning rough drafts into typed copy. To these typists, my thanks.

Finally, my thanks go to the members of my family. Jerry, Melinda, and Randall have supported me with their interest, questions, and ob-servations along the way. The book is dedicated to my parents, whose support has always seemed to know few bounds.

Stillwater, Oklahoma   R. F. W.
April 1983

Contents

Selective Nontreatment of Handicapped Newborns

1

Infanticide: Selective Killing, Selective Punishment

> As to the exposure and rearing of children, let there be a law that no *deformed* child shall live, but that on the ground of an *excess* in the number of children, if the established customs of the state forbid this (for in our state population has a limit), no child is to be exposed, but when couples have children in excess, let abortion be procured before sense and life have begun. . . .
>
> ARISTOTLE[1]

> Nowadays we universally condemn practices such as infanticide, incidental and specific abuse, and the torture of infanticidal mothers; and, most importantly, today there is universal agreement that every child born has the right to live. This is a new idea. A true achievement of this century.
>
> MARIA Piers, PH.D.[2]

The contemporary practice of selective nontreatment of handicapped newborns is, in many aspects, a continuation of historical practices of infanticide. The settings and circumstances vary from historical patterns, but infant deaths brought about in neonatal intensive care units (NICUs) often provide parallels to acts of infanticide in earlier times and places. Although dealing with life-and-death decisions in a sophisticated technological context that earlier generations could not have imagined, current debates about selective nontreatment retrace familiar ground when they focus on the attitudes of parents toward anomalous newborns, the rights and limits of parental discretion, the appropriate roles of physicians in neonatal cases, the proper function of the law in cases of infant homicides, and the morality of terminating the lives of some infants with serious congenital anomalies.

This chapter will provide an overview of infanticide in order to establish a historical backdrop for the discussion of selective nontreatment. We will begin with some general features of the practice of infanticide, compare historical patterns of infanticide, explore some of the motivating reasons for terminating the lives of infants, and focus on the selectivity that seems always to have characterized the killing of infants and the punishment of the persons who did the killing.

General features of infanticide

To modern minds the word "infanticide" suggests an easily performed, despicable act of killing once tolerated by developing societies but rarely practiced in the contemporary world. In many respects this general under-standing of infanticide is correct. Infanticide has traditionally been an easy act of killing to perform, given the obviously helpless condition of infants and small children when the destructive impulses of adults turned in their direction. Infanticide has also been tolerated by the great majority if not all of the world's societies, for reasons ranging from the need of population control in times of scarcity to the sheer inability of govern-ments to prevent parents from killing their defenseless babies. Moreover, infanticide has come to be regarded, given modern perspectives on the value of children, as a homicidal act bordering on the unthinkable. Yet the practice persists and, in the age of neonatal medicine, takes on new and sophisticated forms.

Infanticide has for centuries meant the intentional destruction of young children ranging in age from newborns to children just under the "age of discretion." In English criminal law, for instance, an "infant" has usually been defined as a child nine years old or younger.[3] To gain greater clarity in analyzing acts of child destruction, some authors have suggested distinguishing between two chronological categories of infanticide, with "neonaticide" referring to parental murder of infants within 24 hours of their births and "filicide" denoting parental murder of children older than a day.[4]

This distinction is too sharply drawn in that it limits the four-week neonatal period to one day. Nevertheless, the distinction is helpful in pointing out one of the general features of infanticide: the younger the child, the more vulnerable to acts of destruction. The selectivity evident in many historical patterns of infanticide and in some current practices in NICUs clearly indicates that the chances of continued living greatly increase once a neonate has survived the first few days or weeks of life. If "neonaticide" can be expanded to include intentional acts of child de-struction during the first month of life, it may indeed sharpen our understanding of the total helplessness of the neonate and its complete dependence on adults for protection and survival.

A second general feature of infanticide is the diversity of means used to bring about the deaths of young children. In addition to laying bare the vulnerability of neonates to the destructive impulses of parents, the history of infanticide reveals that the means used for child destruction have been limited only by human imagination and the available technology of particular times and places. Children have been killed through starvation, drowning, strangulation, burning, smothering (often by "accidental" overlaying in the parent's bed), poisoning, exposure, and a variety of lethal weapons. With the advances of medical technology and the establishment of NICUs over the years since the early 1960s, new means of killing neonates—or at least hastening their dying—can be added to the list: lethal injections, overdoses of sedatives, and "accidental" coughs or sneezes over neonates highly susceptible to infection.

A third general feature of the practice of infanticide is that, as with abortion, governments have often displayed considerable uncertainty in dealing with it. Is the killing of infants by their parents to be legally acceptable and possibly even promoted for eugenic reasons, or are such homicidal acts to be legally prohibited and the killers actively prosecuted and punished? In earlier centuries many governments appear to have been indifferent toward infanticide, and some of them (e.g., Sparta in ancient Greece) even required the killing of weak and deformed infants. Since the Enlightenment, virtually all governments in developed societies have moved toward the current consensus on infanticide: regard it as an illegal act, but have uncertain punishment for those who actually commit the crime. The reasons for the current uncertainty of punishment in the United States are several: enormous weight is given to parental autonomy, importance is placed on medical discretion when infant deaths occur in clinical settings, infants (especially neonates) are often believed to have a lesser legal status than do older children and adults, no laws exist that specifically proscribe infanticide, and parents (usually mothers) tried for child homicide are often acquitted for reasons of temporary insanity.

Historical patterns of infanticide

The vulnerability of the very young, the multiplicity of death-causing actions, and the uncertainty of governments in handling child deaths caused by parents are perennial features of infanticide. Once these features are laid out as a general framework, the history of infanticide becomes more diverse and indicates the customs, beliefs, and laws of differing cultures and significantly different historical periods. Reflected in a wide range of literary works—including Euripides' *Medea*, Chaucer's *The Canterbury Tales*, Swift's *A Modest Proposal*, Goethe's *Faust*, Eliot's *Adam Bede*, Dickens' *Oliver Twist*, and Chekhov's story "Sleepyhead"— the history of infanticide contains far more material than we can analyze here. However, a look at infanticidal practices in diverse social settings will provide a helpful background for the current debate regarding medical treatment of neonates with serious congenital anomalies.

Tribal societies in various parts of the world have practiced infanticide for centuries. The ancient Hebrews, for instance, accepted the killing of firstborn children as religious offerings and signs of religious obedience, as suggested by the biblical story of Abraham and Isaac (Gen. 22). Other biblical passages reveal infanticidal practices during the periods of Moses (thirteenth century B.C.E.) and Manasseh, one of the kings of Judah during the seventh century B.C.E. (Num. 31:17–18; 2 Kings 21:6). The selective destruction of children continued among the Hebrews at least until the sixth century B.C.E., for the writer of Isaiah 57:5 criticizes his people for slaying "your children in the valleys, under the clefts of the rocks."

The Bedouin tribes of ancient Arabia also practiced infanticide, with infant girls most frequently selected for destruction. Because only sons were highly prized, the birth of a daughter was a shameful event that often resulted in a simple homicidal act: the parents buried the girl in the desert sand. By the time of Muhammad (570–632 C.E.), female infanticide was a widely accepted practice in the area. Although such acts of child destruction were opposed in the Quran (Surah 16:58–59), they remained a part of Bedouin tribal life for centuries.[5]

The customs of some tribal groups regarding the destruction of infants have changed only in the modern era. The Eskimos have only in recent years begun to move away from their traditional practice of setting infants out on the ice to freeze whenever the father or tribal elder decided that the tribe could not support them.[6] Several Polynesian tribes have ceased the long-standing custom of killing all infants after the third or fourth child in a family. Australian tribes have also stopped their traditional practice of killing infants who could not be carried on long marches. Because the carrying limit for each mother was one child, any infants born before the older child could walk were killed by starvation and exposure.[7]

In addition to these traditional tribal practices, major civilizations have permitted and sometimes encouraged the destruction of infants thought to have little value. In the ancient cultures of China and India, such infants have generally been females. For the Chinese, whose traditional culture was largely shaped by the Confucian tradition, female infanticide was not only a means of controlling population growth but also a way of reflecting their belief in the basic inferiority of females. Because "the most excellent daughter is not worth a splay-footed son," the practice of killing infant girls remained until recent centuries an acceptable way of managing family size and limiting financial hardship. The ideal ratio of five sons to two daughters often led to endemic female infanticide, especially in the poorer areas of China.[8]

India's version of female infanticide has traditionally served other purposes in addition to population control. The practice of offering female infants (and occasionally firstborn males) as a sacrifice to the gods was widely accepted among some Hindus until the nineteenth century. For other Hindus, the destruction of female infants was merely an easy way of lessening a family's liabilities. Because the birth of a daughter was sometimes viewed as a punishment for sins committed in a former state of existence, the moral status accorded female infants was minimal. If not offered as a sacrifice, they were often drowned, sometimes smothered in milk, and occasionally killed by means of opium smeared upon the mother's breasts.[9]

In the West, infanticide has been practiced from antiquity to the present day. Societies as different as ancient Greece, classical Rome, Renaissance Italy, and western Europe societies in more recent centuries have had infanticide as part of their moral landscape and have displayed inconsistent legal patterns in dealing with the problem of child destruction.

In ancient Greece, as reflected in the quotation from Aristotle at the beginning of the chapter, infanticide was a widely accepted practice in conformity with prevailing legal standards. For example, Euripides (ca. 480–406 B.C.E.) dramatized infanticide in *Medea* by having Medea kill her two sons.[10] Young children, weak children, female children, and especially children regarded as being defective were regularly strangled, drowned, buried in dunghills, "potted" in jars to starve to death, or exposed to the elements (with the belief that the gods had the responsibility of saving exposed infants). Concerned that defective infants would, once grown, pass on their defects to the next generation, the Greeks actively promoted the destruction of anomalous infants. Euripides commented that such children were often left as "a prey for birds, food for wild beasts to rend."[11]

Although girls were killed more often than boys, the major issue in determining whether an infant lived or died was its normalcy rather than its gender or its legitimacy. In fact, the issue of normalcy was so dominant in Greek thinking that infants were often denied the benefit of the doubt: infants who appeared normal but were products of "inferior" parents were also killed. Such infanticidal practices were advocated by Plato in *The Republic*:

> The proper officers will take the offspring of the good parents to the pen or fold, and there they will deposit them with certain nurses who dwell in a separate quarter; but the offspring of the inferior, or of the better when they chance to be deformed, will be put away in some mysterious, unknown place, as they should be.[12]

This attitude toward defective infants was a dominant theme in the ancient world. By the second century C.E., it was a regular feature of medical works. For example, Soranus of Ephesus had a section in his gynecological manual entitled "How to Recognize the Newborn that Is Worth Rearing." In his view, worth depended on normalcy:

> The infant which is suited by nature for rearing will be distinguished by the fact that its mother has spent the period of pregnancy in good health. . . . Second, by the fact that it has been born at the due time, best at the end of nine months. . . . Furthermore by the fact that when put on the earth it immediately cries with proper vigor; for one that lives for some length of time without crying, or cries but weakly, is suspected of behaving so on account of some unfavorable condition. . . . Also by the fact that it is perfect in all its parts, members and senses. . . . And by conditions contrary to those mentioned, the infant not worth rearing is recognized.[13]

In classical Rome, an infant worth rearing was a firstborn male without observable abnormalities. Female infants and defective neonates were usually victims of drowning, strangulation, or exposure. The diversity of death-causing actions was described by Philo, a first-century Jewish philosopher who was one of the early opponents of infanticide in the Roman world. He distinguished between acts of direct killing and acts of exposure:

> Some of them do the deed with their own hands; with monstrous cruelty and barbarity they stifle and throttle the first breath which the infants draw or throw them into a river or into the depths of the sea, after attaching some

heavy substance to make them sink more quickly under its weight. Others take them to be exposed in some desert place, hoping, they themselves say, that they may be saved, but leaving them in actual truth to suffer the most distressing fate. For all the beasts that feed in human flesh visit the spot and feast unhindered on the infants, a fine banquet provided by their sole guardians, those who above all others should keep them safe, their fathers and mothers.[14]

The Romans had two fundamental reasons for permitting these infanticidal practices. The first reason, patriarchal authority, was a common feature in the world of antiquity. The *patria potestas*, the father's absolute legal authority over members of his family, included the right to destroy a young child if that was what a father willed. Even a Roman law forbidding the murder of a relative exempted fathers from the criminal code: a mother or some other relative might be charged for the murder of an infant, but a Roman father could kill his daughter or son with impunity until early in the fourth century.[15] The second reason for permitting infanticide among the Romans was simply that they regarded it a reasonable course of action whenever an infant turned out to be anomalous. Just as one would not want to preserve the life of a seriously diseased animal, so the Romans thought it made no sense to preserve the life of a weak, sick, or defective infant. The rationality of this approach was defended by Seneca, a first-century Roman philosopher:

> Mad dogs we knock on the head; the fierce and savage ox we slay; sickly sheep we put to the knife to keep them from infecting the flock; unnatural progeny we destroy; we drown even children who at birth are weak and abnormal. Yet it is not anger, but reason that separates the harmful from the sound.[16]

In time this Roman pattern of infanticide began to moderate mostly as a result of the influence of Christianity and the changing Roman legal system. The *Didache*, an early second-century document setting forth a code of Christian conduct, specifically opposed Roman infanticidal practices by exhorting Christians, ". . . do not murder a child by abortion or kill a newborn infant. . . ."[17] Tertullian, Lactantius, the writer of *The Letter of Barnabas*, and other early Christian writers joined Philo in vigorously opposing infanticide in the Roman world. One of the results of this opposition by Christianity, with its emphasis on the inherent value of all humans, was the gradual revision of Roman laws governing infanticide. In 318, under Constantine, the law of parricide was extended to include the killing of a daughter or a son by the father. In 374 the direct killing of an infant—including females and defective newborns—was ruled to be an act of homicide punishable by death regardless of who did the killing.[18] Exposure and abandonment of infants, however, continued to go unpunished because the Romans believed these actions were less serious than drowning or strangulation, the difference being the remote chance that someone would save an exposed or abandoned child from death. When such a child was saved, it often was reared for slavery or prostitution.

This distinction between directly killing an infant and "merely" abandoning an infant became an important feature of the history of infanticide. With infanticide as a punishable crime restricted to acts of direct killing, parents and their accomplices in numerous societies abandoned unwanted infants with no possibility of being criminally charged for the child's death. The result was that during the Middle Ages, exposure through abandonment "was practiced on a gigantic scale with absolute impunity, noticed by writers with most frigid indifference and, at least in the case of destitute parents, considered a very venial offense."[19]

By the fifteenth century, Renaissance Italy had institutionalized the process of abandonment. In response to widespread acts of infanticide directed against bastard children and defective children, Milan, Rome, and Florence had as early as the eighth century established foundling hospitals for the care of infants who otherwise would have been killed by their mothers. The majority of infants admitted to these hospitals were illegitimate males. By contrast, defective neonates and infant females, whether legitimate or not, were usually abandoned by being turned over to a *balia* (wet nurse) who took the infant into the countryside and, while ostensibly feeding the child, killed it. Having killed their own infants first, the *balie* could either sell their milk to prosperous parents or receive payment for arranging the deaths of "abandoned" infants. This "putting out system" was a convenient way of circumventing Roman law and the Church's teachings on infanticide.[20] The system also provided professional killers for infanticidal mothers who wanted to avoid all legal and ecclesiastical problems connected with the deaths of their infants:

> It seems that everywhere infanticidal *mothers were punished by death. Wet nurses were not.* They played the role of the executioner, whose deeds were difficult to prove and were silently condoned. An execution of a wet nurse is never mentioned in the pertinent literature. And the only mention of any punishment at all concerns a 1415 law that forbade *balie* to "relinquish their charges before they were thirty months old." The punishment inflicted on the guilty *balia* was a fine or a public whipping. Not, however, the death penalty.[21]

In contrast to the *balie*, many women who committed infanticide in Italy were severely punished. Unwed mothers and older women believed to be witches were special targets for prosecution and punishment. Because of the difficulty of proving cases of infanticide within the family home, parents could easily claim that the deaths of their children came as the result of accidental suffocation. Unwed mothers, however, were often presumed to have committed infanticide unless they could prove that an infant had been stillborn or accidentally overlain. Older women, often labeled as witches by demonologists, had even greater difficulty establishing their innocence. It was somehow more reasonable—or at least more convenient —to assume that "witches passed through locked doors in the dead of night to suffocate infants than to believe that man and wife . . . would do such a thing."[22]

The punishment meted out to unwed mothers and "witches" convicted of child destruction had few moral or legal limits. In Italy, Germany, France, and other European countries prior to the nineteenth century, punishment for intentionally killing an infant took a number of gruesome forms: drowning, burial alive, impalement, and decapitation. The most imaginative and cruel form of punishment was known as "sacking." Representing the ritual sacrifice of a human scapegoat, sacking involved stuffing an infanticidal mother into a black sack together with a dog, a cat, and a rooster or poisonous snake. The sack was then submerged in water for six hours, while a choir at this public spectacle sang Psalm 130 ("Out of the depths I cry to Thee").[23]

If the purpose of these public killings was to inflict cruel and unusual punishment on infanticidal mothers at the lower end of the social scale, they unquestionably succeeded. If, however, the purpose of these events was to deter acts of child destruction, they failed. Illegitimate and defective infants continued to be the victims of parental violence on a broad scale well into the nineteenth century, and both governmental and ecclesiastical authorities were severely limited in their ability to curtail the murderous actions directed toward infants. Some church people even revived an antiquated justification for some of the infant killings. Just as demonologists claimed that older, unmarried women were "witches," so they claimed that physically deformed and mentally retarded children were "changelings." Thus labeled, defective infants were often believed to be supernatural substitutes or "demon-children" who had taken the place of "real" children. Having been tricked in this manner by the devil, parents resorted to the only recourse available to them: "beat the devil out" of the child until the child itself was destroyed.[24]

During the eighteenth century, infanticide became almost epidemic in western Europe. In France, with unprecedented population growth, migration of the poor to the cities, unemployment, hunger, and illness, the parenting population engaged in "an all-out war against infants."[25] Even the foundling hospitals run by religious orders became so over-burdened and understaffed that they, in spite of their avowed purpose of saving the lives of abandoned infants, ended up practicing a legally accepted form of infanticide. Children in these hospitals died in large numbers as a result of neglect, inadequate medical care, and direct acts of violence. In contrast to the vicious punishments directed against unwed mothers who killed their children in the cities and countryside of France, persons who worked in the Paris foundling hospitals were rarely prose-cuted for the deaths in their institutions. Men, also, were exempt from prosecution. The father of a murdered infant, regardless of the father's social standing or marital status, was "not held responsible, either legally or morally, for the concealed pregnancy or the committed infanticide."[26]

In Germany during the same century, infanticide was a troubling legal problem. In a society that traditionally had allowed parents to toss newborns into icy rivers to test the infants' hardiness, court records indicate that dozens of unmarried women were drowned or decapitated for having killed their infants.[27] Yet acts of infanticide continued. One indication of the extent of infanticide in Germany is Goethe's *Faust*. Written over a period of 60 years and completed in 1832, this work depicts an unmarried pregnancy, Gretchen's shame at being pregnant, the drowning of her infant, and her subsequent imprisonment. When Faust, Gretchen's lover, reprimands Mephistopheles for having concealed Gretchen's plight from him, Mephistopheles cynically states that "she's not the first one." Faust's response reveals the commonness of infanticide at the time: "The misery of this one woman surges through my heart and marrow, and you grin imperturbed *over the fate of thousands!*"[28]

England was no exception to the infanticidal practices common to Europe in the eighteenth century. In fact, given the amount of research on infanticide in England, it is possible to get a fairly good idea of infanticide practices in England prior to the eighteenth century and to see how eighteenth-century English practices influenced attitudes toward infanti-cide in the American colonies.

In the medieval English context, the most common form of infanticide was smothering or overlaying an infant in the mother's bed and then concealing the dead child's body in a rural location. Although both legal and ecclesiastical authorities condemned these incidences of child murder, the secrecy of the crime and the ease of concealing the evidence (the child's corpse) meant that the authorities did little for centuries to suppress the crime. Few cases of infanticide were tried in the king's courts.[29] Church officials, in turn, regarded infanticide as a venial sin that could be handled under the requirements of penance established as early as the seventh century by Columban. The traditional requirement for intentional smothering of an infant was three years' penance: one year on bread and water, and two more years without wine or meat. If the overlaying was accidental, the penance was lowered to two years. Given that the traditional penance for accidentally killing an adult was five years, it is obvious that the intentional death of an infant was regarded as substantially less serious than homicide.[30]

Victims of parental destruction traditionally were neonates, bastards, and/or infants thought to be defective in some manner. As in other European countries, some of the anomalous infants were believed to be "changelings." English parents tried to rid themselves of these children as soon as possible, lest they be regarded as accomplices of the devil. Physically deformed and mentally retarded infants were also regarded as subhuman parasites who, if fed, sucked "whitened blood" (milk) from the mother's breast at every feeding.[31] In addition, illegitimate infants and seriously deformed infants fell outside the category of "freemen" in medieval England, as evidenced by a legal commentary of the time:

> Among freemen there may not be reckoned those who are born of unlawful intercourse, such as adultery and the like . . . and others begotten of unlawful intercourse, nor those who are procreated pervertedly, against the way of human kind, as for example, if a woman bring forth a monster or a prodigy. Nevertheless, the offspring in whom nature has in some small measure, though not extravagantly, added members or diminished them— as if he should have six fingers or only four—he should certainly be included among freemen.[32]

In the seventeenth century, after hundreds of years of virtually ignoring infanticidal practices, English legal authorities decided to do something about the destruction of children—at least bastard children. In part, the changed political climate regarding infanticide was in response to ecclesiastical upheavals. With the separation of the Church of England from Rome, the traditional warnings to church members about the sin of infanticide fell on increasingly deaf ears. Also in part, the changed political climate regarding infanticide was an effort by royal authorities to punish immoral women for killing the illegitimate products of their promiscuous sexual affairs. The result was the 1624 infanticide law enacted under James I, which stipulated the death penalty for any woman found guilty of having killed a bastard infant:

> Whereas, many lewd women that have been delivered of bastard children, to avoid their shame, and to escape punishment, do secretly bury or conceal the death of their children . . . be it enacted by the authority of this present parliament, that if any woman . . . be delivered of any issue of her body, male or female, which being born alive, should by the laws of this realm be a bastard, and that she endeavour privately either by drowning or secret burying thereof . . . the said mother so offending shall suffer death as in the case of murther [murder].[33]

The selectivity of this law is obvious, in that it applies only to the deaths of certain infants (bastards) and threatens only one segment of the parenting population with punishment (unwed mothers). Several consequences of this law are worth noting. First, it meant that during the seventeenth and eighteenth centuries an infanticidal mother was unlikely to be prosecuted if she was married. Second, it established a legal climate in which a mother "of good reputation" who killed her legitimate infant was almost always acquitted on the grounds of temporary insanity (because she appeared to have no motive), even if she was prosecuted. Third, it encouraged unwed, infanticidal mothers to have conspirators (e.g., their parents, their lovers) do the killing and to go to great lengths to conceal the corpses (by putting them in trunks, haystacks, stairwells, coalbins, and vaults). Fourth, it produced novel pleas on the part of unwed mothers trying to gain acquittal for temporary insanity. The most interesting of these defenses was the "benefit-of-linen" argument: if the mother had made linen for her infant before its birth, she could establish either the accidental nature of the infant's death or her own insanity while killing it.[34]

By the early nineteenth century, it was obvious that two major attempts by the English to curtail infanticide had failed. The 1624 law had proved so discriminatory and harsh that juries regularly refused to convict defendants even when there was sufficient evidence to do so. Furthermore, the London foundling hospital, established in 1739 to combat "frequent Murders committed on poor Miserable Infant Children at their Birth by their Cruel Parents," had for all practical purposes collapsed from the sheer number of children needing care after Parliament mandated an unrestricted admissions policy in 1756.

The social consequences of these two failures were enormous. In terms of the law, the 1624 statute was repealed in 1803 and replaced by the Ellenborough Act, which made prosecution for infanticide more difficult and allowed juries to opt for the lesser crime of concealment of birth (carrying the penalty of two years' imprisonment) when there was insufficient evidence of infanticide. Throughout the rest of the century, there were several infanticide laws passed—including the first Infant Life Protection Act in 1872—in an effort to come up with a workable legal solution for the increasingly visible crime. These legal efforts continued into the present century, with one infanticide law enacted in 1922 and another in 1938.[35]

In spite of these efforts, child destruction was widely practiced in England during most of the nineteenth century. Infanticide was called "the great social evil of the day," and statistical data for 1864 reveal an infanticide rate of 27.4 murders per 100,000 children in their first year of life.[36] William Burke Ryan, a London physician, stated at the time that

> the feeble wail of murdered childhood in its agony assails our ears at every turn, and is borne on every breeze . . . turn where we may, still are we met by the evidence of a widespread crime. In the quiet of the bedroom we raise the box-lid, and the skeletons are there. In the calm evening walk we see in the distance the suspicious-looking bundle, and the mangled infant is within. By the canal side, or in the water, we find the dead child. In the solitude of the wood we are horrified by the ghastly sight; and if we betake ourselves to the rapid rail in order to escape the pollution, we find at our journey's end that the mouldering remains of a murdered innocent have been our traveling companion; and that the odour from that unsuspected parcel truly indicates what may be found within.[37]

This graphic description illustrates that although infanticide was condemned by church and state in England, many people "regarded it as a lesser offence than murder, in part because less value was placed on an infant's life and in part because women committing this crime were seen as acting under the pressures of poverty and social stigma."[38] In fact, certain segments of the population institutionalized infanticide. As Italy had earlier institutionalized infanticide through the system of *balie* and eighteenth-century France through the foundling hospitals, so England during the past century saw the rise of burial clubs and "baby farms." Burial clubs thrived on parental purchases of burial insurance for their infants. If a child was thought to have died of natural causes at least three months after the insurance policy was purchased, the parents received an insurance payment. Because parents could insure their infants in several

burial clubs, the temptation to kill infants for profit was significant—to
the point that neighbors would sometimes comment, "Aye, aye, that child
will not live, it is in the burial club!"[39] To supplement these domestic
infanticidal practices, some individuals established "baby farms." Merely
an updated version of the abandonment practices of classical Rome and
Renaissance Italy, these farms provided infanticidal parents a place to
"put out" their infants for a fee with the expectation that the children
would be killed and their bodies concealed. Until the execution of some
baby farm owners stopped this business of infanticide for profit, the
mortality rate at some of the farms reached 90%.[40]

Many of the European, and especially British, attitudes toward infanticide affected the practices of child destruction that developed in America.
Overlaying was the most common form of child destruction in the colonies,
unwed mothers and their accomplices did most of the killing, and most of
the trials for infanticide involved the defendant arguing that a child's
death either was accidental or had been caused by temporary insanity. In
New England, "suspicion of attempted infanticide brought swift and
severe chastisement . . . and trials for the crime were major communal
dramas."[41] Although there was no established state church with jurisdiction over public sin, Puritan conceptions of sin significantly influenced
attitudes toward child destruction. In this religious context infanticide
was regarded as wrong not only because it destroyed a child's life, but also
because infanticide violated "God's law" by encouraging sexual im-
morality, concealing the effects of sin (the body of a bastard infant), and
promoting female disobedience of authority.[42] Beyond the borders of
New England, American state courts periodically dealt with cases of
infanticide during the eighteenth and nineteenth centuries.

If American practices of infanticide paralleled much of the British
experience with infanticide over the past two centuries, the response of
the American legal system to infanticide has proved to be quite different.
For one thing, law in the United States does not distinguish between
homicide and infanticide. For another thing, the United States adopted a
federalist system of government, meaning that there is no national
homicide law because each state has its own penal code and homicide
statutes. The result is that "no laws proscribing infanticide exist, no
legislative battles as to its status have ever been waged in the U.S.
Congress as they were in the British Parliament, and the crime is wholly
under the aegis of state homicide statutes."[43]

Motivating reasons for infanticide

Although there have been some government-sponsored infanticide programs—for example, the biblical accounts of the Egyptian-sponsored
male infanticide effort (Exod. 1) and the similar Roman program during
Jesus' infancy (Matt. 2)—the great majority of infanticides have been acts
of destruction by parents acting alone or with the help of accomplices.
What are the circumstances and reasons that led these parents to kill their
newborn infants, or at least to allow them to die through abandonment
and exposure? Because most infanticides appear to have been committed
by mothers, the question can be raised in another way: why would a
mother choose death for an infant she had carried throughout its fetal
development?

These questions of motivation are of course difficult to answer in
individual cases apart from substantial psychological data related to
particular acts of child destruction. Motivation for individual acts of
infanticide has undoubtedly been as varied as the personalities of the
women and men involved in the acts and the situations in which they
found themselves. Nevertheless, despite the limitations we have in getting
at a range of psychological variables (including those that may cause
temporary insanity), it is possible to sort out several recurring patterns of
reasons for infanticide in various times and places. These patterns of
motivating reasons cluster together in three general groups.

Some mothers (and fathers) have chosen death for their infants for
economic reasons. Especially in times of ineffective birth control, rapid
population growth, high unemployment, and widespread scarcity of food,
mothers have often opted for child destruction as the lesser of two evils: if
the child lived, it would inevitably increase the hardships experienced by
the mother and, if she was married, by other members of the family. By
contrast, a dead child would mean one less mouth to feed. In periods of
economic crisis, such a calculation represented a realistic assessment of
severely limited options for an impoverished mother.

Similar cost–benefit calculations continue to be made in the modern
world. In impoverished sections of South American cities, for example,
mothers and fathers who do not practice effective birth control often have
more children than they can support. If the additional infant is female,
she represents "the girl one-too-many" who may be doomed to die through
starvation and neglect so that the older children can live.[44]

A different version of this traditional calculation is beginning to appear in North American hospitals. At a time when neonatal care for a premature or anomalous infant easily runs into the thousands of dollars, questions are increasingly being asked about the withholding of treatment from some infants on the grounds of excessive cost. For parents of a severely defective neonate, who may be uninsured or have limited eligibility for programs providing aid for handicapped children, the prospect of paying for long-term institutionalized care exceeding $400,000 may be a sufficient motivating reason to withhold medical treatment so that the infant will die.[45]

Other mothers have been motivated to choose death for their infants because of *social customs and pressures*. In numerous traditional societies, there have been socially accepted standards regarding the marital status of mothers, the number of children in a family, and the gender ratio of children in a family. If an infant was illegitimate or represented an "extra" child beyond the correct family size or happened to be female in a family already having one girl, the pressure of social convention often led to the child's death at the hands of its mother.

Of these social standards, the one regarding marital status has unquestionably been the most important. From ancient societies to those in the modern world, illegitimacy has ranked with poverty as a leading contributing cause of child destruction. For an unmarried woman, the birth of a child outside social conventions has frequently represented too great a price to pay for her sexual activity. Rather than lose her job (e.g., if she was a domestic slave in eighteenth-century England or France) or her reputation, it was much easier simply to conceal the pregnancy, kill the illegitimate infant in its first hour of life, and dispose of its body. In this kind of situation, the immediate motivations for a child's death may have been shame, anger, or self-interest.

Social attitudes have also contributed to the deaths of infants in some societies. To many citizens of ancient Greece and Rome, for example, the lives of children had little value. The birth of an infant—even a normal male—was often greeted with ambivalence if not indifference. There was no more celebration, excitement, or thanksgiving than if a family pet had reproduced. Once devalued in this manner, an infant's life was easily— indifferently—destroyed as a matter of social custom through strangulation, drowning, or exposure.

Others have engaged in death-causing actions because of the *abnormality of their infants*. Expecting a normal infant to appear at birth, mothers past and present have recoiled at the sight of infants with physical deformities. In earlier historical periods, congenital defects were interpreted as works of the devil, portents of coming events, signs of fate, punishment for the sins of the parents, or tricks played by witches. Regardless of which of these interpretations was used, the infant was regarded more as a supernatural sign or symbol than as a real child. For example, Martin Luther and Philip Melanchthon, two of the Protestant reformers, jointly published a tract in 1523 called *Der Papstesel*. In this work they interpreted the appearance of a strange ass-like newborn in the Tiber as a sign from God signaling the downfall of the papacy.[46]

One traditional way of explaining the existence of an abnormal infant was the "changeling" theory. By believing that a physically deformed infant was only a temporary substitute for the normal or "true" child, distraught mothers were motivated to carry out a variety of cruel acts against a defective infant: beat it, place it in a basket over a fire, hold it under water for a lengthy period, or expose it at a crossroads at midnight. The intended purpose of these acts was not the infant's death. Rather, these abusive mothers were attempting to treat the child so badly that the supernatural power (the devil, or perhaps a malevolent elf) who originally switched the children would feel sorry for the changeling and return the real child. Of course, few infants survived these maternal struggles with unseen powers.[47]

Two other traditional theories about abnormal infants motivated mothers to kill their offspring to remove their "blame" for having produced such children. One theory, that of maternal impressions, explained congenital malformations by means of certain "photographic" impressions the mother had during pregnancy. By having had the wrong kind of thoughts or seen the wrong kind of things during pregnancy, the mother was believed to have caused the malformation in her infant. An infant with a harelip, for example, signified that its mother had looked at—and perhaps been frightened by—a rabbit during pregnancy. The resemblance between monkeys and microcephalic or anencephalic infants suggested that women should not look at monkeys during pregnancy. The second theory, known as the hybridity theory, attempted to explain abnormal infants as semihuman creatures. Based on a widespread belief that members of different species were fertile with one another and would produce offspring resembling both sexual partners, the theory suggested that abnormal children—often simply called "monsters"—were the consequence of bestial sexual activity.[48]

The existence of these theories, which were still being used in nineteenth-century America, provided ample reason for mothers and fathers to kill their abnormal infants immediately after birth. Otherwise, the parents might have been ostracized as collaborators with the devil or persecuted for having produced a monstrous infant through their own misguided behavior.

The role of selection in infanticide

Although all kinds of children have been killed by their parents, most victims of infanticide have been singled out in a selective manner. In virtually every society, the chances of an infant's surviving to experience adolescence and adulthood have been significantly improved when the infant was male, legitimate according to societal standards, a member of the racial or religious majority, several weeks or months (or even years) old, and apparently normal according to physical appearance and mental performance. By contrast, female infants, bastard infants, minority group infants, neonates, and anomalous infants have been high-risk candidates for destruction. Infants at the greatest risk have been those combining several of these features, with illegitimate or anomalous female neonates the least likely to survive.

Of these features, the two most important ones for the contemporary debate about selective nontreatment are those of age and deformity. The history of infanticide is replete with examples indicating that newborns and defective infants have been easy targets for abuse and destruction. The rationale often used for killing these infants has been the claim that their deaths represent a lesser harm to themselves, their parents, and society than would be the case with the deaths of older and/or normal children. To cite one example, Charles Mercier, an English physician, attempted in 1911 to justify the killing of neonates by appealing to the minimal harm caused by the act:

> In comparison with other cases of murder, a minimum of harm is done by it. . . . The victim's mind is not sufficiently developed to enable it to suffer from the contemplation of approaching suffering or death. It is incapable of feeling fear or terror. Nor is its consciousness sufficiently developed to enable it to suffer pain in any appreciable degree. Its loss leaves no gap in any family circle, deprives no children of their breadwinner or their mother, no human being of a friend, helper or companion. The crime diffuses no sense of insecurity. No one feels a whit less safe because the crime has been committed. . . .[49]

Similar attitudes have produced mistreatment and death for anomalous infants. As late as the 1939 World's Fair in New York, there were "incubator-baby sideshows" displaying premature and deformed infants for the curious public who paid to see the shows.[50] Numerous societies have, as a matter of social custom, encouraged the selective killing of defective infants at birth. The Nuer tribe, for instance, has traditionally defined defective neonates as nonhuman "hippopotamuses" who were mistakenly born to human parents. With little apparent thought to the harm being done to these infants, they have simply returned the "hippopotamuses" to their natural habitat by throwing them into a river.[51]

The process of selection in the history of infanticide has meant not only the singling out of easily expendable children but also the making of certain distinctions with regard to socially acceptable means of securing an infant's death. Beginning with the Romans, numerous societies have distinguished between acts of direct killing and more passive or subtle acts of child destruction (e.g., abandonment, exposure). Even if the thought of parents strangling, drowning, smothering, or stabbing their infants was morally reprehensible and possibly prohibited by law, it has often been possible to bring about the death of an infant (and avoid legal punishment) by choosing other means. In ancient Rome, selectivity meant leaving an infant exposed in a deserted place rather than directly killing it. In Renaissance Italy, it meant turning an unwanted infant over to a wet nurse. In eighteenth-century France, it meant admitting an unwanted infant to an obviously understaffed and overburdened foundling hospital. In the United States in the latter part of the twentieth century, it has sometimes meant parents abandoning a premature or defective infant to the medical staff in an NICU, with decision making about the infant's life or death being left to the physicians.

Selectivity has also characterized societal efforts at prosecuting and punishing individuals for having committed infanticide. As an ongoing example of inequality before the law, the history of infanticide indicates clearly that some individuals are much more likely to be punished for acts of child destruction than are other persons who commit the same kinds of acts. In societies having laws against infanticide, certain kinds or classes of persons have been selected as targets for active prosecution: unwed mothers, impoverished mothers, and older women thought to be witches. When prosecuted for infanticide, these individuals have traditionally been convicted (unless they could establish temporary insanity) and until the mid-nineteenth century were often sentenced to death. By contrast, numerous societies have chosen neither to prosecute nor punish fathers, married mothers, members of wealthy families, or socially accepted professional killers such as the *balie* in Renaissance Italy. In somewhat the same manner, and perhaps because there is no national infanticide law, prosecutors in the United States have at the time of this writing been very selective in enforcing the various laws that apply to the deaths of defective neonates. If the death of an infant has occurred inside a hospital, neither the parents nor the physicians have been prosecuted for whatever roles they may have had in the child's death.

An ancient act in modern contexts

Infanticide is not as widely practiced in the modern world as in earlier historical periods, for several reasons. Many societies, especially in the last few centuries, have tried through their religious institutions, governments, and medical communities to curtail or even eliminate infanticidal practices. No society has been completely successful in this effort, but contemporary societies—and infants born in them—benefit from earlier attempts to combat the destructive impulses of parents directed against their young children.

Christian churches in Europe and North America took a variety of steps against infanticide. By making child destruction a sin, requiring infanticidal parents to participate in penance, publicly humiliating infanticidal persons for their sinful deed, in some places interpreting infanticide as a heinous crime, and occasionally requiring midwives to take a church oath not to "destroy the child born of any woman," Catholic and Protestant churches tried with moderate success to deter infanticidal acts. At times, however, these ecclesiastical efforts were ineffective, in that they merely encouraged infanticidal parents to conceal their violent acts rather than endure a public punishment for them.

In recent centuries the governments of several countries have tried to curtail infanticide. In eighteenth-century Europe, several governments had a role in establishing foundling hospitals as an outlet for parents who otherwise would have killed their children. These institutions, although effective for awhile, finally collapsed as a result of the sheer numbers of infants admitted to them. Another governmental effort against infanticide has involved the enactment of laws prohibiting child destruction and establishing punishment for persons convicted of such acts. England's most recent attempt, the Infanticide Act of 1938, is directed against infanticidal mothers:

> (1) Where a woman by any wilful act or omission causes the death of her child being a child under the age of twelve months, but at the time of the act or omission the balance of her mind was disturbed by reason of her not having fully recovered from the effect of giving birth to the child or by reason of the effect of lactation consequent upon the birth of the child, then, notwithstanding that the circumstances were such that but for this Act the offence would have amounted to murder, she shall be guilty of felony, to wit of infanticide, and may for such offence be dealt with and punished as if she had been guilty of the offence of manslaughter of the child. . . .
>
> (3) Nothing in this Act shall affect the power of the jury upon an indictment for the murder of a child to return a verdict of manslaughter, or a verdict of guilty but insane. . . .[52]

Individual physicians and medical associations have also joined the effort to combat infanticide. England again provides a helpful example. In the second half of the nineteenth century, when condoms and diaphragms were increasingly used for contraceptive purposes and when abortions under moderately antiseptic conditions also slowed the birthrate, leading medical authorities in England actively opposed the widespread abuse and destruction of children. Thomas Wakley, founder and editor of the *Lancet* for almost 40 years, used his position as a member of Parliament to campaign against infanticide. Edwin Lankester, one of England's first medically qualified coroners, opposed the practice of "baby farms" and worked for the compulsory registration of all births. The *British Medical Journal* campaigned for legislation to protect infants. Many activist physicians, under the leadership of John Curgeven, joined together to form the Infant Life Protection Society in 1870, a group whose goals included securing better infanticide legislation and promoting better medical care for infants.[53]

Despite these efforts, infanticide continues in the modern world. In England, there have been approximately 20 women convicted of infanticide each year since the passage of the 1938 law.[54] In the United States, it is estimated that over 100 infants are killed by their parents each year in nonclinical settings.[55] In Yugoslavia, to cite an example outside the Anglo-American sphere, there are also approximately 100 infanticide cases each year.[56]

Virtually all of these infanticide cases are only updated versions of traditional ways of killing children. Many of them take place in modern cities. Some of the cases are reported in newspapers and on television. Rarely is there anything significantly different about an infanticide case that distinguishes it in an important way from earlier cases in Greece, Rome, Italy, France, or England. Some examples follow.

In Columbus, Ohio, a mother was indicted for the multiple murder of her three infants (1976).

In Farmington, Connecticut, a newborn was abandoned under a bed in a girls' boarding school (1976).

In Washington, D.C., a teenage mother was acquitted by reason of temporary insanity for having beaten her three-month-old son to death to exorcise "Satan" (1976).

In Miami, a teenage mother beat her two-month-old daughter to death (1978).

In Chicago, a mother was convicted in a state court for having dumped her one-month-old daughter into an apartment building incinerator (1978).

On Mother's Day, 1982, a mother abandoned her newborn son in a plastic trash bag in a Silver Spring, Maryland, apartment building only to have him rescued by another woman.

In June, 1982, a mother in Oklahoma City killed her newborn infant by tossing it in a trash dumpster at an apartment complex.[57]

In contrast to these cases, there is a modern context for instances of infanticide that is entirely new and in many respects significantly different from cases in earlier historical periods. Rather than being a private home, an isolated rural location, a river, an alley, or some other traditional setting, this modern context is, of course, the NICU (or less well-equipped maternity ward) in contemporary hospitals. Staffed by pediatricians and pediatric nurses, filled with the sophisticated technological arsenal of neonatal medicine, antiseptically clean, and backed up by diagnostic labs and an extensive medical support team, the NICU is now the preeminent setting for the life-and-death decisions regularly made about premature and congenitally anomalous neonates.

The extent to which decisions about life and death are made in NICUs was made public in a 1973 article in *The New England Journal of Medicine*. Raymond Duff and A. G. M. Campbell's widely discussed article, "Moral and Ethical Dilemmas in the Special-Care Nursery," reported a policy of selective nontreatment of infants in the Yale–New Haven Hospital. Over a period of 30 months, this NICU admitted 1615 infants born at the hospital and accepted 556 infants transferred from community hospitals in Connecticut. Between January 1970 and June 1972, 299 of these infants died; of these deaths, 43 infants died because of the withdrawal of medical treatment. Most of the infants who died because of nontreatment had multiple anomalies (34.9%), whereas others had trisomic conditions (18.6%), cardiopulmonary problems (18.6%), meningomyelocele (16.3%), other central nervous system defects (7%), or short-bowel syndrome (4%).[58]

The remainder of this book is about these decisions to withhold or withdraw medical treatment from certain infants because they have severe congenital anomalies. Perceptive readers will observe several continuities with the history of infanticide as we analyze the issue of selective nontreatment:

the role of a special institution or protective haven (the NICU) in which decisions about infants' lives can be made and carried out apart from public scrutiny (with the foundling hospital as a historical parallel);

the great discretion granted a professional class (physicians) to take irreversible steps in bringing about selected infants' deaths (although there are significant differences, the traditional role of the *balie* has some similarities);

the distinction between directly killing infants and securing their deaths in less direct and less active ways (the Roman pattern provides a parallel);

the practices of concealment of the actual means used to bring about infant deaths in NICUs (concealment has been a feature of infanticide for centuries);

and the difficulty experienced by legal institutions in the United States and elsewhere in determining which acts of neonaticide are permissible and which should be prosecuted and punished.

The focus of the rest of the book, however, will be on the present and future rather than the past. A number of important but vexing questions will be raised about the selective nontreatment of neonates, and attempts made to answer them. Why and in what ways do pediatricians disagree about which infants should be "selected out" for nontreatment? When should the law be used to override parental authority and medical discretion in decisions not to treat anomalous newborns? To what extent can ethical principles provide guidance for these decisions? Is there a moral difference between killing neonates and allowing them to die? Is it possible to put forth a reasonable argument for the claim that some defective neonates would be "better off dead" than alive? Can an infant be suffi- ciently harmed by congenital defects and medical treatment that death is in that infant's best interests? Who should make these agonizing decisions about selective nontreatment and death?

Notes

1. Aristotle, *Politics*, in Richard McKeon, ed., *The Basic Works of Aristotle* (New York: Random House, 1941), bk. 7, chap. 16, p. 1302.
2. Maria W. Piers, *Infanticide* (New York: W. W. Norton & Co., 1978), p. 126.
3. Peter C. Hoffer and N. E. H. Hull, *Murdering Mothers: Infanticide in England and New England 1558–1803* (New York: New York University Press, 1981), p. xiii.
4. Ibid., pp. 147–48.
5. See A. M. Carr-Saunders, *The Population Problem* (Oxford: Clarendon Press, 1922), chap. 10.
6. William L. Langer, "Infanticide: A Historical Survey," *History of Childhood Quarterly* 1 (Winter 1974): 354.
7. Carr-Saunders, *Population Problem*, p. 217.
8. Denise Lardner Carmody, *Women and World Religions* (Nashville, Tenn.: Abingdon Press, 1979), p. 68; see also Olga Lang, *Chinese Family and Society* (New Haven, Conn.: Yale University Press, 1946).
9. See K. M. Kapadia, *Marriage and Family in India* (London: Oxford University Press, 1958); and S. Chandrasekhar, *Infant Mortality, Population Growth, and Family Planning in India* (Chapel Hill: University of North Carolina Press, 1972).
10. Euripides, *Medea*, in C. A. Robinson, Jr., ed., *An Anthology of Greek Drama* (New York: Holt, Rinehart & Winston, 1949).
11. Quoted by Lloyd deMause, "The Evolution of Childhood," in Lloyd deMause, ed., *The History of Childhood* (New York: The Psychohistory Press, 1974), p. 25.
12. Plato, *The Republic*, trans. Benjamin Jowett (Cleveland: Fine Editions Press, 1946), bk. 5.460, p. 181.
13. Soranus of Ephesus, *Gynecology*, trans. Owsie Temkin (Baltimore: Johns Hopkins University Press, 1956), bk. 2.10, pp. 79–80.
14. Quoted by deMause, "Evolution of Childhood," p. 28.
15. John T. Noonan, Jr., *Contraception* (New York: New American Library, 1967), p. 113.
16. Quoted by deMause, "Evolution of Childhood," p. 27.
17. From Cyril C. Richardson et al., eds., *Early Church Fathers*, Vol. I of the *Library of Christian Classics* (Philadelphia: Westminster, 1953), p. 172.
18. Noonan, *Contraception*, pp. 114–15.

19. From W. E. H. Lecky, *A History of European Morals from Augustus to Charlemagne*, quoted by William A. Silverman, "Mismatched Attitudes about Neonatal Death," *Hastings Center Report* 11 (December 1981): 12.

20. Richard C. Trexler, "Infanticide in Florence: New Sources and First Results," *History of Childhood Quarterly* 1 (1973): 98–115.

21. Piers, *Infanticide*, p. 51.

22. Trexler, "Infanticide in Florence," p. 105.

23. Piers, *Infanticide,* pp. 69–70.

24. Mary Martin McLaughlin, "Survivors and Surrogates," in deMause, *History of Childhood*, pp. 120, 155.

25. Piers, *Infanticide*, p. 63.

26. Ibid., p. 64.

27. Langer, "Infanticide: Historical Survey," p. 356.

28. Goethe, *Faust*, trans. Walter Kaufman (Garden City, N.Y.: Anchor Books, 1963), p. 401, emphasis added; see Maria Piers' discussion of this passage in *Infanticide*, pp. 75–76.

29. Hoffer and Hull, *Murdering Mothers*, p. ix.

30. Barbara A. Kellum, "Infanticide in England in the Later Middle Ages," *History of Childhood Quarterly* 1 (1974): 369–70.

31. Ibid., p. 380.

32. Quoted by Catherine Damme, "Infanticide: The Worth of an Infant under Law," *Medical History* 22 (1978): 7.

33. Hoffer and Hull, *Murdering Mothers*, p. 20.

34. Ibid., pp. 68–71.

35. Damme, "Infanticide: Worth of an Infant," pp. 13–16.

36. George K. Behlmer, "Deadly Motherhood: Infanticide and Medical Opinion in Mid-Victorian England," *Journal of the History of Medicine* 34 (October 1979): 422.

37. Quoted by Behlmer, ibid., p. 404.

38. R. Sauer, "Infanticide and Abortion in Nineteenth-Century Britain," *Population Studies* 32 (March 1978): 92.

39. Ibid., pp. 87–88.

40. Ibid., p. 87.

41. Hoffer and Hull, *Murdering Mothers*, p. 42.

42. Ibid., pp. 49–59.

43. Damme, "Infanticide: Worth of an Infant," p. 17.

44. Piers, *Infanticide*, pp. 15–17.

45. See Marcia J. Kramer, "Ethical Issues in Neonatal Intensive Care: An Economic Perspective," in Albert R. Jonsen and Michael J. Garland, eds., *Ethics of Newborn Intensive Care* (Berkeley: University of California, Institute of Governmental Studies, 1976), pp. 75–93.

46. John Fletcher, "Attitudes toward Defective Newborns," *Hastings Center Studies* 2 (January 1974): 21–22.

47. Carl Haffter, "The Changeling: History and Psychodynamics of Attitudes to Handicapped Children in European Folklore," *Journal of the History of the*

Behavior Sciences 4 (1968): 55–61; see also Leo Kanner, *A History of the Care and Study of the Mentally Retarded* (Springfield, Ill.: Charles C Thomas, 1964), p. 7, where he points out that Martin Luther believed that changelings were merely a mass of flesh with no soul, because they were possessed by the devil. He also indicates that Luther once recommended that a 12-year-old mentally retarded boy be drowned in the Moldau River.

48. Josef Warkany, "Congenital Malformations in the Past," *Journal of Chronic Diseases* 10 (1959): 87–91; see also John Locke, *An Essay Concerning Human Understanding*, bk. 3, chap. 6.23, where he says that "if history lie not, women have conceived by drills. . . ." For additional historical information on teratology, see George M. Gould and Walter L. Pyle, *Anomalies and Curiosities of Medicine* (Philadelphia: W. B. Saunders, 1896); and Josef Warkany, *Congenital Malformations* (Chicago: Year Book Medical Publishers, 1971).

49. Quoted by Glanville Williams, *The Sanctity of Life and the Criminal Law* (New York: Alfred A. Knopf, 1968), p. 18.

50. See William A. Silverman, "Incubator-baby Side-Shows," *Pediatrics* 64 (1979): 127–41.

51. Tom L. Beauchamp and James F. Childress, *Principles of Biomedical Ethics* (New York: Oxford University Press, 1979), p. 121.

52. In Marvin Kohl, ed., *Infanticide and the Value of Life* (Buffalo, N.Y.: Prometheus Books, 1978), pp. 219–20. For a discussion of the practical effects of this law, see Williams, *Sanctity of Life*, pp. 26–31.

53. Behlmer, "Deadly Motherhood," pp. 403–27; see also Sauer, "Infanticide and Abortion," pp. 89–90.

54. Nigel Walker, *Crime and Insanity in England* (Edinburgh: Edinburgh University Press, 1968), p. 133.

55. Hoffer and Hull, *Murdering Mothers*, p. 161.

56. Janez Milcinski, "Abortion and Infanticide in Yugoslavia," in H. Karplus, ed., *International Symposium on Society, Medicine, and Law* (Amsterdam: Elsevier Scientific Publishing Co., 1973), pp. 163–71.

57. *Columbus Dispatch*, November 11, 1976; *New York Post*, December 4, 1976; *Washington Post*, September 16, 1976; *Miami Herald*, July 28, 1978; *Chicago Tribune*, April 26, 1978; *Washington Post*, May 10, 1982. Four of these cases come from Hoffer and Hull, *Murdering Mothers*, pp. 160–61; one case is taken from Damme, "Infanticide: Worth of an Infant," p. 1.

58. Raymond S. Duff and A. G. M. Campbell, "Moral and Ethical Dilemmas in the Special-Care Nursery," *The New England Journal of Medicine* 289 (October 25, 1973): 890–94.

2

The Neonatal Intensive Care Unit: Locus for Problematic Cases

Pediatrics within our lifetime has attained a near-utopian state. We have the means to guarantee the health and vigor of all but the severely defective or irreversibly damaged children. . . . Unlike the obstetricians, we are not asked to destroy life, but merely to consider whether or under what circumstances we might refrain from actively supporting it when the survival of an otherwise doomed child may be a greater misfortune than death.
WOLF ZUELZER, M.D.[1]

How does a nurse react and what are her feelings when she is asked to carry out an order for an infant who is on the respirator, not responding to medical treatment and the order reads, "place in head hood at 40 percent oxygen?" Should she execute the physician's order even though she may not agree with it nor understand why the decision was made to "let the infant go?"
DAGMAR CECHANEK, R.N.[2]

Diagnostic and therapeutic procedures used in the medical care of infants have changed significantly since the early 1960s, as has the location where these procedures are often carried out. Before that time, the organization of infant care in hospitals was based on the premise that staphylococcal infections were airborne in nurseries. In an effort to avoid these infections, which in earlier years had caused epidemics the world over, physicians isolated and dispersed infants throughout hospitals. Infected infants were placed in isolation nurseries reserved for contagious disease, infants with unproven but suspected infection were put in observation nurseries, low-birthweight newborns were located in premature nurseries, postoperative neonates were treated in surgical areas along with other children, and uninfected infants of normal weight were cared for in full-term nurseries.

After several studies proved that it was epidemiologically safe for most severely ill infants to share the same clinical environment, comprehensive nurseries began to be established for the purpose of coordinating and improving the care of infants with neonatal disorders.[3] Known variously as neonatal intensive care units (NICUs), special-care units (SCUs), newborn centers, perinatal centers, or special-care nurseries, these clinical settings for neonatal medicine have since the early 1960s functioned as comprehensive diagnostic and treatment centers for premature, low-birthweight, and otherwise anomalous neonates.

Coupled with improved prenatal care and advanced perinatal technology (e.g., amniocentesis, ultrasonography, fetal monitors), the application of intensive care to neonates has had significant success in reducing infant mortality and improving the neurological and developmental conditions of many infants who survive a high-risk neonatal period. Hospitals with NICUs have been able to cut the infant mortality rate in half when compared with hospitals without such units.[4] For example, the mortality of low-birthweight neonates in NICUs has been reduced in one Tennessee hospital from 11.5 to 5.9% and in another hospital in the same state from 21.8 to 6.6%; and in Arizona the mortality of infants with hyaline membrane disease has been reduced from 59 to 32% when the neonates have been transferred to hospitals with NICUs.[5]

Key features of the NICU

Today there are approximately 600 hospitals with NICUs in the United States. These units admit approximately 200,000 newborns annually, representing 6% of all live births in this country. The estimated length of stay for newborns in NICUs is 8–18 days, with a national mean of 13 days per NICU patient. Costs per patient in the NICU range from $2000 to well over $40,000, with an average expenditure per NICU patient of approximately $8000. The combination of these figures places the annual national cost of neonatal intensive care in the area of $1.5 billion.[6]

Hospitals with NICUs form a loosely organized perinatal and neonatal care system throughout the country. The NICUs are generally classified according to three levels of intensive care. Level I hospitals provide minimal or normal newborn care for uncomplicated cases. Level II hospitals provide a full range of maternal and neonatal services for uncomplicated patients and offer intermediate care through their NICUs for limited types of neonatal illnesses. Level III hospitals have NICUs that provide the most intensive care available, serve as regional referral centers for difficult cases, and offer continuing education programs for pediatric specialists.[7]

The cases to be discussed in this book typically take place in level II or level III hospitals, and most of the cases end up in level III NICUs even if the births occurred in smaller, less sophisticated hospitals. The key features of these NICUs are several and are worth mentioning before we discuss problematic cases.

Neonatologists

Concentrating on knowledge and treatment of the human newborn, neonatology has become a major subspecialty of pediatrics. Beginning with Alexander Schaffer's *Diseases of the Newborn*, Clement Smith's *Physiology of the Newborn Infant*, and the establishment of the National Institute of Child Health and Human Development in 1962, neonatology has now moved beyond its early emphasis on premature infants to study an expanding range of medical problems presented by infants in their first month of life.[8] With an increasing awareness of the antepartum factors (e.g., maternal infection, drug use, metabolic problems) and intrapartum factors (e.g., asphyxia during labor, fetal hemorrhage) that can cause congenital abnormalities, some neonatologists refer to their subspecialty as perinatology or simply perinatal pediatrics. In using this terminology, they emphasize the need for medical care throughout the biological continuum of conception, gestation, labor, birth, and neonatal life. In recent years, almost 200 training programs in the United States have graduated more than 800 certified specialists in perinatal and neonatal medicine.[9]

The views of neonatologists and other pediatricians regarding selective nontreatment will be discussed in chapter 3. At this point it will suffice to observe that the neonatologists who are in charge of NICUs are convinced that the human newborn represents a unique challenge for medicine. In the words of Sheldon Korones, director of the newborn center at the City of Memphis Hospital, it is "as inappropriate to consider the neonate a small child as it is to consider the child a small adult."[10] For one thing, the neonate has to make a rapid adjustment from an aquatic thermoneutral intrauterine environment to a gaseous environment that demands respiration and body heat for survival. For another, care of the neonate necessitates an accurate interpretation of physical signs and laboratory data that may differ significantly from those of older infants. An example is hemoglobin concentration: hemoglobin levels that are normal for older infants indicate critical fetal blood loss when the same readings appear during the early postnatal hours.[11]

The effective management of an NICU is a demanding task. Although the team orientation of neonatology keeps the task from being shouldered by one person—as though that were possible—the demands of managing a unit that may admit 1000 high-risk infants a year are nevertheless arduous. The primary order of business centers on the scientific and intensely personal aspects of a wide range of problematic cases. In addition to the continual flow of life-and-death situations, however, the head neonatologist also bears responsibility for coordinating the complex neonatal team, evaluating new equipment, overseeing neonatal residents and interns, scrutinizing publications for new developments in the field, having budget negotiations with the hospital administration, and so forth. Referring to the management of an NICU as "akin to administration of a small hospital within a hospital," Gordon Avery observes that the ideal neonatologist for today's NICUs "is a multitalented superman or superwoman who never sleeps."[12]

Specialized nurses

Nurses who work in NICUs also have difficult jobs because of the constant pressures that attend their work. Confronted with the minute-to-minute responsibilities of caring for high-risk infants, NICU nurses often experience psychological problems caused by burnout. Another indication of the pressures involved with NICU nursing is the unusually high turnover rate of nursing personnel, with some units reporting turnover rates of over 100% per year.[13]

In spite of these problems, nurses who regularly work in NICUs are, in at least three respects, the heart of such units. First, nurses bear responsibility for the ongoing routines of the NICU. With nurse-to-neonate ratios ranging from 1:4 to as low as 1:1, nurses are responsible for evaluating the gestational age of new arrivals, stabilizing body temperature, watching for shock, carefully noting respiration and circulation, starting intravenous infusions, suctioning at a moment's notice (especially with infants receiving ventilatory assistance or premature infants whose secretions and vomit place them in danger of asphyxia), bathing the infants, feeding them, weighing them, providing oxygen for some of them, controlling infection (e.g., by thorough handwashing before and after handling an infant, wearing a cover gown whenever holding an infant), cleaning and disinfecting the neonate's living environment, and in every possible way immediately being aware of any significant change in a neonate's condition.[14] The critical importance of this constant patient observation on the part of well-trained nurses is evident from the fact that numerous neonatal conditions (e.g., jaundice, abdominal distention, edema, pallor and early cyanosis, infectious skin lesions) cannot be detected by monitors.[15] At times, observations by alert nurses may save a neonate's life:

> The staff must be so organized and oriented that the nurses know each baby individually. . . . The description by a competent and conscientious nurse that an infant "is not doing well" in the absence of any specific findings is probably the most frequent first "tip-off" of sepsis or other important illness in the premature infant.[16]

Second, nurses carry the emotional freight in the NICU. While neonatologists, pediatricians, pediatric surgeons, and other medical consultants come and go, nurses in the NICU spend long hours thinking about and caring for the vulnerable patients entrusted to them. Such thinking and caring is not emotion-free, in spite of the nurses' professional objectivity. In the midst of monitors, alarms, thermoregulatory devices, and other technological equipment, the art of nursing high-risk neonates often comes down to very human acts of care: watching, listening, touching, cleaning, rocking. For infants requiring a prolonged stay in the NICU, acts of care also frequently involve using family snapshots, greeting cards, posters, and stuffed toys to create a warmer, more homelike environment for the infants and their visiting parents.

Third, nurses are more closely involved with the parents of neonates than are the other persons associated with the NICU. For parents who are physically and psychologically able to visit their children during their intensive hospitalization, nurses provide a daily source of information regarding the progress and general condition of their anomalous babies. This kind of regular contact with the nurses establishes a trusting relationship not often possible through limited encounters with physicians, and it provides anxious parents with an outlet for their questions, anger, and guilt. For other parents, other possibilities exist. If an infant's mother is hospitalized elsewhere, the NICU nurses may send her a picture of the baby and encourage her to call the nursery at any time to talk with the nurses caring for her baby. If an infant's parents have difficulty coping with the lost expectation of a perfect child, the nurses may encourage them to touch and fondle their baby during their infrequent and stressful visits. And if an infant's survival is in doubt, the nurses can provide needed counsel and support. In such situations "the nurse is continuously the support figure, the one who consoles, and the one who can best help in constructing some sort of future from shattered expectations."[17]

As a consequence of the prolonged contact with their neonatal patients—and their less frequent, but emotionally charged encounters with parents—nurses occasionally have difficulty with the decisions by physicians and/or parents to withhold medical treatment from infants with serious congenital defects. As "baby advocates," NICU nurses sometimes find themselves in serious disagreement with nontreatment decisions.[18] As "surrogate mothers," they occasionally experience antagonism toward some attending physicians and want to ask, "Why don't you stay in the nursery when you write a specific order for an infant's demise?"[19] And if, for reasons of job security, they neither try to change a nontreatment decision with which they disagree nor request to withdraw from the case, they may perceive themselves as being accomplices to murder.[20] The moral bind of such a situation is illustrated by James Gustafson's analysis of the nurses' role in the Johns Hopkins case involving a neonate with Down's syndrome and duodenal atresia (see case 2.2 later in this chapter):

> If they had not known that the infant could have survived, the depth of their frustrations and feelings would not have been so great. Feelings they would have had, but they would have been compassion for an infant bound to die. The actual range of decision for them was clearly circumscribed by the role definitions in the medical professions; it was their duty to carry out the orders of the physicians. Even if they conscientiously believed that the orders they were executing were immoral, they could not radically reverse the course of events; they could not perform the required surgery. It was their lot to be the immediate participants in a sad event but to be powerless to alter its course.[21]

Advanced diagnostic and therapeutic procedures

The establishment of NICUs has coincided with important advances in electronics, biochemistry, and surgery. As a consequence NICUs offer premature infants and congenitally anomalous infants the benefits of an increasingly sophisticated approach to medical care. That medical care is partially based on technological equipment now so routinely used that large NICUs retain teams of technicians around the clock to service the equipment. Divided into general categories, the technology of intensive care includes the following:

monitoring equipment for key neonatal signs (respiration, heart rate, brain activity, blood pressure, blood chemistry, and temperature)

therapeutic equipment (incubators with servo-controlled temperature, infusion pumps for intravenous fluids, phototherapy lamps, and radiant heaters)

equipment for oxygen administration (head hoods, humidifier warmers, and several types of respirators)

resuscitation equipment (insufflation bags, endotracheal tubes, and laryngoscopes).[22]

Medical care in NICUs is also based on procedures and treatments that are so regularly performed in specific situations that they are often taken for granted. As infants progress from the acute section of an NICU through other graduated care areas in the NICU, their survival and continued development depend on dozens of diagnostic and therapeutic procedures that are continually being updated. Some of these procedures are performed on newborns in all hospitals prior to the use of intensive care; others require the specialized equipment and personnel of an NICU, supported by appropriate medical specialists in several areas.[23] Some examples are listed below.

The *Apgar score* is a simple, relatively quantitative method for clinically evaluating the medical conditions of neonates immediately after birth. The score gives numerical values of 0, 1, and 2 to each of five observed physiological signs: heart rate, respiration, muscle tone, reflex response, and color. Evaluations are made at one and five minutes after birth. The score indicates which infants are in need of particular resuscitation methods and intensive care.

Resuscitation at birth is required for newborns who are moderately to severely depressed in the delivery room. Moderately depressed infants (with Apgar scores of 4–6) usually respond to oxygen by mask, whereas severely depressed infants (scores of 0–3) require immediate intubation and admission to an NICU.

Oxygen therapy is necessary for neonates with respiratory distress. Involving the use of a plastic head hood for an infant who breathes spontaneously or mechanical ventilation for one who cannot breathe without

support, the administration of oxygen is a crucial but potentially dangerous aspect of intensive neonatal care. With the aid of an oxygen analyzer,
the lowest possible concentration of oxygen is used that can effectively
prevent apnea (cessation of breathing) or cyanosis (a bluish discoloration
caused by reduced hemoglobin in the blood). If too much oxygen is
administered, retrolental fibroplasia (blindness) or bronchopulmonary
dysplasia (chronic lung damage) may result.

Continuous positive airway pressure (CPAP) was initiated in the early
1970s for the treatment of infants with hyaline membrane disease. By
maintaining a gas pressure greater than atmospheric pressure throughout
the respiratory cycle of a spontaneously breathing infant, neonatologists
can prevent the neonate's lungs from totally deflating once they are
evacuated. Initially administered through an endotracheal tube, CPAP is
now widely utilized via the neonate's nose. Especially helpful with premature infants, CPAP used during the expiratory phase of mechanically
assisted ventilation is known as PEEP: positive end-expiratory pressure.

The *computerized cranial tomography* (CT) scan has greatly simplified
the radiological evaluation of a neonate's brain and spinal canal. As a
noninvasive study of a completely immobilized infant, CT provides early
detection of intracranial pathology such as intracranial cysts and tumors.
In addition, CT provides helpful diagnostic information that was not
previously available: evidence of early edema (excessive fluid in intercellular tissues), hemorrhages, and calcification.

Drugs and surgery represent alternate ways of treating one of the more
common cardiovascular defects in neonates, patent ductus arteriosus
(PDA). A fetal channel connects the pulmonary artery to the descending
aorta; this is a natural shunt or bypass that normally closes a day or two
after a full-term birth. In premature infants, however, the channel often
remains open and pours too much blood back through the lungs instead
of routing it through the rest of the body. The condition can be corrected
surgically, but a newer treatment involves the use of antiarthritic medication to hasten the closing of the shunt.

Ventricular shunts are widely used for the treatment of hydrocephalus. As
a surgical method of removing cerebrospinal fluid and thus reducing head
size, shunts have greatly reduced the mortality and morbidity of infants

and young children with hydrocephalus. Of the two possible ventricular shunt procedures, the most common method (the ventriculoperitoneal shunt) drains fluid into the membrane lining of the abdominal cavity. The alternate shunting method (the ventriculoatrial shunt) takes the fluid into one of the heart's chambers.

Other advances in *neonatal surgery* represent an important aspect of intensive neonatal care. Neonates who once would have died or at least been severely handicapped because of congenital defects can now often be treated with the combination of surgery followed by intensive care during the postoperative period. Surgical treatment is used for many congenital problems, especially in newborns whose surgical needs are not complicated by other factors such as congenital heart disease, low birthweight, or other major anomalies. Among the operations that can now be performed on neonates are several that are often the focal point of selective nontreatment decisions: operations to correct esophageal atresia, duodenal atresia, perforations of the gastrointestinal tract, meconium ileus, an imperforate anus, meningomyelocele, abdominal wall defects, and congenital heart disease (see cases 2.1, 2.2, 2.3, and 2.8).

Consultants and support staff

In the ongoing battle against neonatal disease, deformity, and death, the personnel connected with an NICU function in some ways like a military unit. Without stretching the analogy too far, it is evident that even with its team orientation, the NICU calls for the head neonatologist to function as the commander of the unit and requires nurses to carry out important but often mundane tasks somewhat along the lines of the unromantic jobs often assigned to ground troops in time of war. And as a military commander can call for a variety of military support during a battle, so the chief-of-staff in an NICU has a number of consultants and "support troops" available when they are needed.

The support staff includes a range of medical specialists who often help in the diagnosis and treatment of anomalous neonates: neurologists, neurosurgeons, cardiologists, cardiac and thoracic surgeons, geneticists, orthopedic surgeons, and so forth. Other specialists in hematology, immunology, urology, endocrinology, ophthalmology, and dermatology are also available as consultants in problematic cases. In addition, the support staff includes respiratory therapists, physical therapists, pharmacologists, lab technicians, chaplains, and social workers, each of whom plays an important role in the treatment of defective infants or in meeting the needs of troubled parents.

Beyond simply listing the professional specializations of the support staff, it is important to point out two features of their work with the NICU that affect decisions regarding diagnosis and treatment of problematic cases. First, some of the decisions about treatment depend on the availability of specialists and support personnel on a 24-hour basis. For example, because it is sometimes necessary to move an infant directly from the NICU or the catheterization lab to the operating room, "no neonatal cardiac unit can function safely without 24-hour thoracic surgical backup."[24] Second, many decisions about diagnosis and treatment depend on laboratory personnel who can handle requests from the NICU quickly and efficiently. Whether the request is for bilirubin and protein for a jaundiced infant, serum electrolytes for a premature infant, or a dozen or more sets of blood gas measurements in a 24-hour period for an infant with respiratory distress, the situation confronting the laboratory personnel is the same: "Everything must be in a hurry and must be done on the smallest possible sample."[25]

Neonatal anomalies

The 6% of neonates requiring intensive care present an assortment of anomalous conditions to the neonatal team. A partial list of the conditions is presented here to indicate the types of cases handled in an NICU. Some of the cases result from maternal factors, whereas others are at increased risk because of labor complications or nonmaternal congenital defects.

Maternal factors
    Mother under 16 or over 35 years
    Mother's weight less than 100 or more than 200 pounds
    History of problematic pregnancies (e.g., multiple births, premature births, infants with malformations)
    Diabetic or drug-addicted mother
    Mother with infectious disease (e.g., syphilis, tuberculosis, herpes, rubella)
    Other medical problems (e.g., anemia, toxemia, Rh incompatibility, sickle cell disease, hyperthyroidism, major surgery during pregnancy, heart disease)

Labor-related or other congenital defects
  Prolonged labor
  Complications in cesarean section
  Apgar score of 5 or less at one minute of life
  Low-birthweight infants (under 2500 grams)
  Preterm or Postterm infants (more than 42 weeks gestation)
  Infants requiring resuscitation
  Infants with sepsis (generalized infections)
  Infants with postdelivery distress (cardiac, respiratory, or gastroin-
  testinal)
  Infants with demineralized and fractured bones
  Infants with jaundice
  Infants with birth injuries or significant malformations[26]

Beyond this general listing of congenital anomalies, there are several conditions that call for a more complete description. Some of the conditions have probably motivated parents in previous centuries to commit acts of infanticide; other conditions are problems only because modern medical technology, regional referral systems, and advances in neonatal surgery now make them compatible with live birth. Either way, whether traditional malformations or complications of modern neonatal medicine, the conditions present parents and physicians with difficult decisions regarding treatment.[27] Several of the conditions will subsequently be presented as cases and discussed in this and other chapters.

Prematurity. According to current medical definitions, a premature or preterm infant is one born before the thirty-seventh week of gestation. *Moderately premature* neonates are born at 31–36 weeks and comprise 7% of all live births; at least half of them have birthweights over 2500 grams. *Extremely premature neonates* are born at 24–30 weeks, comprise less than 1% of all live births, and generally have birthweights of 500–1500 grams. The survival rate in NICUs for extremely premature infants ranges from 25% at 26 weeks to approximately 90% at 29 weeks, with neonatal deaths usually resulting from intrauterine infections, asphyxia at birth, respiratory distress, or gradual physical deterioration during the first weeks of postnatal existence. Treatment decisions for premature infants cover a range of medical conditions: asphyxia at birth, heat loss, respiratory distress, metabolic acidosis, hypocalcemia and/or hypoglycemia, anemia, patent ductus arteriosus (PDA), infections (pneumonia, meningitis, urinary tract), and apneic spells. Preterm infants with serious respiratory problems present especially difficult treatment decisions, because those given endotracheal intubation and respiratory assistance with CPAP are always at some risk of dying from intraventricular hemorrhage or bronchopulmonary dysplasia.

SGA infants. Both preterm and term infants can be small for gestational age (SGA), which according to the World Health Organization means that they weigh less than 2500 grams (5½ pounds) at term. Regardless of the timing of their births, SGA infants suffer from intrauterine growth retardation, which may be caused by maternal factors (nutrition deficiencies, alcohol consumption, smoking), fetal infections, fetal undernutrition, a small or diseased placenta, metabolic problems, or chromosomal anomalies. Because SGA infants have a significantly higher mortality rate than full-birthweight infants (e.g., they are 10 times more likely to die from intrapartum asphyxia), perinatal treatment decisions involve electronic fetal monitoring, resuscitation at birth, prevention of heat loss, respiratory assistance, and prevention of infection. Such treatment decisions are made more difficult by the fact that SGA infants often have congenital anomalies in addition to low birthweight, are likely to have slower physical growth (i.e., be more slim, less tall) than children born with normal birthweight, and often have a somewhat slowed neurological development pattern in their early years compared with other children.

Hyaline membrane disease (HMD). Also known as respiratory distress syndrome (RDS), hyaline membrane disease is an acute disorder that is symptomatic at birth or within six hours after birth. As a failure of expansion of the lungs, HMD occurs almost exclusively in premature infants. From 25 to 35% of all premature neonates have HMD, premature infants weighing less than 1500 grams are especially susceptible to it, and 60% of all premature infants with HMD die from it. The condition is a developmental disorder in which premature lungs have difficulty coping with a gaseous environment and undergo stress attempting to do so. Clinical signs of the condition include an increased respiratory rate, respiratory grunts, severe retractions, decreased body temperature, edema, and occasional apneic episodes in severe cases. Patent ductus arteriosus is a frequent complication of the disease. Although successful management of HMD includes multiple procedures, the major treatment decisions involve oxygen therapy and ventilation support. Warm and humid oxygen must be administered to an affected infant by means of a head hood, CPAP apparatus, or mechanical ventilator, while careful monitoring is done to avoid hypoxia (oxygen deficiency) and hyperoxia (oxygen excess). If too much oxygen is administered, the infant is more likely to develop the iatrogenic conditions of retrolental fibroplasia and/or bronchopulmonary dysplasia.

Congenital heart disease. The significance of cardiac anomalies in neonates is increasingly obvious. Congenital heart disease occurs at the rate of 8 per 1000 births and accounts for one-third of all neonatal deaths. At least 20 types of cardiac lesions cause serious disability among neonates and, given various combinations of lesions, it is possible that 100 different cardiac anomalies occasionally occur during the neonatal period. Infant prematurity contributes to some of the anomalies; other cardiac defects accompany congenital syndromes such as trisomy 21. Six heart defects occur more frequently than others: ventricular septal defect, patent ductus arteriosus, transposition of the great arteries, hypoplastic left ventricle, coarctation of the aorta, and tetralogy of Fallot. Early clinical signs of these anomalies include cyanosis, difficulty or excessive rapidity in breathing, tachycardia (excessively rapid heart activity), the detection of a heart murmur, feeding difficulties, and unusual fatigue. Standard treatment consists of surgical repair done either as a single-stage operation in infancy or as a series of operations in childhood following a palliative operation during infancy. Decisions regarding treatment often hang on a risk–benefit analysis: Is survival without surgery likely? Will a delay in surgery bring about a precipitous decline in the infant's condition? Will cardiac catheterization cause serious injury or death? Will surgery cause permanent central nervous system damage to the infant? Is surgery more likely to prolong life or merely hasten death?

Anencephaly. As one of the congenital defects involving the central nervous system, anencephaly represents a condition of arrested development of the anterior neural tube. In some cases the cerebral hemispheres are absent; in other cases the brain (including the brain stem) is totally absent. Anencephaly is a relatively common disorder, occurring once in approximately every 1000 births. The condition is usually lethal before birth or in the first hours or days after birth. Because no treatment is possible, nursing care consists of holding the anencephalic infant or gently touching it through isolette portholes. A somewhat similar condition is *hydranencephaly.* In this congenital anomaly, the entire cranium can be transilluminated because the once-existing brain was destroyed by a major vascular event or inflammatory disease during pregnancy. Although most hydranencephalic infants die during the neonatal period, a few such children survive for years.

Hydrocephalus. This condition, a progressive enlargement of the head from increased amounts of cerebrospinal fluid in the ventricles of the brain, often results in brain damage from neural tube depression. The condition is caused by a pathological obstruction along the pathway of cerebrospinal fluid circulation, and may be congenital or acquired (e.g., meningitis). Hydrocephalic infants are characterized by increased head size, lack of appetite, vomiting, lethargy and/or excessive irritability, and irreversible brain damage in untreated cases. Treatment decisions concern whether to shunt the condition, which shunting procedure to use, and whether complicating factors call for a selective nonuse of shunting. For most hydrocephalic infants with little or no evidence of brain damage, shunting is likely to produce survival for a limited number of years and, in the majority of cases, little if any mental retardation. For hydrocephalic infants evidencing irreversible damage to the brain or other major organs (e.g., cerebral atrophy secondary to meningitis, multiple congenital anomalies), parents and/or physicians may decide to withhold shunting operations because of the uniformly poor prognosis for such infants.

Intraventricular hemorrhage. Intraventricular bleeding in the first 24–48 hours after birth is a distinctive disorder that frequently occurs in premature infants weighing less than 1500 grams or in term SGA infants who have hyaline membrane disease or pneumonia. Some forms of intraventricular bleeding are so severe that they cause rapid deterioration to the point of coma and respiratory arrest; other forms are less severe, can be definitively diagnosed with ultrasound or a CT scan, and can be treated. Treatment decisions depend on the severity of the condition, with four grades of hemorrhage being possible. In cases of moderate hemorrhage, treatment includes drainage of cerebrospinal fluid, assisted ventilation, frequent transfusions, and a combination of anticonvulsants and antibiotics. In severe cases (grade 4 hemorrhage), 90% of the infants die, and those surviving through aggressive medical management often end up with mental retardation and blindness.

Spina bifida cystica. Perhaps 25% of the population is born with *spina bifida occulta*, a minor neural tube defect along the spinal axis; this vertebral defect is unsymptomatic and unproblematic because there is no visible exposure of meninges or neural tissue. By contrast, *spina bifida cystica* accounts for the great majority of serious neural tube defect cases, occurs at the rate of 1 per 1000 live births, and represents a recurring problem of medical management. Some spina bifida cases involve decisions about treatment of a *meningocele*, a hernial protrusion of membrane tissue and fluid in the lumbosacral region of the spinal column. Most spina bifida cases concern treatment of *meningomyelocele*, an opening in the thoracic, lumbar, or lumbosacral region of the back that exposes both membrane tissue and nerve tissue and often leaks cerebrospinal fluid. Caused by the failure of the neural tube to close during the first trimester of pregnancy, spina bifida with meningomyelocele differs in its severity depending on the size of the lesion, the location of the defect along the spinal column, and the associated congenital anomalies present (hydrocephalus, neurological dysfunction, sensory loss below the lesion, paralysis or muscle weakness below the defect, incontinence of bowel and bladder). Treatment decisions for neonates with spina bifida concern surgical closure of the spinal lesion in the first 24 hours after birth, shunting and other surgical procedures for neurological problems, control of infection, and whatever surgical procedures may be necessary for orthopedic and urological abnormalities. Such treatment decisions are complicated by the knowledge that some spina bifida infants left untreated remain alive for a year or more after birth, that severe cases of spina bifida require numerous operations over several years, and that children treated for spina bifida often have to go through life with severe physical handicaps.

Esophageal atresia with tracheoesophageal fistula. Ninety percent of the congenital malformations of the esophagus consist of esophageal atresia with associated tracheoesophageal fistula. This condition exists when a neonate's upper esophagus ends in a blind pouch rather than connecting with the stomach. In addition a fistula, or abnormal passage, connects the distal part of the trachea with the lower part of the esophagus, thereby causing an abnormal connection between the trachea and the stomach. Newborns with the condition are diagnosed initially by nurses who observe several clinical signs (choking, coughing, excess salivation, cyanosis, inability to pass a nasogastric tube); definitive diagnosis is supplied by radiology. Management of the condition involves antibiotics to combat the threat of pneumonia, suction of the esophageal pouch, and intravenous feeding. The decision to correct the malformation surgically depends on the neonate's maturity, the condition of the lungs, and (for some physicians) the presence of other major anomalies such as Down's syndrome. Surgery is corrective in 85% of the cases.

Duodenal atresia. As one of the forms of intestinal obstruction, duodenal atresia is another congenital malformation often associated with Down's syndrome. It involves either the absence or the obstruction of a portion of the duodenum. Because swallowed air cannot pass beyond the duodenal obstruction, a secondary feature of the condition is a distended stomach filled with ingested air. Vomiting is the earliest clinical indication of the defect. Management of the condition consists of nasogastric drainage, resuscitation with intravenous fluids and electrolytes, and surgical correction of the defect. The surgery represents a significant treatment decision only when other major anomalies are present. Without corrective surgery, affected infants die; with surgery, the great majority of them live.

Trisomy 21. Commonly called Down's syndrome (Langdon Down first described the features of the syndrome in 1866), trisomy 21 is the most common major pattern of congenital malformation. The general incidence rate is 1 per 660 births, but this figure varies significantly depending on maternal age: mothers under the age of 30 have an occurrence risk of 1 in 1500, whereas mothers over 40 have a risk of 1 in 130 for a Down's child. Caused by a faulty chromosome distribution in the ovum, sperm, or early cell division of the fertilized egg, a trisomic 21 infant generally has 47 chromosomes in each cell, with the variance from the normal chromosome complement being an extra chromosome 21. Over 90% of Down's syndrome cases involve a *full trisomy 21*, with three number 21 chromosomes in every cell. Approximately 4% of Down's cases are *mosaics*, with some cells containing the normal 46 chromosomes and other cells having the abnormal 47. Another 4% of Down's cases are known as *translocation trisomy 21*, with the extra chromosome being composed of portions of two different chromosomes (typically 14 or 15 plus 21). Neonates with trisomy 21 are easily diagnosed at birth (prior to definitive chromosome studies), because they present several of the physical characteristics of the syndrome: hypotonia (muscle weakness), smaller than average head, slanted eyes, relatively flat face, a short neck with excess skin, short fingers, a simian crease on the palms, and a thick tongue. Treatment decisions regarding such infants are made difficult by two principal factors: the inherent but variable mental deficiency associated with the condition and the serious physical problems that often accompany the condition. The mental deficiency is such that older children and adults with trisomy 21 typically have an I.Q. ranging between 25 and 60, with some Down's individuals being severely defective and some attaining an adult I.Q. of 60 or above. Because they fail to keep up with normal peers, Down's individuals display progressively slower mental growth with the passage of years. Coupled with the unpredictable factor of how severe the mental deficiency will be in any case is the fact that one-third to one-half of neonatal trisomy 21 cases have one or more complicating physical problems: higher than normal susceptibility to infection (pneumonia, gastroenteritis), esophageal or duodenal atresia, a congenital heart defect (in 40% of the cases), and a 1% chance of developing childhood leukemia. When life prolongation requires surgery, parents sometimes choose to forego treatment because of the prospect of lifelong mental retardation or because the surgery itself (open-heart surgery in some cases) may not work and might threaten the infant's life.

Trisomy 18. First diagnosed by J. H. Edwards and colleagues in 1960, trisomy 18 (or Edwards syndrome) is the second most common multiple-malformation syndrome. It occurs on the average of once in 3500 births, with female neonates three times more likely to have the genetic defect than males. Caused by a faulty chromosome distribution resulting in an extra chromosome 18, the condition usually produces death in embryonic or fetal life. Trisomic 18 individuals surviving to birth may have full, mosaic, or translocation forms of the syndrome. Diagnosis of the condition at birth is relatively easy because of the multiple physical abnormalities associated with the syndrome: incompletely developed, low-set ears; narrow, elongated skull; hypertonia; clenched hand, with overlapping fingers and malformed thumb; rocker-bottom feet; low birthweight; short sternum; congenital heart disease; and severe gastrointestinal and renal deformities. Trisomic 18 neonates also display severe mental deficiency, difficulty in breathing, apnea, cyanosis, a poor sucking reflex, and a high-pitched cry. Life expectancy for such infants is short: 50% die in the first two months, only 10% survive the first year (with severe mental and physical retardation), and only 1% have a chance of surviving 10 years even with aggressive treatment and institutionalization. Parents and physicians often choose not to prolong life with medical treatment once definitive chromosome studies have been completed.

Trisomy 13. Originally described by Bartholin in 1657 (as "a monster without eyes") but not clearly diagnosed until 1960 by Klaus Patau and colleagues, trisomy 13 is also known as Patau syndrome and trisomy D_1 syndrome because the extra chromosome may be any one of the D group of chromosomes (numbers 13–15). It occurs on the average of once in every 5000 births and, as in trisomy 21 and trisomy 18, maternal age is a factor in its occurrence. Neonates with the syndrome present several clear clinical signs: holoprosencephaly (incomplete development of the forebrain with midline facial defects), cleft lip and palate, major eye abnormalities ranging from absent eyes or extremely small eyes to abnormal iris and retina, severe mental deficiency, deafness, polydactyly of the hands and feet, congenital heart disease (in 80% of the cases), apneic spells, and seizures. Because of the severe cardiac and central nervous system abnormalities, life expectancy is short: 44% die in the first month, 70% die by six months, and the 16% who survive the first year do so with ongoing severe mental defects, seizures, and failure to thrive. Parents and physicians usually elect not to provide life-prolonging medical treatment.

Diaphragmatic hernia. In 1 of approximately every 3000 births, a defective opening in the neonate's diaphragm results in an extensive protrusion of the abdominal organs into the thoracic cavity. Infants with a congenital diaphragmatic hernia have severe respiratory distress, cyanosis, a collapsed lung on the side of the defect (usually the left side), a relatively large chest, and heart sounds on the right side. On diagnosis by physical exam and radiology, immediate surgical correction is necessary to save the neonate's life. Done as a one- or two-stage procedure, the surgery involves relocating the organs in the abdominal cavity and repairing the diaphragmatic defect. If the surgery is withheld, death is inevitable within a few days or weeks. Even if surgical intervention is done expeditiously, mortality is nevertheless high because aggressive management cannot in some cases overcome the combination of pulmonary hypoplasia, hypoxia, cardiac tamponade (acute compression of the heart), and pulmonary hypertension.

Abnormalities of the abdominal wall. Developmental arrest of the abdominal wall causes several abnormalities in neonates that require treatment decisions. An *omphalocele* is a herniation of the abdominal organs at the point where the umbilical cord connects with the abdomen. The defect is covered by a translucent membrane that encases the extended abdominal viscera. The size of the sac varies significantly, and in rare cases the sac ruptures. *Gastroschisis* is a similar defect, except the portion of the intestinal tract extending through the abdomen wall is sac-less.

Once a hopeless anomaly, gastroschisis consists of edematous, matted intestinal loops hanging outside an opening at the base of the umbilical stalk. *Prune-belly syndrome* is a rarer condition involving congenital hypoplasia of the abdominal musculature. Because of the deficiency of abdominal muscle, the abdomen has a wrinkled and flabby appearance somewhat like that of a prune. The condition produces abnormalities in the urinary tract (large bladder, dilated and tortuous ureters, hypoplastic kidneys) that often lead to urinary tract infection. In cases involving any one of these anomalies, treatment decisions focus on the prospects of surgical reconstruction. Surgical closure of an omphalocele is usually recommended (unless a neonate has other anomalies such as exstrophy of the cloaca or congenital heart disease) and is usually successful (depending on the size of the omphalocele). With gastroschisis, prompt surgery is successful in 50% of the cases in returning the intestinal loops to the abdomen and closing the defective opening. Nutritional support is often necessary in these cases through intravenous alimentation. Surgery on neonates with prune-belly syndrome consists of attempting to shorten the lax abdominal musculature and to reconstruct the defective portions of the urinary tract. The mortality in such cases is 50%, with most of the deaths resulting from urinary tract infection.

Exstrophy of the cloaca. In the embryonic development of some neonates, there is failure of cloacal septation, with persistence of a common cloaca into which the ureters, ileum, and a rudimentary hindgut open. Because there is no cloacal membrane, the resulting common passage for urinary, fecal, and reproductive discharge is completely exstrophic (turned inside out). Cloacal exstrophy (or vesicointestinal fissure) has several features: exstrophy of the bladder, omphalocele, prolapse of the intestine, imperforate anus, lumbosacral myelocele, and incomplete genital development. A relatively rare condition, cloacal exstrophy sometimes also has neurological features such as hydrocephalus and occasionally produces malformed feet and legs. Treatment decisions regarding surgery are complicated by the knowledge that many patients fail to survive the surgical efforts and that, for those who do survive aggressive early surgical treatment, long-term rehabilitation measures and physical handicaps remain. If surgery is attempted, it involves neurosurgical repair of the myelocele and an ileostomy (a surgical opening into the ileum through a small opening in the abdominal wall) during the neonatal period, repair of the exstrophied bladder and reconstruction of the urinary system when the patient is two years old, and possibly orthopedic surgical efforts to correct malformations in the lower limbs. Mortality from the condition is at least 50% even with aggressive early surgery, but survivors often have normal intelligence and manageable physical limitations.

De Lange syndrome. Some small-for-gestational age neonates have the fairly common set of malformations known as Cornelia de Lange syndrome. With an as yet unknown cause, this condition consists of several anomalies: small head, hirsutism (shaggy, excessive hair), synophrys (meeting eyebrows), conically tapering limbs (with the proximal portion of limbs foreshortened in severe cases), severely retarded growth, and severe mental deficiency. With 10% of these infants having congenital heart disease and all of them being unusually susceptible to infection, most de Lange infants die in their first year of life. The children who survive infancy have I.Q. scores below 50, are speechless and expressionless, and sometimes engage in self-mutilation (although in less severe forms than for children with Lesch-Nyhan syndrome). In cases without congenital heart disease, treatment decisions during the neonatal period consist of combating infection, careful tube feeding to avoid aspiration, and surgical efforts in some instances to correct hand or feet abnormalities.

Apert's syndrome. This set of physical deformities is inherited as an autosomal dominant condition, with advanced paternal age a factor in its occurrence. Although a few cases of Apert's syndrome involve mental retardation, the majority of cases are limited to physical abnormalities of the head and extremities. Neonates with this syndrome have a pointed head caused by craniostenosis, a premature fusion of the cranial sutures. They also have a progressive synostosis (fusion of adjacent bones) affecting various sections of the skeleton. The most obvious feature of the syndrome is the symmetrical syndactyly of the hands and feet: the second, third, and fourth digits on the hands and feet are webbed to give the appearance of "mitten hands" and "sock feet." The first and fifth digits are sometimes free, sometimes joined to the middigital mass of bone. Treatment decisions center on surgical efforts to correct the craniostenosis and syndactyly. If done in the early months of life, the surgery on the head is usually effective in preventing brain damage.

Genetic conditions with late onset dates. Two congenital anomalies that will be discussed in later chapters present unusual treatment decisions because of the late onset dates of symptoms and the severe prognosis for individuals inheriting the diseases. *Lesch-Nyhan syndrome* and *Tay-Sachs disease* are genetic conditions that differ in their inheritance pattern (Lesch-Nyhan is inherited as an X-linked recessive condition, Tay-Sachs is an autosomal recessive condition) but otherwise share several general features. The heterozygous carriers of the conditions can be detected through genetic screening programs, and the conditions can be diagnosed prenatally through amniocentesis. Fetuses detected as having either of the diseases are usually aborted; neonates with the conditions often appear mentally and physically normal for approximately the first three to six months after birth, and after that point a progressive cerebral deterioration and assorted physical problems take over until the children die at an early age. For parents having an infant son with Lesch-Nyhan syndrome or Ashkenazic Jewish parents having an infant with Tay-Sachs disease, treatment decisions are made difficult by several factors: the child is probably several months old when diagnosed, there is no treatment that can prolong life beyond a projected four years for Tay-Sachs infants or effective treatment for the neurological or self-mutilative behavioral manifestations of Lesch-Nyhan syndrome, and consequently infants having either disease will progressively and inevitably deteriorate from their medical conditions during the neonatal and early pediatric periods.

Cases

Some of the NICU cases that require parents and/or physicians to make decisions about treatment are presented below. Some cases that have involved legal procedures will be presented in chapter 4. Additional cases will be discussed at appropriate points in other chapters.

Case 2.1

H. R. was a two-day-old male infant for whom pediatric surgical consultation was requested because of vomiting of feedings and large quantities of green fluid. The infant was born to a forty-five-year-old woman who had two normal teenagers and had thought she was through menopause and safely out of range of pregnancy. Both parents were in good health and the pregnancy had been uneventful. The baby had the unmistakable stigmata of Down's syndrome, promptly confirmed by chromosome karyotyping which identified a trisomy of chromosome 21. In addition he had a grade

3/6 heart murmur but no cyanosis or signs of congestive heart failure.

Roentgenographic examination confirmed the clinical impression of duodenal obstruction which could only be relieved by surgery. The parents, both well educated, had expressed their intention to institutionalize the baby prior to the diagnosis of intestinal obstruction. When asked by the physician caring for the baby if they would give consent for operative intervention, the father said, "I have no alternative, do I?" There was no reply, and the father signed the consent form. The surgery was successful, and ten days later the infant was on his way to the state institution.[28]

Case 2.2

THE FAMILY SETTING

Mother, 34 years old, hospital nurse.

Father, 35 years old, lawyer.

Two normal children in the family.

In late fall of 1963, Mr. and Mrs. —— gave birth to a premature baby boy. Soon after birth, the child was diagnosed as a "mongoloid" (Down's syndrome), with the added complication of an intestinal blockage (duodenal atresia). The latter could be corrected with an operation of quite nominal risk. Without the operation the child could not be fed and would die.

At the time of birth Mrs. —— overheard the doctor express his belief that the child was a mongol. She immediately indicated she did not want the child. The next day, in consultation with a physician, she maintained this position, refusing to give permission for the corrective operation on the intestinal block. Her husband supported her in this position, saying that his wife knew more about these things (i.e., mongoloid children) than he. The reason the mother gave for her position—"It would be unfair to the other children of the household to raise them with a mongoloid."

The physician explained to the parents that the degree of mental retardation cannot be predicted at birth—running from very low mentality to borderline subnormal. As he said: "Mongolism, it should be stressed, is one of the milder forms of mental retardation. That is, mongols' I.Q.s are generally in the 50–80 range, and sometimes a little higher [this estimate varies from the information on p. 45]. That is, they're almost always trainable. They can hold simple jobs. And they're famous for being happy children. They're perennially happy and usually a great joy." Without other complications, they can anticipate a long life.

Given the parents' decision, the hospital staff did not seek a court order to override the decision. The child was put in a side room and, over an 11-day period, allowed to starve to death.

Following this episode, the parents undertook genetic counseling (chromosome studies) with regard to future possible pregnancies.[29]

Case 2.3

Matthew Starkey was a "kilogram kid" at birth, weighing 700 grams. He was an extremely premature neonate born at 24 weeks' gestation because his mother's cervix, unable to hold and carry the baby to term, dilated three months early and brought on premature labor. Even an injection of beta mimetic to stop her labor failed to work.

Before Matthew's birth his parents were told that his chances of survival were slim. If he weighed less than 500 grams at birth, the NICU personnel would consider him too small to try to save. If he weighed over 500 grams, he would probably have numerous medical problems because of his prematurity. His mother's comment about this information reflected the severity of the situation: "We didn't want it to survive if it was going to be handicapped beyond a productive life."

Matthew beat the odds for neonates born at 24 weeks, but not easily. He had surgery for patent ductus arteriosus and complications including brain hemorrhage, high bilirubin, dehydration, tube-caused infections, chronic lung disease, and distended bowel from forced feeding. He remained on a ventilator for seven weeks and in the NICU for another four weeks. When he was dismissed at that time to go home, he weighed 1930 grams (4 lb., 4 oz.). At six months of life, he weighed 9½ pounds and had a slight case of RLF disease (retrolental fibroplasia), which may later lead to trouble with reading. His mother believes he survived "through a combination of natural resistance and the doctors' skill."[30]

Case 2.4

Mignon was an extremely premature infant. Born after only 19 weeks' gestation, she weighed 482 grams at birth. Nevertheless, she was admitted to an NICU for treatment.

She encountered multiple problems brought about by her prematurity and low birthweight, but continued to live with aggressive medical treatment. After seven months in the NICU, she was described by her physician in the following manner:

> She has been plagued with frequent kidney failures, liver problems that defy textbook definition, and the usual lung problems . . . at seven months after delivery she is hanging in there. We have kept the [umbilical artery] catheter in her aorta all the way, so her hyperalimentation has been intra-arterial . . . she can't suck because of the endotracheal tube . . . of course, she has been constantly on PEEP. . . . But with no spontaneous breathing, all mechanical ventilation, her lungs are pretty damaged now. . . .[31]

Case 2.5

Gillian and Edward Solem live in Cleveland Heights, within walking distance of University Hospitals. Gillian completed seven months of a first pregnancy under the care of a nurse-midwife at the Kaiser Permanente program, a prepaid medical care plan in the Cleveland area.

At 32 weeks, unexpectedly, Gillian began premature labor. She immediately went to Kaiser Permanente for a preliminary evaluation, and was transferred by ambulance to University Hospitals. The NICU personnel anticipated an infant suffering from hyaline membrane disease (HMD).

Following a spontaneous and routine delivery, Amanda Solem was born with a birthweight of 1460 grams (3 lb., 3 oz.). She immediately developed HMD, or respiratory distress syndrome. She had difficulty breathing and experienced apnea.

Avroy Fanaroff, the neonatologist in charge of Amanda's case, instituted continuous positive airway pressure (CPAP). Sensors were taped to Amanda's skin to provide continuous readouts of oxygen concentration. Such "fine-tuning" of the oxygen therapy was necessary to avoid harming the infant. Fanaroff stated: "Too much oxygen can be damaging to the eyes and the lungs, resulting in continued dependency on mechanical ventilation. On the other hand, it is essential to provide enough oxygen to sustain the brain and other vital functions."

By the fourth day, Amanda was ready to breathe without mechanical assistance, and CPAP was discontinued. She remained in the NICU for 20 days, at a charge of $11,000. Then, past her critical period, she was transferred back to Kaiser Permanente, where she spent another 20 days before going home in good health.[32]

Case 2.6

A girl was born by cesarean section after a 34-week gestation to a 30-year-old mother. The mother had gone through an abortion previously and also had given birth by cesarean section to a live infant with severe Rh disease (anemia caused by antibodies from the mother that destroy red blood cells in the baby) who died two hours after birth.

The amniotic fluid was sampled frequently during this girl's gestation because of the risk of Rh disease. At 32 weeks' gestation there was a marked increase in signs of severe Rh disease, indicating that the child would not survive for long in utero unless treated. At 34 weeks' gestation, the girl was given an intrauterine transfusion. Three days later the mother went into labor and an emergency C section was performed.

At birth the baby girl weighed 1700 grams (3 lb., 12 oz.) and had an Apgar score of 1. She made no respiratory efforts, was blue and limp, had no reflexes, and had a very slow heart rate. She was grossly edematous (swollen with excess fluid); the liver and spleen were very large. Vigorous resuscitation was required, and the parents consented to the resuscitation in part because they had gone to great lengths during the pregnancy to bring the girl successfully to term.

A tube was inserted through the girl's mouth, and she was ventilated with positive pressure; catheters were introduced into both the umbilical artery and vein. At five minutes of age, while she was being ventilated with oxygen, her Apgar score was still essentially 1. Her arterial blood had an extremely low oxygen concentration (20 mm Hg) and a high carbon dioxide concentration; her blood was very acidotic, with a pH less than 6.8 (such blood conditions carry the threat of damage to the brain if not corrected rapidly). At 6½ minutes of age her heart rate was still quite slow (under 100), and a large dose of bicarbonate was infused. At 11 minutes of age her blood pH was still 6.9.

Should resuscitation on this girl be stopped? She is now 11 minutes old, with a blood pH of 6.9, not breathing on her own, and not well oxygenated.[33]

Case 2.7

Baby Girl S was born at a small community hospital, four weeks prematurely, after an uncomplicated pregnancy. At birth the baby breathed spontaneously, but shortly thereafter had an apneic episode in which respiration stopped, and oxygen was required. She also had unusual face and hands and showed little spontaneous motor activity. For these reasons she was transferred to a neonatal intensive care unit. Physical examination showed findings consistent with trisomy 18, a serious genetic defect. The infant continued to have occasional episodes of apnea, which over the next twenty-four hours became sufficiently severe that respirator assistance was considered. A heart murmur was noted and signs of early heart failure (normally treated with a variety of medications) became evident.

Mr. and Mrs. S came to the center thirty-six hours after the birth, having been told that Baby S had multiple birth defects. They met with the pediatrician and geneticist caring for the baby. The infant's primary problem was explained (a chromosomal "accident" resulting in extra genetic material in all of the infant's cells, with diverse manifestations), the immediate difficulties outlined (short periods where the infant "forgot" to breathe, and a heart defect which was probably an opening between the major artery to the body and the large artery to the lungs, with resultant heart failure), the child's abnormal features described (small size, unusual facial features, and deformed hands), and the long-term outlook explored (profound retardation with very high probability of death within the first year).

Within the next day or two decisions will need to be made:

1. Should resuscitative efforts be continued when the baby "forgets" to breathe?
2. Should a respirator be used if that becomes necessary to maintain the baby's life?

3. Should medication to control the potentially life-threatening heart failure be instituted?
4. Should other routine care be given?

Before these decisions are made, should the parents see the baby? Should the physician encourage or discourage them in touching and holding the baby?[34]

Case 2.8

Debbie Caruso had her first pregnancy in 1978. Having always loved children and looked forward to being a mother, Debbie and her husband Randy anticipated the child's birth with great joy. Then, late in her pregnancy, Debbie was given tragic news by her obstetrician. A fetal monitor had failed to pick up the fetal heartbeat. A week and a half later, Debbie delivered a stillborn infant that had been strangled in the uterus by the umbilical cord.

Within months Debbie was pregnant again. She believed that this time "it was going to be perfect." She and Randy selected names for the child, decorated the baby's room, and stocked the closet with diapers. In her joy Debbie began keeping a diary for her child: "Dear baby . . . I hope that when you are old enough to read this you can understand what it's like to love someone that you made."

Debbie went into labor in June of 1980. A cesarean section was necessary because the baby was in breech position. Debbie was given a spinal anesthetic and was wide awake when the doctors made the incision. Suddenly, the medical team tensed and no one looked at her. "What's wrong?" she shouted. No one answered.

Hours later she was informed that her baby son Nicky had spina bifida cystica with meningomyelocele. The doctors told her that developmental problems caused by the spinal deformity would cause permanent paralysis and serious brain damage, even if the lesion was closed surgically. She was told that she had 24 hours to make a decision about the surgery.

The next morning another doctor came to Debbie and told her of the numerous deformities present: Nicky had no control over sphincter nerves, he had clubfeet and dislocated hips, he was hydrocephalic, and he had serious apneic spells. Even if aggressive medical treatment was done, she was told, her son faced a horrible future.

With Randy devastated by the tragic news, Debbie was left to make the decision about the treatment. She decided, in Nicky's interests, not to have the surgery performed. The baby was transferred out of the NICU to a pediatric nursery, and Debbie went home.

Over a period of days, Debbie called numerous friends and doctors for advice. One of the calls she made was to a spina bifida counseling service, where she was emphatically told to "get that baby operated on right away." In the midst of this conflicting advice, she found out that the state attorney's office, acting on an anonymous tip, was considering legal action in her son's case.

Nevertheless, Debbie continued to think that the decision not to treat Nicky was correct. She commented later: "We're not talking about just a handicapped child or a child who wasn't perfect. I wouldn't have cared what he looked like, or lived like. I would have devoted my whole life to that life, to his life, if he could have *had* a life."

When Nicky was four weeks old, Debbie and Randy were told by hospital administrators that there was nothing more to be done with him in the hospital. Nicky was transferred to a nursing home. Debbie and Randy informed the nursing home personnel that when Nicky started to die, they were "to let him go."

One week later, Nicky died. An autopsy confirmed the multiple problems the doctors had diagnosed. Debbie still keeps a plastic bag of Nicky's toys and clothes, just as it was given to her by the ambulance driver who dropped it off on the way to the autopsy.[35]

Notes

1. Wolf W. Zuelzer, "The Problem and Its Limits: Relationship to Pediatrics," in Tom D. Moore, ed., *Report of the Sixty-Fifth Ross Conference on Pediatric Research: Ethical Dilemmas in Current Obstetric and Newborn Care* (Columbus, Ohio: Ross Laboratories, 1976), pp. 16–17.
2. Dagmar Cechanek, "Nursing Reactions," in Moore, *Report of the Sixty-Fifth Ross Conference*, p. 59.
3. Louis Gluck and Joan Richardson, "Newborn Special Care," in Harry C. Shirkey, ed., *Pediatric Therapy* (St. Louis: C. V. Mosby Co., 1975), p. 355. The only infants who should be treated in separate nursery facilities are "infants with open draining lesions, those with infectious diarrhea, and those with frankly contagious diseases such as varicella, vaccinia, and pertussis."

4. See Paul R. Swyer, "The Regional Organization of Special Care for the Neonate," *Pediatric Clinics of North America* 17 (November 1970): 761–76; Joseph R. Christian, "Recent Advances in Perinatal Medicine," in Sudhir Kumar and Mahohar Rathi, eds., *Perinatal Medicine* (Oxford: Pergamon Press, 1978), pp. 1–4; Paul R. Swyer, "The Organization of Perinatal Care with Particular Reference to the Newborn," in Gordon B. Avery, ed., *Neonatology: Pathophysiology and Management of the Newborn*, 2nd ed. (Philadelphia: J. B. Lippincott Co., 1981), pp. 17–47; and Robert H. Usher, "The Special Problems of the Premature Infant," in Avery, *Neonatology*, pp. 230–61.

5. Sheldon B. Korones, *High-Risk Newborn Infants*, 2nd ed. (St. Louis: C. V. Mosby Co., 1976), p. 244.

6. These figures are taken from Peter Budetti et al., *Case Study #10: The Costs and Effectiveness of Neonatal Intensive Care* (Washington, D.C.: Office of Technology Assessment, August 1981), pp. 4–5; see also Lawrence K. Altman, "Health Quality and Costs: A Delicate Balance," *New York Times*, March 30, 1982, pp. 1, 21–22.

7. Budetti et al., *Case Study*, pp. 8–9; see also Albert R. Jonsen and George Lister, "Newborn Intensive Care: The Ethical Problems," *Hastings Center Report* 8 (February 1978): 15–18.

8. See Avery, *Neonatology*, pp. xvii–xx.

9. Ibid., p. xvii; and Budetti, et al., *Case Study*, p. 8.

10. Sheldon B. Korones, "The Newborn: Perinatal Pediatrics," in James G. Hughes, ed., *Synopsis of Pediatrics*, 5th ed. (St. Louis: C. V. Mosby Co., 1980), p. 218.

11. Ibid., pp. 218, 233.

12. Avery, *Neonatology*, pp. xvii–xviii.

13. Mitzi L. Duxbury, "The Role of the Nurse in Neonatology," in Avery, *Neonatology*, p. 50.

14. Mary Beth L. House and Michele M. Dombkiewicz, "Patient Care in the ICU," in Avery, *Neonatology*, pp. 59–77.

15. Korones, *High-Risk Newborn Infants*, p. 245.

16. Gluck and Richardson, "Newborn Special Care," pp. 365–66.

17. Jean Lancaster, "Impact of Intensive Care on the Maternal-Infant Relationship," in Korones, *High-Risk Newborn Infants*, p. 240.

18. Elaine L. Ambrosini, "The Withholding of Treatment of a Defective Newborn: A Quandry," in Gladys M. Scipien and Martha Underwood Barnard, eds., *Issues in Comprehensive Pediatric Nursing* (New York: McGraw-Hill, 1976), pp. 23–24.

19. Cechanek, "Nursing Reactions," p. 60.

20. Elsie L. Bandman, "The Dilemmas of Life and Death: Should We Let Them Die?" *Nursing Forum* 17 (1978): 123.

21. James M. Gustafson, "Mongolism, Parental Desires, and the Right to Life," *Perspectives in Biology and Medicine* 16 (Summer 1973): 548.

22. Korones, *High-Risk Newborn Infants*, pp. 245–46.

23. Information on these medical procedures has been taken from several resources: Avery, *Neonatology*; Hughes, *Synopsis of Pediatrics*; Korones, *High-*

Risk Newborn Infants; Mary Coleman, *Neonatal Neurology* (Baltimore: University Park Press, 1981); and Lutz Wille and Michael Obladen, *Neonatal Intensive Care: Principles and Guidelines* (New York: Springer-Verlag, 1981).

24. Donald C. Fyler and Peter Lang, "Neonatal Heart Disease," in Avery, *Neonatology*, p. 450.

25. Gordon B. Avery, "Neonatal Physiology: Basis for the Laboratory Needs of the Nursery," in Donald S. Young and Jocelyn M. Hicks, eds., *The Neonate* (New York: John Wiley & Sons, 1976), p. 94.

26. See Gluck and Richardson, "Newborn Special Care," p. 356; and Jonsen and Lister, "Newborn Intensive Care," p. 15.

27. Information on congenital anomalies described in this section has been taken from several helpful resources: Avery, *Neonatology*; Korones, *High-Risk Newborn Infants*; David W. Smith, *Recognizable Patterns of Human Malformation* (Philadelphia: W. B. Saunders, 1970); Josef Warkany, *Congenital Malformations* (Chicago: Year Book Medical Publishers, 1971); A. P. Norman, ed., *Congenital Abnormalities in Infants*, 2nd ed. (Oxford: Blackwell Scientific Publications, 1971); and William L. Nyhan and Nadia O. Sakati, *Genetic and Malformation Syndromes in Clinical Medicine* (Chicago: Year Book Medical Publishers, 1976).

28. This case was prepared by Anthony Shaw and is quoted by permission. The case is reprinted from Tom L. Beauchamp and James F. Childress, *Principles of Biomedical Ethics* (New York: Oxford University Press, 1979), pp. 266–67.

29. This case, frequently referred to as the Johns Hopkins Hospital case, is reprinted by permission from James M. Gustafson, "Mongolism, Parental Desires, and the Right to Life," *Perspectives in Biology and Medicine* 16 (Summer 1973): 529–30, published by the University of Chicago Press.

30. This case is adapted from information in Jack Fincher, "Before Their Time," *Science 82* 3 (July–August 1982): 68–78.

31. Originally contained in a *Medical Tribune* report by J. Henahan (September 1979), this case is adapted from William A. Silverman, "Mismatched Attitudes about Neonatal Death," *Hastings Center Report* 11 (December 1981): 15.

32. This case is reprinted by permission from the Robert Wood Johnson Foundation. Amanda's case was described in the foundation's *Special Report* on regionalized perinatal services, no. 2 (1978): 15.

33. This case is an adaptation of a case prepared by Alex Stalcup, M.D. The case originally appeared in Albert R. Jonsen and Michael J. Garland, eds., *Ethics of Newborn Intensive Care* (Berkeley: University of California, Institute of Government Studies, 1976), pp. 20–21. It is used by permission.

34. This case, written by Robert M. Veatch, appeared as Case No. 274: "Nurturing a Defective Newborn," *Hastings Center Report* 8 (February 1978): 13. It is quoted by permission.

35. This case is adapted from information in Bonnie Remsberg, "The Agonizing Decision of Debra Sorenson," *Family Circle*, April 6, 1982, pp. 18, 37–40, 134.

3
Pediatricians and Selective Nontreatment

> Although philosophers may debate the question of whether there is such a thing as a life not worth living, many physicians, including myself, agree that there are such lives and that we, through our applied technology, have perpetuated many of them along with the much larger number of "worthwhile" lives we save.
>
> ANTHONY SHAW M.D.[1]

> It is sometimes said that these infants [with spina bifida cystica] should be left to die (or encouraged to die), mainly because their lives will be nothing but misery and unhappiness due to their disability. Yet extreme disability is not synonymous with unhappiness, and we are only at the beginning of finding ways of developing the capabilities of these patients to the maximum, either in work or recreation.
>
> R. B. ZACHARY, M.D.[2]

In recent years numerous neonatologists, general pediatricians, and pediatric surgeons have written about the problematic cases confronting them in NICUs. As they have deliberated over the appropriate course of action to take with anomalous neonates, they have discussed two related but distinct issues. Some of them have wrestled with the substantive questions of when, if ever, it is morally justifiable not to provide life-prolonging medical treatment for neonates with severe congenital defects and, if the decision is made that not all infants are to be treated, the means that may be used to bring about the deaths of those untreated. Others have focused more on the procedural question of who should make these agonizing decisions regarding life, suffering, and death.

The literature on selective nontreatment produced by these physicians clearly indicates that pediatricians and pediatric surgeons are not in agreement regarding what constitutes "standard medical practice" in caring for neonates with serious congenital defects. In particular, they are not in agreement regarding the ethical criteria for selective nontreatment, the clinical criteria to be used in nontreatment decisions, or the persons who should bear the moral and legal responsibility for such decisions.

59

Nevertheless, it is important to give serious attention to the views of neonatologists and other pediatric specialists on the issue of selective nontreatment. Their technical expertise does not make them moral experts on this or any other issue, but as indicated in chapter 2 they do serve on the "front line" in combating death and disability in NICUs and regularly confront infants having a variety of severe congenital anomalies. In addition, their familiarity with the technical aspects of diagnosing and treating congenital anomalies allows them to establish the clinical framework that has direct bearing on the debate among nonmedical persons regarding the morality and legality of selective nontreatment.

It will be helpful, therefore, to examine the views of several pediatric specialists who have entered the public debate over selective nontreatment. We will concentrate in this chapter on their views regarding the substantive issues involved in selective nontreatment and only note in passing their positions on procedural matters. Along the way it will be evident that these physicians, in spite of their differences on both substantive and procedural matters, often tend to develop their positions on selective nontreatment in the light of the ancient principle of nonmaleficence: *primum non nocere*, "above all, do no harm."

Seven pediatric views on selective nontreatment

Although a few pediatricians and pediatric surgeons had proposed criteria for selective nontreatment of defective neonates during the 1960s, the medical debate over selective nontreatment did not become public until the early 1970s when three widely read articles were published. John Lorber indicated in 1971 that clinical criteria were being used in his hospital in England to determine which spina bifida children were to receive life-prolonging treatment and which were to be left untreated.[3] In 1973 *The New England Journal of Medicine* published two articles stating that selective nontreatment was being practiced with a variety of infants in some hospitals in the United States. Anthony Shaw, Raymond Duff, and A. G. M. Campbell acknowledged that in their respective hospitals in Virginia and Connecticut decisions were sometimes made to withhold medical treatment from neonates with serious congenital defects.[4]

Since the publication of these articles, surveys have indicated that many pediatricians and pediatric surgeons agree in general with a policy of selective nontreatment of seriously defective newborns. A survey of Massachusetts pediatricians found that 54% of the responding physicians do not recommend surgery for an infant with Down's syndrome and duodenal atresia, and 66% of them would not recommend surgery for an infant with a severe case of spina bifida with meningomyelocele.[5] A survey in the San Francisco Bay area indicated that 22% of the pediatricians surveyed favor nontreatment for infants having Down's syndrome with no complications, and over half of them recommend nontreatment in cases of Down's syndrome with duodenal atresia or in cases of trisomy 18.[6] In addition, a national survey of pediatricians and pediatric surgeons revealed substantial agreement with a policy of selective nontreatment. Most of the physicians participating in the survey indicated that they tend to support the decision of parents who refuse to consent to surgery for an infant with intestinal atresia accompanied by other anomalies such as anencephaly, Down's syndrome, meningomyelocele, or cloacal exstrophy. Less than 1% of the pediatricians and only 3% of the surgeons stated that there "is *no* situation in which I would accept such a decision."[7]

In addition to these surveys, several pediatricians and pediatric surgeons have joined Lorber, Shaw, Duff, and Campbell in an ongoing public debate about selective nontreatment. Although each of the physicians to be discussed in this chapter (with the possible exception of Everett Koop) is willing to engage in selective nontreatment in some clinical situations, they have fundamental disagreements about which infants should be left untreated, what should be done with the untreated infants, and who should make these decisions.

Raymond Duff

Raymond Duff, with and without his former medical colleague A. G. M. Campbell, has been a strong advocate of selective nontreatment since 1970. That is the year that Duff and Campbell instituted a policy of selective nontreatment in the Yale–New Haven Hospital, a policy that resulted in the deaths of 43 infants over a period of 30 months because of the withdrawal of medical treatment (see chapter 1 for a statistical breakdown of their cases). As to their reasons for withdrawing treatment from these infants, they simply state that infants with anencephaly and hydranencephaly have a "right to die," that some defective infants need to escape a "wrongful life" characterized by cruel treatment in institutionalized "dying bins," and that families need to be spared the chronic sorrow of caring for infants with little or no possibility for meaningful lives. The principal criterion used in these decisions was the belief that, because the infants had little or no capacity to love or to be loved, the "prognosis for meaningful life was extremely poor or hopeless." The nontreatment decisions were made jointly by the physicians and parents, with the physicians sometimes yielding to parental wishes "as physicians have done for generations."[8]

Duff and Campbell contrast two philosophies of care: a "disease-oriented" approach in which all that matters is the prolongation of life, with death as the supreme failure, and a "person-oriented" approach that places primary emphasis on the quality of life that is to be lived. Allying themselves with physicians in the second category, they indicate that the prolongation of some infants' lives results in net harm being done: such infants face a future of "severely compromised living" that is "worse than death." When confronted with decisions about such tragic cases, they believe "that 'deep down' almost all physicians and those they serve would agree that there are some occasions when death may be a prudent choice and achieving death (in fact, killing) a sorrowful and painful obligation."[9] Once the decision for nontreatment has been made, the means taken do not really matter: "Euthanasia, either passive or active, can be a safe and humane choice in dealing with selected tragedies."[10]

The disease-oriented perspective in neonatal medicine results in what Duff calls "an *unbridled* aggressive approach" in which all seriously defective infants are treated for an indefinite period of time, regardless of patient suffering or the apparent uselessness of the treatment.[11] This aggressive approach, whether promoted by the pediatrician or requested by the parents, can be harmful and possibly even cruel to the infant, as indicated by Duff's comments about Baby Girl U.

Case 3.1

> Apparently in good health at birth, Baby Girl U developed symptoms of bowel obstruction (from a malformation) at 34 hours of age. Her chances of long-term survival were estimated to be very low, perhaps less than one in ten thousand. Nevertheless, her physician chose to go with surgery in which most of her necrotic bowel was removed to save her life. Intravenous nutrition was given in hope of eventual adequate bowel function, even though such substitutions commonly have complications and cannot be effective over a long period.
>
> By four months of age, Baby Girl U's intravenous support was increasingly problematic and her bowel was not functioning. She

had been through several operations and had endured numerous other medical treatments.

The U family, initially supportive of the physician's aggressive approach to treatment, suffered under psychological and financial pressures. They became increasingly aware that they had misunderstood the physician's enthusiasm to treat their daughter as being optimism regarding the treatment's result. They came to regret the choice to treat their daughter because the prolonged treatment was cruel to her and damaging to the family unit. During their daughter's fourth month of life, the parents decided that she would be better off dead than alive in the circumstances she had to endure and rejected further life-sustaining treatment. The baby died slowly of dehydration and starvation.[12]

Duff believes that the physician in this case made a mistake in continuing treatment after the infant's second day of neonatal life. The girl's suffering could have been fully anticipated and the chances of her survival were exceedingly low. After presenting the case, Duff raises several questions:

> Should we (family and health professionals) have chosen to treat her at all? If not, should we have let her cruel disease kill her or should we ease her into death, perhaps by killing her in a more kindly way? Should we continue treatment . . . despite apparent hopelessness? If so, how can we justify our cruelty? If not, should we kill her gently, as some suggested when she was two days of age?[13]

In another collaborative article Duff and Campbell lay out three options for the care of neonates with congenital defects. The first option is "maximal treatment without qualification"; infants whose conditions place them in this treatment category are to receive all available methods of treatment and life support. The second option is "limited treatment" in which emphasis is placed on the alleviation of suffering for infants who are not likely to benefit from aggressive treatment. The third option is "withdrawal of life-sustaining treatment" from infants who are born dying; for these infants "it is imperative that suffering be alleviated and dying not be unnecessarily prolonged."[14]

Because of the vagueness of these treatment options, Duff and Campbell responded to criticism in the *Journal of Medical Ethics* by laying out their criteria of selection in greater detail. Affirming that the "vast majority

of children with handicapping abnormalities or diseases must be treated,"
the pediatricians then address the issue of selective nontreatment:

> In our view the most important medical criterion is the degree of ab-
> normality, disease or damage to the central nervous system, especially the
> brain. If there is little or no prospect of brain function sufficient to allow a
> personal life of meaning and quality or no potential for development in
> harmony with [Joseph] Fletcher's "indicators of humanhood," non-treat-
> ment seems the prudent course of action.[15]

As to when this medical criterion leads to nontreatment, they list
several cases: anencephaly; hydranencephaly; extreme forms of hydrocephalus ("especially if complicated by other abnormalities or by CNS
infection"); chromosomal disorders such as trisomy 13; fully documented
severe brain damage following asphyxia, hemorrhage, or infection; progressive diseases of the brain such as the leukodystrophies; and terminal
cases of intracranial cancer. Additionally, there are borderline cases such
as trisomy 18, Down's syndrome with complications, severe forms of
spina bifida cystica, and major multiple congenital anomalies not necessarily involving the brain. Especially in deciding about these borderline
cases, Duff and Campbell extend their medical criterion to include psy-
chosocial considerations as well (e.g., whether parents are willing to care
for an infant with spina bifida). In this manner they attempt to protect
infants and their families "from caprice and the tyranny of sometimes
cruel technology."[16] They also avoid setting rigid criteria for treatment
and nontreatment, preferring that decisions be made "instance by instance"
by the responsible parties involved.

In his most recent article, Duff again places infants in three categories.
At one "prognostic extreme" are most of the infants admitted to NICUs;
these infants are to be treated, and "no question about fighting for their
lives is ever raised." One minority group consists of borderline children—
"those with spina bifida, Down's syndrome, severe prematurity, brain
damage, and miscellaneous others"—who may or may not be treated
depending on several variables. Another minority group is at the other
prognostic extreme: infants with anencephaly, trisomy 13, trisomy 18,
and "others with an extremely bleak or hopeless prognosis." The conditions in this third group are often lethal, but if they are not lethal in
particular instances the infants "are sometimes sedated and given skilled
nursing and parental care as they wither and die."[17] As to the justification

of nontreatment of infants in the third and sometimes in the second category, Duff states:

> Risking unpopularity, some people reason that while nontreatment appears more unfair to the child, in fact sometimes it is not. Treatment may brutalize the child and yet promise little except better understanding of disease, some good technical practice for the staff, consistent staff orientation to fighting . . . against disease and death, and income. The surviving child's life at home might have such a detrimental effect on the family that the child, too, would suffer excessively. Deprived of a loving home, the severely handicapped child's life in a series of foster homes or an institution would be too miserable. Choosing death sometimes is viewed as an act of love because some life can only be wrongful.[18]

Anthony Shaw

Anthony Shaw, a pediatric surgeon now at U.C.L.A. and the City of Hope Hospital, is another advocate of selective nontreatment. In his original article on the subject, he described several cases involving rapidly lethal lesions: for example, infant A had intestinal obstruction, a heart murmur, and clinical signs of Down's syndrome (see case 2.1); infant B had duodenal obstruction plus Down's syndrome; and infant C had microcephalus and an imperforate anus.

Case 3.2

Baby B was referred at the age of 36 hours with duodenal obstruction and signs of Down's syndrome. His young parents had a 10-year-old daughter, and he was the son they had been trying to have for 10 years; yet, when they were approached with operative consent, they hesitated. They wanted to know beyond any doubt whether the baby had Down's syndrome. If so, they wanted time to consider whether or not to permit the surgery to be done.

Within 8 hours a geneticist was able to identify cells containing 47 chromosomes in a bone-marrow sample. Over the next three days the infant's gastrointestinal tract was decompressed with a nasogastric tube, and he was supported with intravenous fluids while the parents consulted with their ministers, with family physicians in their home community, and with our geneticists. At the end of that time the B's decided not to permit surgery. The infant died three days later after withdrawal of supportive therapy.

Case 3.3

I was called to the Newborn Nursery to see Baby C, whose father was a busy surgeon with three teenage children. The diagnoses of imperforate anus and microcephalus were obvious. Doctor C called me after being informed of the situation by the pediatrician. "I'm not going to sign that op permit," he said. When I didn't reply, he said, "What would you do, doctor, if he were your baby?" "I wouldn't let him be operated on either," I replied. Palliative support only was provided, and the infant died 48 hours later.[19]

In discussing these cases Shaw indicates that the presence of mental retardation and/or severe physical malformation in an infant is an important consideration in deciding whether or not to treat neonates. While stating that he "would not allow an otherwise normal baby with a correctable anomaly to perish for lack of treatment," he does not find it obligatory to engage in life-prolonging treatment for infants with meningomyelocele and hydrocephalus—lives that will be measured by "operations, clinic visits and infections." As to infants with multiple anomalies and crippling deformities, such decisions have to be made according to the circumstances of each case:

> My ethic holds that all rights are not absolute all the time. . . . My ethic further considers quality of life as a value that must be balanced against a belief in the sanctity of life.[20]

In 1977, the same year that he and his colleagues did the national survey of pediatricians, Shaw attempted to define the quality-of-life criterion operative in his decision making about defective neonates. He presents the formula, $QL = NE \times (H + S)$; that is, quality of life equals one's natural physical and intellectual endowment times the contributions made to the individual by family/home and society.[21] Thus an anencephalic infant has no prospect for quality of life because its natural endowment is lacking, whereas an assessment of the potential quality of life of an infant with Down's syndrome depends on parents and home life as well as the child's mental and physical abilities.

In a subsequent article he builds considerations of harm into his quality-of-life formula. He asks: "What, from the *infant's* point of view, could justify letting it die? A qualitatively meaningless life? A life of vegetative, noncognitive existence, or one doomed to early extinction, or a life of constant frustration or pain?"[22] Clearly, in his judgment, some defective neonates are saved from death only to be harmed on balance through an intolerable life. By virtually any definition of "meaningful life," the result is the same: some infants are born with such serious mental and physical defects that they have little or no possibility for lives with quality or meaning.

He acknowledges that attempting to predict an infant's quality-of-life is not easy, especially in borderline cases (e.g., spina bifida, Down's syndrome) involving variable mental and physical disabilities. Nevertheless, such predictions are a necessary aspect of the decisions made jointly by physicians and parents, because

> considerations other than a basic right to life enter into decisions made in the newborn special care unit. There are infants, in my opinion, who should be allowed to die; we have no right to flex the muscles of our supertechnology and pump life into a newborn whose existence will be meaningless to himself or bring constant torment to himself and his family.[23]

John Lorber

John Lorber, in contrast to Duff, Campbell, and Shaw, does not address the issue of selective nontreatment of all birth-defective newborns. Rather, from his perspective as a pediatric surgeon in Sheffield, England, he focuses his attention on only one type of defective neonate: infants with spina bifida cystica. In his original article he indicates that after years of aggressively treating infants with spina bifida cystica, he has adopted a policy of selective nontreatment in order to spare infants with a poor prognosis unnecessary suffering. Basing his position on a study involving 524 infants, Lorber argues that it is possible to use clinical criteria to distinguish between infants whose milder forms of spina bifida cystica allow them the prospect of meaningful lives and infants whose severe forms of spina bifida doom them either to years of tragic suffering if treated in infancy or the likelihood of death in their first year of life if left untreated. From a group of prognostic clinical criteria, he indicates that four are the most valuable: (1) the degree of paralysis, (2) head circumference, (3) the presence of kyphosis or curvature of the spine, and (4) associated gross congenital anomalies. He concludes that "*it is possible to forecast* from a purely clinical assessment with accuracy *the minimum degree of future handicap* in an individual even if *it is impossible to forecast the maximum degree of disability* which he may suffer, if he survives."[24]

In a follow-up report on his selection criteria, Lorber indicates that a study of 270 infants with spina bifida cystica confirms the validity of the "adverse prognostic criteria" defined in his 1971 article. In this report he lists five clinical criteria, adding thoracolumbar lesions to the previous four. He also distinguishes between children having moderate physical handicaps and those with severe physical handicaps. Children with *moderate* physical handicaps

> are incontinent, or have an ileal loop diversion, but do not have chronic urinary tract infection or hydronephrosis; if they are able to walk without the help of calipers, though they may limp, waddle, or need surgical boots; if they have analgesia of their legs or perineum but without chronic ulceration or abscess; if they have hydrocephalus which either required no shunt therapy or hydrocephalus well controlled with a shunt.[25]

In contrast, children with *severe* physical handicaps are those with any handicap more severe than those just listed:

> incontinence with pyelonephritis or hydronephrosis, renal stones, or hypertension; paraplegia requiring calipers, crutches, or wheelchair for locomotion; kyphosis or scoliosis; repeated fractures or unreduced dislocated joints; hydrocephalus under precarious control; blindness, fits, or other less common defects.[26]

Given the technical criteria by which Lorber thinks nontreatment decisions can be made, he is convinced that the primary responsibility of deciding not to treat infants who will have severe physical handicaps lies with the physician. Parents are to be consulted, but rarely do they disagree with the physician's advice against treatment. Accordingly, he indicates that physicians typically have three major concerns when they consider withholding medical treatment from seriously defective infants: (1) the fate of the "few badly affected infants who survive in spite of absence of treatment," (2) the difficulty of having adequate criteria for selection, and (3) fear of criticism by parents, the public, and professional colleagues. Convinced that he has demonstrated adequate selection criteria and thus blunted criticism from medical colleagues, he addresses the first fear by stating that "very few truly untreated, initially severe cases survive for any length of time." He follows by saying that "no treatment" means more than merely "no operation":

> It means the provision of normal tender nursing care . . . with ordinary feeding but no more; no incubators, no oxygen, no tube feeding, and no antibiotic drugs. To deny an infant the potential benefit of an operation and then prolong life by other means is irrational. One should either offer total care or nothing operative at all. . . . An untreated infant should be protected against all pain and discomfort. An occasional initially severe case will survive; if after some months an infant's general condition is good, then he can be brought back to the group given total care.[27]

The following year he reported additional results of his policy of selective nontreatment. He indicates in the *British Medical Journal* that 25 of 37 newborn infants with spina bifida cystica were not treated during a 21-month period because, using his clinical criteria, their conditions were too severe; all died within 9 months. In contrast, only one treated infant died, and the rest are reported to be normal or only moderately handicapped. Selection for treatment is thus "the best but not a good solution to an insoluble problem."[28] One of the advantages of using the criteria for selection is that "infants are so severely affected at birth that no appreciable functional loss can result from failure to treat on the first day."

Lorber repeats his position in a commentary in *Pediatrics*. Physicians should either treat all infants with spina bifida or determine which infants not to treat by using clinical criteria (now expanded to six): "(1) gross paralysis of the legs . . . ; (2) thoracolumbar or thoracolumbosacral lesions related to vertebral levels; (3) kyphosis or scoliosis; (4) grossly enlarged head . . . ; (5) intracerebral birth injury; (6) other gross congenital defects—for example, cyanotic heart disease, ectopia of bladder, and mongolism."[29] Physicians should avoid a combination of treatment and nontreatment, and should not engage in intentional killing, because euthanasia "could be an extremely dangerous weapon in the hands of unscrupulous individuals."

He again argues that if the objective of selective nontreatment is the early, painless death of an infant, then "one must do nothing to prolong life" in a seriously defective neonate: "no antibiotic therapy for infections, no 'intensive care,' no oxygen or tube feeding and infants should be fed on demand, no more."[30] Moreover, no active treatment should be given children who *after* closure develop meningitis or ventriculitis and who already have serious neurological handicap and hydrocephalus, *or later*, if any life-threatening episode occurs in a child who is severely handicapped by gross mental and neurological defects.[31]

As to the reasons justifying this selective nontreatment of spina bifida infants and children, he appeals to the harm awaiting neonates with the most severe cases of spina bifida:

> In spite of the most energetic treatment over half of such infants died, often after years and a long succession of operations. The survivors continue with an unending succession of operations; most will remain incontinent with chronic pyelonephritis or hydronephrosis and severely paralyzed, many will develop severe kyphosis, scoliosis and lordosis, and pathological fractures, more than a few will ultimately present the sequelae of hydrocephalus, especially fits.[32]

Lorber's most straightforward appeal to nonmaleficence appears in a paper delivered to a conference on spina bifida. In that paper he repeats his clinical criteria, saying that if an infant within a few hours of birth presents "any one or any combination" of the clinical features, the outlook is "so uniformly bad" that treatment is not recommended. He then indicates his understanding of the relationship between beneficence and nonmaleficence by stating that a physician's primary duty is to do the best for the patient: "Normally, this means saving his life: but saving or prolonging life is not necessarily the best for all patients and may be actively harmful." Expanding on that statement, he states:

> If, therefore, today a surgeon is faced with a newborn baby with an extensive myelomeningocele, he should not consider this as an immediate tactical problem but should think of the life that lies ahead for the baby. If he would not like such a child of his own to survive, then he should take the logical long-term strategic view and resist the temptation to operate.[33]

John Freeman

We now turn to examine the views of four pediatricians who have serious reservations about the published positions of Duff (and Campbell), Shaw, and Lorber, even though three of them are willing to justify selective nontreatment in some circumstances. John Freeman, a pediatric neurologist at Johns Hopkins School of Medicine, was one of the first physicians to disagree publicly with Lorber's policy of selective nontreatment of infants with severe cases of spina bifida cystica. In an editorial in the *Journal of Pediatrics*, he describes the situation of the pediatric surgeon as being "between the Scylla of treating all children with meningomyeloceles with resultant increase in the number of survivors with severe handicapping conditions, and the Charybdis of not treating some children and permitting nature to take its often long, lingering course."[34] He points out that there are several gradients to "letting nature take its course":

> One could not feed the child and allow him to starve to death; one could feed, but not treat meningitis or infection if they occur; one could close the back so that the child is aesthetically more desirable and could be cared for at home, but not treat the hydrocephalus; one could close the back and shunt the hydrocephalus, but allow the child to die later of renal disease, with or without orthopedic treatment. In short, when one decides not to treat, or to treat only partially, patients survive.[35]

The lingering deaths of some untreated infants cause Freeman to disagree with Lorber on two points. First, he states that although Lorber correctly indicates that most untreated cases of spina bifida do not survive the first year, "the significant factor is that many do not die quickly, but slowly over months or years, dying of meningitis, hydrocephalus, or renal disease." Of equal importance is the fact that the surviving infants are worse off than if they had been given "early, vigorous—optimal—treatment."[36] Second, he argues that if physicians are going to engage in selective nontreatment, they should alleviate additional suffering by the infant by directly killing it:

> Having seen children with unoperated meningomyeloceles lie around the ward for weeks or months untreated, waiting to die, one cannot help but feel that the highest form of medical ethic would have been to end the pain and suffering, rather than wishing the patient would go away.[37]

Freeman retraces the same arguments in another published work. Using statistical data to support his case, he argues against Lorber that "whereas it may be true that the large majority of untreated infants do not live long, a large *minority* do live long, and at best have more neurological deficit than if treated. . . . If one, therefore, elects not to treat the child with a myelomeningocele, he must be prepared to cope with the child who survives."[38] Nevertheless, there are some *severely* affected infants with myelomeningocele. For these infants, "euthanasia might be the most humane course . . . but it is illegal." Given the moral/legal dilemma between nontreatment (legal, but not humane) and euthanasia (humane, but not legal), he says: "in an *ambivalent* fashion, I feel that *virtually* every child should be given optimal, vigorous therapy."[39]

It may be instructive to note the exceptional kind of case that Freeman would decide not to treat. Following his statement of ambivalence, he describes a case of a paraplegic child with multiple anomalies. Considerations of harm to the infant as well as considerations of the Golden Rule led him to withhold treatment.

Case 3.4

> This first child of recently married young parents was transferred to our hospital at 12 hours of age. The child had a large thoracolumbar myelomeningocele; he was also paraplegic with a motor level at L-1 and a sensory level at T-8. There was obvious marked hydrocephalus with 0.5 cm of cortical mantle by echoencephalogram. There was also severe kyphoscoliosis (backward and lateral curvature of the spine).
>
> In view of the ominous prognosis of the severe hydrocephalus, the paraplegia, and the severe spinal anomaly, which would have led to even further progressive scoliosis, respiratory and cardiac impairment, and would have impaired even a sitting existence, the decision was made not to treat the child. The fact that the family was young and capable of having more children, despite the known increased risks, also entered into the decision.
>
> The child was fed and given ordinary care and succumbed to meningitis at three weeks of age. Had this child continued to survive, he would have been shunted, the back closed, and vigorous, total care been reluctantly instituted.[40]

Even though opting for nontreatment in this particular case, Freeman's comment about being ready to institute vigorous treatment if the child had lived illustrates the moral dilemma he believes pediatricians and pediatric surgeons occasionally confront. Believing that "a slow, natural death over weeks or months is not humane for the child, the family, or the staff forced to care for the infant," he finds himself sometimes "in the schizophrenic position of advocating either active euthanasia or vigorous treatment."[41] Another case illustrates his concern over the fate of severely defective infants who are left untreated, cannot legally be killed, and yet linger among the living. For him, the case represents "the worst possible outcome" of untreated cases of spina bifida cystica.

Case 3.5

An eight-year-old boy was recently brought to the Birth Defects Treatment Center for recommendations about future care. He was the third child of middle-class parents and was born and treated elsewhere. At birth he was found to have a large meningomyelocele with a neurologic deficit below T-12. The parents were told that he would die. He was given routine care, did not develop meningitis, and remained at the local hospital until five and a half months of age when he was transferred to a state institution for chronic care. At ten months of age, because of progressive enlargement of the head which made nursing care difficult, he was transferred to another hospital where a ventriculoatrial shunt was placed, and the back was repaired. The child was returned to the state institution.

By two and a half years he was using two-word sentences, but was found to have cortical blindness. Over the next several years he had multiple orthopedic procedures, including replacement of dislocated hips, achilles tendon lengthening, osteotomies, and repair of fractures. He was always returned to the institution. At six years of age he was found to have severe hydronephrosis (a urine-enlarged kidney, due to obstruction of the ureter), and an ileal loop was performed.

At eight years of age he is in a school for the blind and has an I.Q. of 80. He goes home to his parents on weekends, but they have established little rapport with him. It is difficult for him to sit because of the marked paralytic kyphosis, which also interferes with the ileal stoma so that a collecting device cannot be kept in place. . . . His hips have redislocated; the hydronephrosis is of moderate degree. The family is receiving psychiatric help to cope with this child when he is home. The child needs a spinal fusion to allow him to sit without obstructing his loop and revision of the ileal stoma to permit adequate drainage.[42]

Freeman has addressed the issue of selective nontreatment of infants with spina bifida in two subsequent articles. In one article, coauthored with Michael Hemphill, he argues that the complexity of treatment/

nontreatment decisions means that the physician should bear the responsibility for the decision. In rare instances the physician, acting as "the child's advocate," may opt not to use all the available resources to sustain the infant's life—even though the legal implications of such a decision are unclear. Regarding the legal implications, Freeman asks, "Could a child with a major defect who *has* been treated bring . . . a suit for 'wrongful life,' claiming that he should have been allowed to die?"[43] In the second article, coauthored with Kenneth Shulman and William Reinke, he suggests that treatment/nontreatment decisions can be made on the basis of a statistical risk–benefit analysis. Any physician using such an analysis will, they think, end up disagreeing with Lorber's position:

> The authors find the disability of a prolonged wait for death to be high and find greater utility in those who are treated early. They therefore recommend early surgery for most infants with spina bifida.[44]

R. B. Zachary

Another physician who has reservations about the selective nontreatment of infants with spina bifida cystica is R. B. Zachary, a pediatric surgeon and medical colleague of Lorber at Sheffield, England. In fact, his first article on the subject antedated Lorber's now-famous report of his selection policy. According to Zachary, there are three basic options with a spina bifida infant: "(1) he should be killed; (2) he should be encouraged to die, either by giving no treatment at all (e.g., no feeding) or by not treating complications (e.g., no treatment of infection by antibiotics); or (3) he should be encouraged to live."[45] Given these options, Zachary argues that fairness to children born with spina bifida means that they should not be killed, they should usually be given medical treatment to reduce their handicaps, and they should be the recipients of family and community efforts to improve their well-being and happiness. The great majority of these infants should be encouraged to live rather than be encouraged to die. To that end, most spina bifida infants should be given all of the treatments and procedures that comprise ordinary medical care of neonates. To do anything less is wrong:

> To leave a child without food is to kill it as deliberately and directly as if one was cutting its throat. Even the prescribing of antibiotics for infection, such as pneumonia, must now be considered as ordinary care of patients.[46]

One ordinary feature of medical care for most infants with spina bifida is surgery, yet Zachary points out that there is no necessary connection between early surgical treatment and an infant's survival. In spite of "a widely held but mistaken view" to the contrary, he says that the purpose of early operation on an infant with spina bifida is not to save the child's life: "Quite a number of patients with myelomeningocele survive without any operation at all on the back, and some die as a direct result of operation when otherwise they might have survived."[47] Surgery undoubtedly increases the chances of survival for most of these infants, but the fundamental reason for early surgery is the reduction of handicap so that the child may later have as nearly normal life as possible.

Almost a decade later, Zachary entered the public debate over selective nontreatment brought about by the published views of Lorber, Duff, Campbell, and Shaw. In an article published in the *British Medical Journal* in 1976, he distinguishes between two categories of congenital anomalies: those that are in themselves lethal apart from surgery, and those that are not in themselves lethal. As examples of lethal congenital anomalies, he mentions intestinal obstruction, meconium ileus (intestinal obstruction due to gelatinous secretions of intestinal glands), and duodenal atresia associated with Down's syndrome. In instances of the latter case, he comments: "My personal advice to the parents would be to permit operation, but if they do not give consent I would be careful to avoid any comment that would leave them with a longstanding feeling of guilt."[48]

Although he generally advises surgery in cases that are lethal without surgical intervention, he acknowledges that there are exceptions. Occasionally infants are not surgically treated in his ward because an assessment of all circumstances indicates that surgery is not justified. Although "the final decision rests with the parents," he sometimes advises against life-prolonging surgery. For example, in contrast to his recommendation of surgery in cases of infants with duodenal atresia and Down's syndrome, he did not recommend surgery in the following case.

Case 3.6

A baby was admitted with esophageal obstruction which would certainly result in death without operation. The child also had microcephaly, enophthalmos with probably no vision, absent right arm, imperforate anus, and probably kidney anomalies. I did not advise operation on this baby and the baby died within two or three days.[49]

Spina bifida cystica is an example of a congenital anomaly that in itself is not lethal but involves progressive disabilities without surgery. Zachary places such infants in one of three categories. First, there are the infants who are likely to die in a few days, perhaps as a result of congenital heart disease; he does not operate on these infants "because operation would have no bearing at all on whether they lived or died." Second, there are infants who are not dying but present back wounds unsuitable for surgery, perhaps because of the width of the wound or the presence of a severe kyphosis; no surgery is performed in these cases because "the resulting infection would be far worse than if no operation were done at all." Third, there are infants who are unlikely to die in a few days and present a wound suitable for operation; here Zachary advises immediate surgery for less severe cases (where there is some indication of muscle power in the legs) and surgery within 48 hours for the severe cases already having paralysis. As for his reasons for advising surgery in these cases, he argues that extreme disability need not result in unhappiness (see his statement at this chapter's beginning). Moreover, his basic philosophy calls for the surgical treatment of these spina bifida infants:

> I believe that our patients, no matter how young or small they are, should receive the same consideration and expert help that would be considered normal in an adult. Just because he is small and because he cannot speak for himself this is no excuse for regarding him as expendable, any more than we would do so on account of race or creed or color or poverty.[50]

In a subsequent article Zachary repeats his threefold selection criteria and argues against Lorber's position in several ways. He emphasizes that nontreatment is not synonymous with allowing infants to die—for the obvious reason that some untreated infants continue to live reasonably long periods of time. In fact, he has "seen many children with severe lesions that epithelialized spontaneously, who then had the operation to close the back wound at about 18 months."[51] As a consequence, he is convinced that pediatricians claiming a high mortality rate (often 100%) for untreated cases of spina bifida not only withhold treatment from these infants, but also "push the infants towards death" through a method of management involving excessively high dosages of sedative:

eight times the sedative dose of chloral hydrate recommended in the most recent volume of *Nelson's Pediatrics* and four times the hypnotic dose, and it is being administered four times every day. No wonder these babies are sleepy and demand no feed, and with this regimen most of them will die within a few weeks, many within the first week.[52]

He is also convinced that many pediatricians engaging in selective nontreatment of spina bifida infants are unduly pessimistic about the future awaiting such infants. Whereas older children with spina bifida are frequently depicted as living completely miserable and unhappy lives, he often finds them "happy people who can respond to concern for their personal welfare." Typical 10-year-old children with spina bifida spend most of their time in wheelchairs, but make some progress in long calipers (metal leg braces); they have hydrocephalus, but it is controlled with a valve; they have an I.Q. below the mean, but within the normal range and thus can make some intellectual advancement if their hydrocephalus was treated early and if they are given intellectual stimulation.[53] To support his view, he indicates that a 10-year review of 200 cases involving surgical closure of the neural tube opening reveals that 56% of the cases had what he calls a "reasonable result." He then comments: "Were a similar 200 cases to be treated aggressively at the present time, there would be a larger number of survivors because of improved management of infections in the first 3 months of life."[54]

Thus he disagrees with Lorber regarding the application of the principle of nonmaleficence to cases of spina bifida. In Zachary's view, infants with treatable spina bifida who receive aggressive treatment early cannot reasonably be said to have been harmed by that treatment. It is primarily the infants in Zachary's second treatment category (those whose wounds are unsuitable for surgery) who would be harmed by surgical intervention. On one major point, however, he agrees with Lorber. Having treated some infants whom other physicians had tried directly but unsuccessfully to kill with chloral hydrate, phenobarbitone, and/or morphine, he declares that "under no circumstances would I administer drugs to cause the death of the child."[55]

It is obvious that Zachary recommends surgical treatment for some infants who would be left untreated by Duff, Shaw, and Lorber. Yet he acknowledges recommending that surgery not be performed in occasional cases involving lethal conditions and in other cases involving nonlethal conditions. His primary reason for advising against surgery in these instances is his judgment that the surgery would not prove beneficial, either because of a neonate's multiple anomalies (as in case 3.6) or because of the size of a spina bifida lesion. A secondary reason for nontreatment in some of these cases is his judgment that surgery can in extreme cases prove harmful to the infant receiving it: "There are exceptional instances where the residual handicap will clearly be so severe that life would indeed become an intolerable burden—*to the child* who is the patient."[56]

Norman Fost

Norman Fost, a pediatrician at the University of Wisconsin School of Medicine, adds another perspective to the issue of selective nontreatment. He has paid more attention to the legal ramifications of selective nontreatment than the physicians previously discussed, having in 1976 co-authored a law article on the subject with John Robertson.[57] They point out that parents and physicians who engage in selective nontreatment of defective neonates are potentially liable for several crimes, including murder, manslaughter, child abuse, neglect, and conspiracy. They suggest that in the light of the potential legal liabilities, two changes need to be made in selective nontreatment decisions to minimize the possibility of abuses and mistakes: a clear set of criteria by which such decisions are made and a procedural mechanism whereby an individual or group other than the physician and parents make the decision regarding nontreatment.

In a subsequent article dealing with spina bifida infants, Fost indicates that he has several differences with Duff and Lorber. Contrary to Lorber's position, he points out that some untreated infants with spina bifida (perhaps less than 10%) have prolonged survival. Although the total number of such infants is not great, it nevertheless means that, as Freeman has already pointed out, there are some infants who may survive with more intellectual impairment than would have been the case had vigorous treatment been given early in their lives. And if among treated infants suffering is the greatest among those with the highest intelligence, as Lorber has suggested, then Fost argues:

> If this were true, and if one purpose of selection is to prevent the survival of those who will suffer the greatest anguish, then a selection policy would withhold treatment from those whose prognosis for intelligence is best.[58]

Contrary to Lorber and Duff, Fost has reservations about how much harm comes to infants who will go through life with spina bifida. There is a danger of physicians projecting their own healthy, elitist views about life and suffering on persons who will have serious, but not intolerable disabilities:

> The author would certainly not *choose* to spend his life in a wheelchair, or with an ileal loop, but that does not mean that an infant or child, who never knew another life, need necessarily be psychologically overwhelmed by the experience.[59]

In a manner similar to Zachary, Fost argues that some infants with spina bifida will not be as handicapped in the future as some physicians suggest in the literature. Many of them will be confined to wheelchairs, but the degree to which that is a serious handicap depends in part on external factors unrelated to the congenital defects they will have:

> If buildings had ramps; if colleges would not exclude them from dormitories on the grounds that they are fire hazards; and if airlines would not require them to be accompanied by adult companions, many such individuals would not see themselves as significantly handicapped.[60]

Another point of difference with Duff and Lorber is where one draws the line between infants who should be treated and those who should be denied treatment. In response to Duff's acknowledgment of having not treated an infant with Down's syndrome and intestinal atresia, Fost says: "I do not understand what is hopeless about intestinal atresia, and I do not understand what is hopeless about Down's syndrome."[61] At one point he asks about consistency in line-drawing, and extends the question beyond the NICU: "May the hematologist decide which malignancies he will offer therapy for and which not on the grounds of his own social preferences?" Fost agrees that infants with anencephaly or trisomy 18 need not be treated, but contrary to Duff, he argues that infants with Down's syndrome or spina bifida cystica should be treated because the mental retardation and/or physical handicap involved in these conditions do not constitute sufficient harm to justify withholding treatment. He says that Duff's policy

> rests on the assumption that retardation constitutes a sufficient reason for giving validity to parental actions which would be clearly objectionable if applied to a normal child. While such a policy might be defended for

those children so impaired that it is difficult to agree that they have any interests (such as an anencephalic), its rationale is less clear when applied to children who have an excellent chance for a happy, fulfilling life (such as Down syndrome).[62]

Still another disagreement between himself and Duff, as Fost sees it, is the procedural question regarding the extent to which physicians (or courts) may justifiably intrude into parental discretion in life-and-death decisions about their children. Whereas Duff is reluctant to override the wishes of parents, Fost believes that physicians must sometimes intervene when there is a child "whose prospects for a happy life are blocked only by a parental wish or preference that the child die."[63]

As he compares his views with those of other physicians addressing the issue of selective nontreatment, Fost finds himself attempting to establish "an ethically acceptable middle ground." On the one hand, he disagrees with Duff and Lorber because he believes they fail to treat some infants who should be treated. On the other hand, he does not find it "feasible to declare that all human life is sacred and therefore warrants being preserved forever."[64] Given the complexity of the life-and-death decisions involving neonates with congenital defects, he argues:

> Neither a pro-life policy of treating all infants maximally, or a permissive policy of allowing all parents to decide can be defended. The former position leads to the *reductio ad absurdum* of trying to keep everyone alive forever. The latter gives rise to empiric abuses such as starvation of infants with good prospects for happiness and self-sufficiency, as well as the conceptual difficulty of claiming that parental authority over children includes the right to engineer their death if the child's existence threatens parental happiness.[65]

In attempting to carve out a middle ground between these two views, he rejects two recurring arguments for selective nontreatment. Proceeding on the assumption that "a person should not be deprived of life without good reason," he argues that neither an appeal to society's economic interests (withhold treatment when it is not cost effective) nor an appeal to parental desires or wishes (withhold treatment when parents do not want a defective child) is sufficient to justify a decision not to treat an infant. Rather, "the only compelling reason for letting a child die is when there are reasonable grounds for concluding that it is in the child's best interests to die."[66]

Everett Koop

C. Everett Koop, who was the surgeon-in-chief at the Children's Hospital of Philadelphia before becoming Surgeon General of the United States, disagrees with Fost and all the other physicians discussed thus far. Believing in "the sanctity of all life, born or unborn," he thinks that the majority of pediatricians and pediatric surgeons are "sanctioning infanticide" when they withhold medical treatment from neonates with congenital abnormalities. He believes the infanticide rate is on the increase and thinks that many acts of infanticide are "being practiced by that very segment of our profession which has always stood in the role of advocate for the lives of children."[67]

Duff and Campbell are singled out as the leading representatives of a medical speciality that too frequently fails to treat infants who should be given medical treatment. For them, Koop is an example of what they call "an unbridled aggressive approach" to neonatal medicine that treats all seriously defective infants regardless of patient suffering. For him, they are the most obvious examples of neonatologists who sometimes choose death rather than life for young patients who could live if treated, even though the children would be abnormal in some ways.

Koop believes that Duff, Campbell, and all other physicians who engage in selective nontreatment of infants are wrong on several counts. First, they occasionally interpret lesions as being lethal when they are actually subject to surgical correction. Following surgical intervention, infants having such lesions "may not be pristine in their final form," but "they are functional human beings, loved and loving and productive." Koop continues by saying:

> If indeed we decide that a child with a chronic cardiopulmonary disease or a short bowel syndrome or various manifestations of brain damage should be permitted to die by lack of feeding, what is to prevent the next step which takes the adult with chronic cardiopulmonary disease who may be much more of a burden to his family than that child is, or the individual who may not have a short bowel syndrome but who has ulcerative colitis and in addition to his physical manifestations has many psychiatric problems as well or the individual who has brain damage—do we kill all people with neurological deficit after an automotive accident?[68]

Second, Koop thinks that physicians who engage in selective nontreatment of infants often do so primarily to prevent parents from having burdens they do not want to bear. For example, he points out that Duff and Campbell support parental autonomy when parents are unable to bear such deficiencies in their infants as "chronic dyspnea, oxygen dependence, incontinence, paralysis, contractures, sexual handicaps, and mental retardation." Arguing that such problems do not provide parents sufficient reason for terminating a child's life, Koop asks "why not let the family find that deeper meaning of life by providing the love and the attention necessary to take care of an infant that has been given to them?"[69] Third, he argues that Duff and Campbell are engaged in discrimination against abnormal infants. When an infant dies who could have lived if given medical treatment, and when factors in justifying the nontreatment include such matters as the family's socioeconomic status or the stability of the marriage, it is "clear that there has been introduced a discrimination just as deplorable as those of race, creed, or color."[70]

As to his own approach to infants with serious congenital anomalies, Koop chooses to treat all of them who do not have terminal conditions. Acknowledging that "I have many times withheld extraordinary measures from the care of my patients who were terminal regardless of their age," he states that he has never withheld "something as ordinary as feeding" that would keep a patient alive and has certainly never engaged in an action that would intentionally kill a patient.[71] He treats all the infants he can, because death is not an acceptable alternative and because "each newborn infant, perfect or deformed, is a human being with unique preciousness because he or she was created in the image of God."[72] Moreover, he argues that aggressive treatment meets the requirements of beneficence: no family or adult child has come back to him years later to complain about surgical treatment given during infancy, and most families have found rearing an abnormal child to be a positive experience.

Three points highlight Koop's differences with the physicians discussed earlier. When he reflects on his 35 years of pediatric surgical experience, he says that one of the warmest rewards he has had is the case of an infant with multiple congenital defects who went through 37 operations (Koop performed 22 of them). Years later, he asked the mother of the boy about the worst thing and the best thing that had happened to her over the years. Her response to each question was to say, "having our son born with all those defects that required 37 operations to correct."[73]

When he considers the lives ahead of handicapped infants who receive medical treatment, he is even more optimistic than Zachary. On the basis of interviews with former neonatal patients and their parents, he is convinced that "disability and unhappiness do not go hand in hand." In contrast to many normal but unhappy children he encounters, he finds that "there is remarkable joy and happiness in the lives of most handicapped children"—many of whom have handicaps that he personally would find difficult to endure.[74]

When he looks to the future of neonatal medicine, he argues that many neonatologists and other pediatricians simply do not ask the appropriate question when confronted with birth-defective neonates. The appropriate question to ask is not, "Should we treat?" but rather, "How should we treat?"[75] To aid in the asking and answering of this question, he envisions setting up a national computer service that will facilitate aggressive treatment of all nondying infants:

> I would like . . . to investigate the possibility of making available to physicians and parents, for every congenital lesion and syndrome, a comprehensive computerized service which could inform them of the most competent diagnostic service closest to their home, the closest competent therapeutic service, a list of all the available governmental and private agencies which could help parents and children and finally, a readout of parents with similar situations who have managed the problem successfully. If we could make this service available to parents and physicians alike, I think we would remove the terrible fear that the odds are too great against the handicapped child and his family to make any effort worthwhile, and to slay forever the myth that only perfect quality of life is life worth living."[76]

Issues in the current debate

Now, by way of summary of these pediatric views, what can be said regarding these seven positions in the debate among pediatricians and pediatric surgeons about selective nontreatment? In the midst of their public disagreements, about what do they agree on the subject of selective nontreatment? In terms of procedural matters, who do they think should make these decisions about life and death? On the substantive level, where do they draw the line between anomalous newborns who should be treated and those who should be denied treatment? What do they give as the justifying reason or reasons for selective nontreatment? What is their understanding of nonmaleficence, and how does it influence their decision making? And once the decision has been made not to treat certain infants, what do they say about the means used to bring about the death of those untreated?

Six of the pediatricians surveyed are in agreement that some selective nontreatment of defective neonates is necessary. Zachary, Fost, and Freeman are reluctant to make decisions about selective nontreatment, but they nevertheless agree with Duff, Shaw, and Lorber that the congenital anomalies of some infants are so severe that they preclude beneficial medical treatment. Koop obviously disagrees.

All of the pediatricians are in agreement regarding the consequences of nontreatment. For infants having lethal congenital anomalies, the decision to withhold surgery results in the deaths of the infants. For infants whose congenital anomalies are not in themselves lethal, the decision to withhold surgery and other medical treatment leads to an early death for most but not all of them. As Freeman and Zachary point out, a small minority of untreated defective neonates tends to survive as long as ordinary feeding is maintained, and represents an emotionally straining example of progressive handicap in the neonatal unit because their conditions are much worse than they would have been had they received early treatment.

Agreement ceases when the physicians address the procedural question. Deciding who should bear the responsibility of nontreatment decisions is complicated by several factors: the high stakes involved in the decision, the difficulty of making accurate predictions about a child's future handicap, the emotional instability of many parents in the neonatal unit, general uncertainty about the law, differing commitments by parents to care for handicapped children, and frequent disagreements between parents and physicians about whether and when to withhold treatment. Given this complexity in the decision-making process, the physicians are divided in their views as to who should make the decision. Duff, Campbell, Shaw, and Zachary go with parental autonomy in these decisions, even to the point of trying to assuage parental guilt and refraining from seeking a court order to override the decisions of parents with whom they disagree. In contrast, Lorber, Freeman, Fost, and Koop believe that the physician is better prepared to make the treatment/nontreatment decision. Lorber thinks the physician is the only person qualified to understand the technical criteria according to which the decision should be made, whereas Freeman emphasizes the physician's objectivity as the patient's advocate (compared to the parents' emotional involvement). Fost appeals to the physician's greater knowledge of the probable future of specific congenital anomalies and argues that the physician has an obligation (in the context of medical paternalism) to overrule "clearly unacceptable" parental decisions that threaten an infant's best interests. Because some physicians cannot or will not override parental wishes, Fost at one point suggests that an objective third party (e.g., another physician, a judge, a hospital committee) may be needed to cut down on abuses and mistakes.

Regarding substantive issues, Duff, Campbell, and Shaw think that decisions about selective nontreatment are largely contextual. Shaw is particularly vague about which defective neonates should be treated and which need not be treated. Duff and Campbell, because of the emphasis they place on parental autonomy, indicate that decisions have to be made "instance by instance." Nevertheless they (especially Duff) do indicate several medical conditions that call for nontreatment: anencephaly, hydranencephaly, extreme forms of hydrocephalus accompanied by other anomalies, trisomy 13 and trisomy 18, fully documented cases of severe brain damage or progressive brain disease, terminal cases of intracranial cancer, and "miscellaneous conditions" with a bleak or hopeless prognosis. Additionally, there are borderline cases that are decided on contextually: spina bifida cystica, Down's syndrome with complications, severe prematurity, and cases involving multiple congenital anomalies.

Lorber, Freeman, Zachary, Fost, and Koop do not discuss this range of cases. Rather, Lorber discusses only cases of spina bifida and draws the line for treatment or nontreatment using his five to six "adverse prognostic criteria." Freeman thinks that, given the current status of the law on euthanasia, virtually every infant with spina bifida should be treated. Zachary thinks the line for selective nontreatment of infants with spina bifida should be drawn to exclude from treatment only those who are dying or whose wounds are untreatable; as to other defective neonates, he treats infants with intestinal obstructions or Down's syndrome accompanied by duodenal atresia, but chooses not to treat infants with surgical problems accompanied by multiple gross anomalies. Fost treats infants with Down's syndrome or spina bifida, but follows a policy of nontreatment for infants with anencephaly or trisomy 18; he does not discuss other medical conditions. Koop offers surgical treatment to all infants who do not have terminal conditions.

There are several reasons for selective nontreatment mentioned in the published works of most of these physicians. Zachary, and presumably the other physicians as well, sometimes engages in selective nontreatment for either of two simple reasons: the infants are irretrievably dying or have a medical condition that would not respond to current medical treatments. On a few occasions he and Lorber seem to justify their decisions by using the distinction between ordinary and extraordinary means of prolonging a patient's life, although it is clear that they have serious disagreements as to what medical procedures count as "ordinary means" even after a nontreatment decision has been made. Zachary, for instance, thinks that untreated spina bifida infants should be given antibiotics to combat infection; Lorber argues that a decision not to operate on a spina bifida infant entails leaving the child without antibiotics as well. Koop also finds the ordinary/extraordinary distinction useful. Fost, in contrast, finds the distinction hopelessly vague and believes the reference point should be changed to the patient (an "extraordinary patient") rather than to the medical means used to prolong life.

Other reasons are also involved in nontreatment decisions. For Duff, Campbell, and Shaw, parental refusal to consent to surgery or other medical treatments is often a sufficient reason for nontreatment. They, along with Lorber and Freeman, also try to project an infant's probable quality of life in deciding to treat or withhold treatment. Shaw is the most explicit about using quality-of-life judgments in nontreatment decisions, although Duff and Lorber also project quite negative futures for many infants with severe congenital anomalies. In contrast, Zachary and Fost suggest that such negative quality-of-life projections can often be tempered by means of early medical treatment and ongoing efforts by society to minimize the suffering inflicted on handicapped persons through external physical constraints.

Considerations of suffering, especially the suffering that will accompany treatment and that may only be prolonged through treatment, are a crucial part of nontreatment decisions. All of the physicians surveyed (except Koop) agree that there are instances in which medical treatment for defective neonates is itself harmful (in producing iatrogenic conditions) or does harm to the neonates by prolonging what will be an intolerable existence. Of course most medical treatment inflicts harm as well as benefit on the patient, but these physicians are convinced that a detriment–benefit analysis of treatment options for severely defective newborns occasionally indicates that such infants will be harmed on balance if treated. Duff, Shaw, Freeman, and Zachary specifically indicate that medical treatment can "brutalize" an infant, inflict "cruelty" on an infant, or place an infant in a medical condition that is worse than if treatment had been withheld.

In their appeals to the principle of nonmaleficence, however, these physicians are not in agreement on what "harm" means or on what the principle of nonmaleficence requires. Duff and Campbell regard harm to newborns almost exclusively in terms of neurological deficiency. Lorber, in contrast, judges harm in terms of physical impairment and the inability of a child to achieve a minimal quality of life. Shaw, Freeman, and Zachary all interpret harm in the context of neonatal medicine as involving the pointless prolongation of lives characterized by multiple severe (and largely untreatable) anomalies. Fost suggests that harm can also be understood as a condition of prolonged institutionalization in the absence of caring parents.

As to the principle of nonmaleficence, Duff, Shaw, Lorber, and Freeman think that "doing no harm" has quality-of-life implications: do not prolong the lives of neonates who lack the prospect of a minimally acceptable quality of life. Zachary and Fost think that "doing no harm" involves detriment–benefit considerations in the context of life-and-death decisions: do not prolong the lives of newborns whose overwhelming mental and physical handicaps make death, not torturous existence, in their best interests. By contrast, Koop has another perspective on "doing no harm": do not allow any nondying infants to die, because to do so would be to subject them to death as the ultimate form of harm.

What is to be done with untreated infants who remain alive for months or, in rare instances, years? As the physicians write about cases they have encountered, they raise questions about the problematic nature of partial treatment and comment about intentional killing as a means of hastening the deaths of these untreated children. Duff, Campbell, and Freeman clearly indicate that they think direct killing of untreated infants should be a legal option, and Freeman in particular suggests that if neonatal euthanasia were legal he would kill some defective neonates he now ambivalently treats and, he thinks, harms through treatment. In contrast, Lorber, Zachary, Fost, and Koop do not think the law should be changed. Lorber refers to the harm that would follow if "unscrupulous" physicians had the legal right to kill, and Zachary and Fost suggest that they find significance in the moral distinction between killing and allowing to die. For them, allowing some defective infants to die as a consequence of selective nontreatment is sometimes a regrettable moral option; the intentional killing of infants, in contrast, is never an option for them.

Notes

1. Anthony Shaw, "Who Should Die and Who Should Decide?" in Marvin Kohl, ed., *Infanticide and the Value of Life* (Buffalo, N.Y.: Prometheus Books, 1978), p. 105.
2. R. B. Zachary, "The Neonatal Surgeon," *British Medical Journal* 2 (1976): 869.

3. John Lorber, "Results of Treatment of Myelomeningocele: An Analysis of 524 Unselected Cases, with Special Reference to Possible Selection for Treatment," *Developmental Medicine and Child Neurology* 13 (1971): 279–303.

4. Anthony Shaw, "Dilemmas of 'Informed Consent' in Children," *The New England Journal of Medicine* 289 (October 25, 1973): 885–90; and Raymond S. Duff and A. G. M. Campbell, "Moral and Ethical Dilemmas in the Special-Care Nursery," *The New England Journal of Medicine* 289 (October 25, 1973): 890–94.

5. David Todres et al., "Pediatricians' Attitudes Affecting Decision-Making in Defective Newborns," *Pediatrics* 60 (1977): 197–201.

6. "Treating the Defective Newborn: A Survey of Physicians' Attitudes," *Hastings Center Report* 6 (April 1976): 2.

7. Anthony Shaw, Judson G. Randolph, and Barbara Manard, "Ethical Issues in Pediatric Surgery: A National Survey of Pediatricians and Pediatric Surgeons," *Pediatrics* 60 (October 1977): 588–99.

8. Duff and Campbell, "Moral and Ethical Dilemmas in the Special-Care Nursery," pp. 890–94. For a follow-up to this article, see Raymond S. Duff and A. G. M. Campbell, "Moral and Ethical Dilemmas: Seven Years into the Debate about Human Ambiguity," *Annals of the American Academy of Political and Social Science* 447 (January 1980): 19–28.

9. Raymond S. Duff and A. G. M. Campbell, "On Deciding the Care of Severely Handicapped or Dying Persons: With Particular Reference to Infants," *Pediatrics* 57 (April 1976): 489.

10. Ibid., p. 492.

11. Raymond S. Duff, "A Physician's Role in the Decision-Making Process: A Physician's Experience," in Chester A. Swinyard, ed., *Decision Making and the Defective Newborn* (Springfield, Ill.: Charles C Thomas, 1978), pp. 194–219.

12. This case is adapted from Raymond S. Duff, "Deciding the Care of Defective Infants," in Kohl, *Infanticide and the Value of Life*, pp. 97–98.

13. Ibid., p. 97.

14. A. G. M. Campbell and Raymond S. Duff, "Deciding the Care of Severely Malformed or Dying Infants," *Journal of Medical Ethics* 5 (1979): 67.

15. A. G. M. Campbell and Raymond S. Duff, "Authors' Response to Richard Sherlock's Commentary," *Journal of Medical Ethics* 6 (1979): 141.

16. Ibid.

17. Raymond S. Duff, "Counseling Families and Deciding Care of Severely Defective Children: A Way of Coping with 'Medical Vietnam,'" *Pediatrics* 67 (March 1981): 315.

18. Ibid., p. 316.

19. These cases are quoted by permission from Shaw, "Dilemmas of 'Informed Consent' in Children," pp. 885–86.

20. Ibid., p. 889.

21. Anthony Shaw, "Defining the Quality of Life," *Hastings Center Report* 7 (October 1977): 11.

22. Shaw, "Who Should Die and Who Should Decide?" p. 104.

23. Anthony Shaw, "Conditions in Newborns that Pose Special Problems," *Contemporary Surgery* 11 (October 1977): 51.

24. Lorber, "Results of Treatment of Myelomeningocele," p. 300.
25. John Lorber, "Spina Bifida Cystica: Results of Treatment of 270 Consecutive Cases with Criteria for Selection for the Future," *Archives of Disease in Childhood* 47 (1972): 856.
26. Ibid.
27. Ibid., p. 871.
28. John Lorber, "Early Results of Selective Treatment of Spina Bifida Cystica," *British Medical Journal* 4 (1973): 201.
29. John Lorber, "Selective Treatment of Myelomeningocele: To Treat or Not to Treat," *Pediatrics* 53 (March 1974): 307.
30. Ibid., p. 308; see also idem, "The Doctor's Duty to Patients and Parents in Profoundly Handicapping Conditions," in David J. Roy, ed., *Medical Wisdom and Ethics in the Treatment of Severely Defective Newborn and Young Children* (Montreal: Eden Press, 1978), pp. 9–23.
31. Lorber, "Selective Treatment of Myelomeningocele," p. 307.
32. Ibid.
33. John Lorber, "Ethical Concepts in the Treatment of Myelomeningocele," in Swinyard, *Decision Making and the Defective Newborn*, p. 66.
34. John M. Freeman, "Is There a Right to Die—Quickly?" *Journal of Pediatrics* 80 (1972): 904.
35. Ibid.
36. Ibid.
37. Ibid., p. 905.
38. John M. Freeman, "To Treat or Not to Treat: Ethical Dilemmas of Treating the Infant with a Myelomeningocele," *Clinical Neurosurgery* 20 (1973): 137.
39. Ibid., p. 143.
40. Ibid., p. 145. The case is reprinted by permission.
41. John M. Freeman, ed., *Practical Management of Meningomyelocele* (Baltimore: University Park Press, 1974), p. 21.
42. This case is reprinted by permission from John M. Freeman, "The Shortsighted Treatment of Meningomyelocele," *Pediatrics* 53 (1974): 311–13.
43. Michael Hemphill and John M. Freeman, "Ethical Aspects of Care of the Newborn with Serious Neurological Disease," *Clinics in Perinatology* 4 (March 1977): 208.
44. John M. Freeman, Kenneth Shulman, and William Reinke, "Decision Making and the Infant with Spina Bifida," in Swinyard, *Decision Making and the Defective Newborn*, p. 110.
45. R. B. Zachary, "Ethical and Social Aspects of Treatment of Spina Bifida," *The Lancet* 2 (1968): 274.
46. Ibid.
47. Ibid.
48. Zachary, "The Neonatal Surgeon," p. 869.
49. Ibid. The case is reprinted by permission.
50. Ibid.
51. R. B. Zachary, "Life with Spina Bifida," *British Medical Journal* 2 (1977): 1461.
52. Ibid.
53. Ibid., p. 1460.

54. James Lister, R. B. Zachary, and R. Brereton, "Open Myelomeningocele—A Ten-Year Review of 200 Consecutive Closures," in *Progress in Pediatric Surgery* 10 (Baltimore-Munich: Urban & Schwarzenberg, 1977), p. 175.

55. Zachary, "Life with Spina Bifida," p. 1462.

56. R. B. Zachary, "To Save or Let Die," *The Tablet* 232 (February 1978): 175.

57. John A. Robertson and Norman Fost, "Passive Euthanasia of Defective Newborn Infants: Legal Considerations," *Journal of Pediatrics* 88 (1976): 883–89.

58. Norman Fost, "How Decisions Are Made: A Physician's View," in Swinyard, *Decision Making and the Defective Newborn*, p. 224.

59. Ibid.

60. Ibid.

61. Ibid., p. 247.

62. Norman Fost, "Counseling Families Who Have a Child with a Severe Congenital Anomaly," *Pediatrics* 67 (March 1981): 324.

63. Ibid.

64. Norman Fost, "Ethical Issues in the Treatment of Critically Ill Newborns," *Pediatric Annals* 10 (October 1981): 16.

65. Norman Fost, "Proxy Consent for Seriously Ill Newborns," in David H. Smith, ed., *No Rush to Judgment: Essays on Medical Ethics* (Bloomington, Ind.: The Poynter Center, 1978), p. 16.

66. Fost, "Ethical Issues in the Treatment of Critically Ill Newborns," p. 21. Fost presents the same conclusion in a discussion of selective nontreatment in "Ethical Problems in Pediatrics," *Current Problems in Pediatrics* 6 (October 1976): 13–17.

67. C. Everett Koop, "The Slide to Auschwitz," *Human Life Review* 3 (Spring 1977): 103; see also idem, "The Sanctity of Life," *Journal of the Medical Society of New Jersey* 75 (January 1978): 62–69.

68. Koop, "The Slide to Auschwitz," p. 107.

69. Ibid. Koop's views on a surgeon's responsibility to the parents of neonatal surgical patients are presented in idem, "The Seriously Ill or Dying Child: Supporting the Patient and the Family," in Dennis J. Horan and David Mall, eds., *Death, Dying, and Euthanasia* (Washington, D.C.: University Publications of America, 1977), pp. 537–39.

70. Koop, "The Slide to Auschwitz," p. 108.

71. Ibid., p. 113.

72. C. Everett Koop, "The Handicapped Child and His Family," *The Linacre Quarterly* 48 (February 1981): 23.

73. Ibid., pp. 28–29.

74. C. Everett Koop, "Ethical and Surgical Considerations in the Care of the Newborn with Congenital Abnormalities," in Dennis J. Horan and Melinda Delahoyde, eds., *Infanticide and the Handicapped Newborn* (Provo, Utah: Brigham Young University Press, 1982), p. 91.

75. Ibid., p. 93.

76. Koop, "The Handicapped Child and His Family," p. 29.

4

Selective Nontreatment and Criminal Liability

> This article . . . takes the position that under existing law, parents, physicians, and hospital staff commit several crimes in withholding care [from defective infants], and that on the whole, with few exceptions, criminal liability may be both desirable and morally compelled.
>
> JOHN A. ROBERTSON, J.D.[1]

> There is an old legal maxim that the law does not require performance of impossible conditions: *lex neminem cogit ad vana seu inutilia*—the law will not force anyone to do something that will be vain and fruitless. In those situations in which a child cannot be cured by surgery and in fact the first operation immediately after birth is the precurser of 15 or 20 to follow . . . it can be argued that refusal to begin a long and painful course of treatment with no hope of success cannot constitute neglect, and that sparing the child the pain of further surgery throughout childhood is a reasonable exercise of parental discretion.
>
> ANGELA RODDEY HOLDER, J.D., LL.M.[2]

Are neonates with serious congenital anomalies to be treated, occasionally left untreated by withholding surgery and other medical procedures, or in some cases directly and intentionally killed? These options, often debated in the quasi-privacy of an NICU, are increasingly coming under public scrutiny. A number of attorneys, as yet representing a small percentage of the legal profession, have recently begun to explore the uncertain legal terrain brought about by neonatal medical technology and the life-or-death decisions imposed by that technology. Several legal battles over the care and treatment of handicapped infants have taken place in recent years, with cases involving infants with Down's syndrome, spina bifida cystica, Tay-Sachs disease, joined bodies (Siamese twins), and multiple congenital anomalies receiving considerable publicity.

This publicity is, of course, partially due to the novelty of the cases and their emotional "pull." It is also due to the fact that each of the cases explores the issue of neonatal rights, raises fundamental questions about parental authority and medical discretion, and breaks new legal ground regarding the medical practice of selective nontreatment. The United States, as was pointed out in chapter 1, differs from England in not having a national infanticide law. There is no legal distinction in this country between homicide and infanticide; there are no laws specifically proscribing infanticide, and acts of child destruction are prosecuted under the various state homicide laws. When cases occur in which infants are not directly killed by their parents outside a hospital setting but instead die as a consequence of nontreatment in an NICU, important questions are immediately raised in the news media regarding the legal status of these nontreatment decisions and the legal penalties, if any, that should be attached to such decisions.

Most parents and physicians recognize that directly killing an infant, whether inside or outside a hospital setting, is prohibited by state homicide laws. In contrast, many parents, physicians, and hospital administrators display considerable uncertainty regarding the legal status of nontreatment decisions. Some parents conclude that the law gives them "no alternative" but to choose treatment for a defective infant (see case 2.1); other parents make decisions not to continue medical treatment, apparently believing either that the law permits such decisions or that the appropriate legal authorities will not prosecute them if they find out what has happened in the NICU (see cases 2.2 and 2.8). Some physicians (e.g., Freeman, Fost, and Koop) are apparently careful to operate within the requirements of the law in their decisions about treating anomalous neonates; other physicians (e.g., Duff, Campbell, and Shaw) engage in a form of conscientious objection to laws they believe to be unjust, and they publicly call for the enactment of laws granting greater discretion—or possibly legal immunity—to parents and physicians confronted with difficult decisions about treatment or nontreatment. Hospital administrators, in turn, decide in some instances not to seek a court order overriding parental authority (as in case 2.2); other administrators in other legal jurisdictions occasionally secure court-mandated treatment for infants and thereby override parental authority to decide against treatment (see cases 4.1 and 4.5).

In the midst of this uncertainty regarding selective nontreatment, it is important to examine the legal implications of decisions made by parents and/or physicians not to provide certain kinds of medical treatment for birth-defective infants. We will begin with some cases and examine the potential legal liability of parents and physicians involved in such nontreatment decisions. We will then explore the current debate among legal scholars regarding how the law—in theory and in enforcement—should handle nontreatment decisions.

Cases

As is evident from the cases in the previous chapters, most decisions to withhold treatment from anomalous neonates are never subjected to legal scrutiny. Some cases, however, involve the threat of legal prosecution (see cases 2.8 and 4.4), and a few cases are finally adjudicated in a court hearing (see cases 4.1, 4.4, and 4.5). Additional cases involving the law will be presented in chapter 5.

Case 4.1

A male child was born to Lorraine and Robert Houle on February 9, 1974, at the Maine Medical Center. Medical examination of the neonate revealed the absence of a left eye, a rudimentary left ear with no ear canal, a malformed left thumb, and a tracheoesophageal fistula. The fistula necessitated intravenous feeding and allowed fluid to enter the child's lungs, bringing about pneumonia and other complications. One physician suspected brain damage in the child and stated that such brain damage would render the child's life not worth preserving.

The recommended medical treatment was surgical repair of the fistula to allow normal feeding and respiration. On February 11, Robert Houle directed the attending physician not to proceed with the proposed surgery and to cease the intravenous feeding.

Several physicians involved in the case, including the attending physician and the pediatric surgeon scheduled to perform the operation, disagreed with the decision not to treat the child. They and the administrators at the medical center initiated a neglect case in the superior court. Judge David Roberts heard the case and stated that "the existence of the child herein gives the court equitable jurisdiction to fulfill the responsibility of government in its character as parens patriae to care for infants and protect them from neglect."

Judge Roberts ordered the surgery to be performed. Unable to know that the child would die the day after the operation, he made several comments in mandating the surgery:

Recent decisions concerning the right of the state to intervene with the medical and moral judgments of a prospective parent and attending physician may have cast doubts upon the legal rights of an unborn child; but at the moment of live birth there does exist a human being entitled to the fullest protection of the law. The most basic right enjoyed by every human being is the right to life itself. . . . The measures proposed in this case are not in any sense heroic measures except for the doctor's opinion that probable brain damage has rendered life not worth preserving. . . . However, the doctor's qualitative evaluation of the value of the life to be preserved is not legally within the scope of his expertise. . . . Being satisfied that corrective surgery is medically necessary and medically feasible, the court finds that the defendants herein have no right to withhold such treatment and that to do so constitutes neglect in the legal sense. Therefore, the court will authorize the guardian *ad litem* to consent to the surgical correction. . . .[3]

Case 4.2

A court order was obtained for Baby E. . . . This infant, with Down's syndrome, intestinal obstruction and congenital heart disease, was born in her mother's car on the way to the hospital. The mother thought that the retarded infant would be impossible for her to care for and would have a destructive effect on her already shaky marriage. She therefore refused to sign permission for intestinal surgery, but a local child-welfare agency, invoking the state child-abuse statute, was able to obtain a court order directing surgery to be performed. After a complicated course and thousands of dollars worth of care, the infant was returned to the mother. The baby's continued growth and development remained markedly retarded because of her severe cardiac disease. A year and a half after the baby's birth, the mother felt more than ever that she had been done a severe injustice.[4]

Case 4.3

An infant with spina bifida cystica was born to a young Arizona couple. The parents and the physician agreed, given the severity of the child's condition, not to proceed with surgery. Moreover, they agreed to withhold food and liquids from the infant so that it would die.

The decisions made in the NICU became known outside the hospital, received considerable publicity, and led to the calling of a coroner's jury after the baby died. The jury ruled that the baby had died from natural causes (meningitis) and not from the parents' decision to withhold food and liquids. The Arizona Attorney General's office, which still had the option to prosecute the parents and physician, declined to do so, because the coroner's jury had reached a "reasoned verdict."[5]

Case 4.4

On May 6, 1981, Pam Mueller, a registered nurse, gave birth to Siamese twin boys in Danville, Illinois. The boys, together, weighed 9 pounds, 12 ounces at birth, were joined with a single trunk below the waist, and shared three legs. As soon as the boys were delivered, the obstetrician commented, "Don't resuscitate, let's just cover the babies." The boys' father, Robert Mueller, an emergency room physician in the same hospital, seemed to agree with the obstetrician's decision. After the boys began to breathe spontaneously, an order that the twins not be given food or water—"Do not feed in accordance with parents' wishes"—was written on the medical chart. A family physician present in the delivery room, as well as the anesthesiologist, apparently agreed with the decisions by the attending physician and parents not to resuscitate the infants and then not to feed them. The boys were taken to the newborn nursery to die.

The nursing staff received the medical orders with mixed feelings. Some of the nurses agreed with the decision not to feed the infants. Other nurses disagreed, and at least one nurse surreptitiously fed the boys with a mixture of sugar and water, sometimes at the end of a pacifier, and failed to record the feedings on the children's charts. After a week the boys' weight had dropped to 6 pounds.

On May 13, an anonymous telephone caller told the Illinois Department of Children and Family Services that Siamese twins at Lakeview Medical Center in Danville were being neglected. A social worker investigated and reported, "I saw their ribs sticking out— which indicated to me that they had not been fed."

On May 15, the Family Services staff filed a petition of neglect against the parents, asking that it be given custody of the children. Two attorneys were appointed to represent the boys, with each attorney having responsibility for one of the boys in the event that the boys' interests came into conflict. Several nurses agreed to testify at the hearing only after being granted a waiver of immunity from any possible criminal charges. One nurse testified that the twin boys represented a "horrible" situation:

> It's got three legs, one a half-foot with seven toes—two legs are sticking out of one side, one on the other. . . . I love children, but God forgive me, it should have died right there. . . . I've been in this business for 20 years, but it's the first time I've ever broke down. . . . This woman [the mother] wasn't the type who would abuse children . . . this was the type who was dedicated to children.

The judge found that the infants had been neglected during their eight-day stay in the hospital, and ordered that temporary custody be given to Family Services. The twins were moved, over the Muellers' objections, to Children's Memorial Hospital in Chicago for evaluation and treatment.

On June 11, criminal charges were filed (for the first time in the history of the United States) against the parents and the attending physician for withholding food and medical treatment from a neonate with congenital defects. The charge was conspiracy to commit murder. The district attorney of Vermilion County, Illinois, stated:

> The state of Illinois defines murder as the taking of a human life without justification, and the only justification is self-defense. . . . The quality of human life or the lack of it is not the issue. . . . Most terrible crimes are often committed for lofty ideals. . . . One could easily imagine the pain of the parents. . . . But you also have to feel sorry for the children, hearing the nurses' statements; how they cried in pain because they were hungry; how the cries dwindled down to whimpers as they were starved. . . . These were two infant human beings, that feel things just like any other human does.

On June 17, a preliminary hearing was held to determine whether there was probable cause that the defendants had committed the crime. None of the nurses testifying at the hearing was willing or able to link the parents and physician directly with the order to withhold food from the twins. Based on the lack of evidence, the judge found no probable cause and dismissed the charges.

On September 16, after the state had had temporary custody of the boys for four months, the court ruled that the children could return home with their parents. The boys' health picture remains uncertain.[6]

Case 4.5

Jennifer and Albert Daniels were the parents of a healthy three-year-old son. In June 1981, Jennifer gave birth to a daughter in Miami's Variety Children's Hospital. The daughter, named Elin, was born with spina bifida cystica.

Irwin Perlmutter, the attending physician, advised the couple against neurosurgical treatment. At best, the operation would be the first of many surgical efforts to help Elin cope with her life of paralysis and incontinence. At worst, the operation would not successfully take care of her hydrocephalus and she would go through life mentally retarded. Given this medical advice, the Daniels decided against the surgery and chose to let nature run its course.

Some other physicians at the children's hospital disagreed with the Daniels' decision and sought a court order to have the surgery performed. Persons attending the subsequent hearing in a Dade County courtroom heard conflicting medical testimony about Elin and the probable future awaiting her. Dr. Perlmutter testified that survival for Elin would mean a lifetime of painful surgical procedures and enormous psychological and social pressures, given her predicted paralysis below the waist and inability to control her bladder and bowels. A physician testifying for the hospital acknowledged the probable paralysis and incontinence, but argued that treating her hydrocephalus successfully would prevent mental disability.

Given the conflicting medical advice, Judge Ralph Ferguson ruled in favor of the hospital and ordered surgery. Elin promptly underwent an operation to implant a ventricular shunt to remove excessive cerebrospinal fluid from her head. Judge Ferguson believed his decision was correct: "The child deserves the best opportunity for qualitative and quantitative life." Elin's parents disagreed, but decided not to appeal the decision. Jennifer's comment reflected her anguish over the judge's decision: "It's difficult for us to realize that we may be condemning our daughter to a life of surgical procedure after procedure."[7]

The legal status of selective nontreatment

As John Freeman's comments in the previous chapter clearly indicate, any parents and/or physicians who intentionally kill an infant in an NICU or other hospital setting run the risk of criminal prosecution for murder. No parents or physicians have thus far been prosecuted for neonatal euthanasia in this country, but there have been a few cases in which parents were prosecuted for directly killing an abnormal child who had survived the neonatal period.

But what about cases in which a neonate is not directly killed? Is the widespread uncertainty concerning the legality of nontreatment of anomalous neonates due to a basic ignorance of the law on the part of some parents, physicians, and hospital administrators, or is the uncertainty about the law traceable to certain ambiguities in the law itself? Was the attempted prosecution of the Muellers in Illinois (case 4.4) a legal aberration, or is it an indication that there are criminal laws in Illinois and elsewhere that alert prosecutors can bring to bear against parents and physicians who withhold lifesaving medical treatment from neonates with serious congenital defects? Could the parents in the Houle and Daniels cases (4.1 and 4.5) not only have had their decisions to withhold treatment overruled by judicial verdict, but found themselves prosecuted by a local district attorney on criminal charges?

Given the variety of congenital anomalies, conflicting medical views regarding the effects of nontreatment and the benefits of certain types of treatment, and the diversity of state laws that might be brought to bear in nontreatment cases, it is little wonder that there is considerable uncertainty concerning the legal status of selective nontreatment. However, most legal commentators agree that selective nontreatment is legally risky for parents and physicians because, depending on the circumstances of particular cases, it probably violates one or more existing laws. Most legal scholars writing about selective nontreatment also agree with John Robertson's detailed analysis of the current legal situation.[8]

Robertson, a professor of law at the University of Texas, believes that under traditional principles of criminal law any parents, physicians, or nurses who fail to give ordinary lifesaving medical treatment to a newborn infant are liable for a number of crimes ranging from murder and manslaughter to conspiracy and child abuse. In particular, parents who decide to withhold treatment from a neonate are liable under state homicide or state neglect statutes. State homicide laws have bearing on nontreatment cases whenever parents, through either premeditation or gross negligence, decide to withhold lifesaving medical treatment from a neonate with a lethal condition (e.g., duodenal atresia), and it can be shown that their failure to provide the treatment was the proximate cause of the child's death. In such cases the parents are criminally liable for charges of homicide by omission. If the omission of treatment is intentional, the parents can be prosecuted for first- or second-degree murder depending on their premeditation and deliberation. If, in contrast, the omission of treatment is the result of gross carelessness, the criminal charge directed against them will likely be involuntary manslaughter.[9]

Parents who decide to withhold important corrective treatment from a neonate may also be prosecuted under state neglect statutes that require that parents provide necessary medical care for minor children. Although there are cases in which parents can refuse corrective surgery for a minor child without being liable for neglect (especially if the child also opposes the treatment), parents who refuse medically recommended corrective surgery for a neonate are legally liable for neglect. Especially in cases involving serious congenital defects (e.g., spina bifida) that are not in themselves lethal but require surgical treatment to correct or lessen major medical problems, parental refusal of the recommended surgery is tantamount to neglect and may, should there be a court hearing, warrant the appointment of a guardian who will consent to the surgical correction.[10]

Because of the possible criminal charges against parents, Robertson argues that responsible physicians should inform parents not only of the medical prognosis for their abnormal infant but also of the legal risks involved should they decide not to consent to medical treatment for the neonate. He believes that Duff, Campbell, and other pediatricians who do not inform parents of these matters are themselves negligent.[11]

Additionally, he points out that physicians and other members of hospital staffs are also liable when lifesaving medical treatment is withheld from neonates. It is possible for interns, residents, nurses, chiefs of staff, and hospital administrators to be charged with criminal actions in such cases, but the attending physician is clearly the member of the hospital staff who faces the greatest potential liability because he or she incurs a legal duty to treat a patient upon consenting to undertake that patient's medical care. Therefore, if in a neonatal case the attending physician withholds medical treatment apart from parental consent or persuades the parents to refuse consent to treatment, the physician may be liable for charges of murder or involuntary manslaughter if the child dies. Alternatively, the physician may be regarded legally as an accessory before the fact to a homicide by the parents because of the advice given them prior to their commission of a felony. Even when the attending physician merely acquiesces to the parents' decision to refuse treatment, he or she may still be liable for violating neglect statutes, child abuse reporting laws, accomplice statutes, or conspiracy laws.[12]

What legal defense could parents or physicians make if they were prosecuted under one or more of these criminal charges? Robertson, writing several years before the 1981 preliminary hearing involving the Muellers and their physician (case 4.4), suggests three defenses that might be attempted depending on the circumstances of a given case. One possible defense would be an appeal to the distinction between ordinary and extraordinary means of prolonging a patient's life, with the defendants arguing that the medical treatments withheld from an anomalous infant would not have significantly prolonged the infant's life or corrected the infant's defective condition and would have caused excessive suffering to the infant. Another possible defense would involve arguments about causation, with the defendants attempting to prove that the infant would have died even with the omitted medical care. A third possible defense would center on the legal doctrine of necessity, with the defendants arguing that withholding certain medical treatments from a defective infant was necessary in order to avoid imminent harm: the infant, had it lived, would have been harmed in ways that exceed the harm ensuing from the infant's death.[13]

If Robertson's analysis is correct, and I have no reason to think that it is not, why are there not frequent prosecutions of parents and physicians who withhold medical treatment from neonates and thereby often bring about their deaths? The reasons are several. First, the law is notoriously slow in responding to developments in medical science and technology. In both its legislative and judicial forms, the law tends by its very nature to respond with deliberation to unprecedented changes in society. The relatively recent developments in neonatal medical technology and the resulting decisions about nontreatment have thus been discussed by some legal experts in some law journals, but the legal implications of the decisions being made in NICUs have only begun to be seriously debated in legislative chambers and courtrooms.

Second, the decisions to withhold treatment or directly to kill defective infants are made in the quasi-privacy of NICUs. Few persons know about the decisions, and those who do know—parents, physicians, nurses—are often in agreement that bringing about the deaths of these infants is the best course of action available. Some physicians also succeed, as R. B. Zachary indicates, in concealing their actions by occasionally giving neonates they do not want to live "analgesics" for their pain, whereas in fact the infants are given sleep-inducing drugs (e.g., chloral hydrate, phenobarbitone), fed on demand, and thus starved. No one reports these low-visibility cases to the appropriate legal officials; furthermore, district attorneys, who do not usually read medical journals, have little way of finding out that the law has been violated.

Third, there is a gap between what the criminal law says in theory and how the law works in practice. Whereas parents and physicians are theoretically at risk for criminal prosecution for withholding treatment from defective neonates, the enforcement pattern actually allows considerable room for discretionary decisions by parents and physicians. The result is that to date, although courts in several states have overridden parental authority to mandate surgery for newborn infants (as in cases 4.1 and 4.5), no parents have been criminally prosecuted or convicted of a crime for having withheld lifesaving medical treatment from a seriously defective neonate. The closest we have come to this legal watershed is the Mueller case in Illinois. In that case (case 4.4), charges of conspiring to commit murder were brought against the parents and the attending physician, but the charges were subsequently dropped for lack of evidence.

It is also true that, despite the publicity given to Duff, Campbell, and Shaw in this country's news media, no physician has yet been prosecuted for having withheld ordinary medical treatment from an infant with a serious birth defect. However, the 1975 Edelin case in Massachusetts, involving the conviction (later overturned on appeal) of an obstetrician for having failed to ventilate an aborted but possibly viable fetus, and the 1981 Mueller case, in which food and drink were apparently denied the twin boys, indicate that the gap between legal theory and legal practice occasionally narrows.

Fourth, there is, in terms of legal practice if not legal theory, some ambiguity about a defective infant's legal status. According to constitutional law, and in particular the Fourteenth Amendment, there is no doubt that an infant is legally a person with all of the rights, including the right to life, generally accorded persons in our society. Any infringement of an infant's right to life is a violation of fundamental legal precepts just

as surely as a similar act would be infringement of any other person's right
to life. Yet, as Catherine Damme points out, there "is no special law or
statute in any state setting forth penalties for killing an infant of less
than twelve months." And the absence of criminal prosecutions of parents
and physicians in medical cases involving the deaths of infants leads her
to conclude:

> The infant does indeed have lesser status in law than the adult. Such status
> does not represent an erosion of ethical or religious values nor is it evidence
> of a brutal society, but rather demonstrates society's continued ambivalence
> toward the inherent sanctity of life and realistic judgment on the quality of
> life.[14]

Fifth, there are a number of practical considerations that work against
the enforcement of legal penalties when parents and physicians withhold
treatment or directly kill neonates with serious congenital defects. Even if
prosecutors are informed anonymously that a seriously handicapped
infant is being starved in a local hospital or hear about the questionable
circumstances of an infant's death, they may decline to file charges for a
variety of reasons. Depending on the circumstances and location of a
particular case, prosecutors may respect parental autonomy, find themselves in agreement with the parents' position, be reluctant to press
criminal charges because such a prosecution might prove politically un-
popular, be hesitant to challenge the discretion of the physicians in the
case, believe that the presiding judge in a court hearing would agree with
the decision made in the NICU, be concerned about the emotional stress
on all parties in the case, feel that a criminal procedure would be disproportionate for the circumstances, or simply conclude that they lack
sufficient personnel to do the amount of legal work required to get a
conviction in the case. The Mueller case (case 4.4) illustrates the difficulty
of such a prosecution. Involving criminal charges against individuals
widely respected in their community and running aground when the
nurses proved reluctant to testify at the preliminary hearing, the Mueller
case "does not appear to have played well in Danville, and may have cost
the prosecutor political support."[15]

Such is the current status of the law regarding birth-defective neonates
and the decisions made about prolonging their lives, withholding medical
treatment from them, or bringing about their deaths. Parents and/or
physicians who decide for any number of reasons that it is preferable for
an abnormal infant to die rather than live are potentially liable for a range

of criminal charges, yet the chances are that neither the parents nor the physicians will be prosecuted for their decision not to treat the child. It remains to be seen whether greater public awareness of occasional non-treatment and starvation in hospital nurseries, a more vocal role for nurses who oppose nontreatment practices, new laws enacted at the state level, greater political pressure imposed on hospitals by federal agencies, and increased activity by advocacy groups for handicapped individuals (e.g., the Spina Bifida Association) will lead to more active prosecution of parents and physicians, at least in especially egregious nontreatment cases.

In the meanwhile the ambiguity of the law—potential criminal liability but uncertain prosecution—adds to the psychological and moral burden shared by parents and physicians. The uncertainty of some parents and physicians in not knowing for sure what the law permits and prohibits, as well as the inconsistency in legal practice from one jurisdiction to another, sometimes results in a combination of wrongs being done. Some infants (as in case 2.2), who on medical and moral grounds should live, are left to die untreated; other infants (as in case 2.4) who on medical and moral grounds should be left untreated and die, are forced to undergo extensive medical treatment in part, one suspects, because the parents and physicians are anxious about their legal liability.

The debate about the law among attorneys

Even though most attorneys seem to agree with Robertson's analysis of the current legal situation, many of them do not agree with his statement (quoted at the beginning of this chapter) that the current risk of criminal liability is, in the majority of cases, "both desirable and morally compelled." In fact, attorneys who have written about the legal implications of selective nontreatment offer a wide range of possible legal alternatives for cases involving neonates with serious congenital defects.

Continue the present legal system

Robert Burt, a professor of law at Yale, says that "formal criminal law proscription but only occasional application is . . . the best choice among bad choices."[16] In arriving at this conclusion, he suggests that existing laws should neither be changed nor be more strictly enforced. By keeping the law as it is, decisions by parents and physicians to terminate treatment will continue to carry risks of criminal liability—risks that might "more or less unpredictably" end up in criminal proceedings should local prosecutors decide to take action against the parties involved. He acknowledges that there will continue to be selective nontreatment of defective newborns (and thus, some unreported crimes), but argues that "the continued regime of many ignored law violations when treatment is withheld" is necessary to avoid inflicting needless cruelty on those exceptional infants who are "terribly, tragically deformed." Even if there are few prosecutions, the risk of such prosecutions will continue to serve the important purpose of deterrence:

> The true enormity of these actions to withhold life from newborns . . . will remain in high visibility only if advance social authorization is withheld, and only if the parents and physicians who wish to take this action are willing to accept some significant risk that they will suffer by such action.[17]

Enforce present criminal sanctions

Dennis Horan, a professor of law at the University of Chicago, disagrees. He argues that the law should be enforced more rigorously, thereby removing whatever ambiguity there may be regarding legal penalties for selective nontreatment. Continuing the present enforcement pattern will only ensure that numbers of defective infants (e.g., those with Down's syndrome plus duodenal atresia) who could be treated will instead be starved to death in NICUs as a consequence of two decisions made by parents and physicians. The first decision, not to operate on an infant whose condition calls for lifesaving or corrective surgery, is a decision of medical management. The second decision, not to feed an infant who has been denied surgery, is a "decision to kill." And the sequence of the two decisions means that the first decision is in actuality also a decision to kill, because "it must of necessity be followed with a refusal to give any sustenance even by intravenous feeding." When an infant dies as a result of this failure to feed, the decision makers should be vigorously prosecuted because, in Horan's words, "I submit the case becomes murder."[18]

Terminate parental rights and obligations

There are cases, as Robertson points out in another article, in which treatment is withheld from a defective newborn not because the treatment would be useless or harmful to the infant, but because the infant's continued living represents a severe burden for the parents. Such cases, as described by Duff, Campbell, Shaw, and other pediatricians, often seem to offer parents only two alternatives: break the law by withholding treatment that might benefit the infant, or follow the legally prescribed course and end up burdened with a mentally retarded and/or physically handicapped child for life. There is, according to Robertson, a third alternative: parents who find the prospect of continued custody of a severely handicapped infant an intolerable burden "may simply use the statutory procedure existing in most jurisdictions to transfer these burdens to the state, thus spreading the cost among all taxpayers."[19]

If the court terminates parental rights and obligations, guardianship and legal custody of the infant is transferred to another family or to a state agency. This alternative removes parents from a legal bind and allows the handicapped infant to be treated and to continue living, although probably in a state institution. The prospect of prolonged existence in an institution for the mentally and/or physically handicapped is certainly not the most desirable possibility for a child, but neither is nontreatment followed in most instances by a lingering death. For Robertson, even though the wards for retarded children in state institutions are often "an apt description of hell," the termination of parental rights in a custody hearing and assignment of a child to an institution "is not clearly a worse alternative than death" for the child.[20]

Give parents and physicians greater discretion

The previous positions, while significantly different in some respects, would maintain the present criminal liabilities potentially involved in selective nontreatment. The basic reason all three attorneys have for maintaining the law in its present form is the hope of deterring acts of treatment termination. In contrast, a number of physicians and some attorneys are convinced that the law should allow for greater discretion by parents and physicians directly involved in making the difficult decisions about treatment and nontreatment. Rather than constraining them through the threat of criminal prosecution, the law should be interpreted and enforced in a manner that would allow greater latitude in determining what counts as ordinary, obligatory medical treatment for all neonates and what counts as the sort of extraordinary treatment that no physician is obligated to give an infant with serious congenital anomalies. One legal scholar who holds this view is Frank Grad, a professor of law at Columbia, who states:

there is an area where a physician clearly has discretion, and that is that a
physician is under an obligation to render ordinary, prudent, accepted
medical care. If in the instance of a particular infant, what is required or
what would be required to save the situation are extraordinary, heroic
measures, the author does not believe that there is any legal obligation to go
that far.[21]

Allow nontreatment decisions in limited situations

Two other legal commentators think it is possible to employ the traditional ordinary/extraordinary distinction in specifying certain limited
situations in which nontreatment is legally permissible. For Elizabeth
MacMillan, an attorney in private practice in Virginia, it seems obvious
that the traditional distinction is applicable to neonatal nontreatment
cases because no court is likely to convict parents or physicians for
withholding treatment that is judged medically nonbeneficial to an infant.
Moreover, some treatments for some infants may actually be harmful: for
these infants treatment will not lead to a relatively normal and healthy
life, but may cause brain damage and further deterioration. As to which
clinical situations may permit nontreatment, she rejects quality-of-life
arguments and opts instead to lay out the conditions under which nontreatment could be said to be "in the infant's best interests." Therefore,
instead of grounding nontreatment decisions in subjective predictions of
the type of life an infant would have if treated, she argues that nontreatment decisions should be made according to a "medical-feasibility
standard" which focuses on "the infant's existing medical condition and
the availability of treatment for that condition."[22]

There are, she believes, two situations in which medical treatment of a
defective neonate will be either useless or harmful (in the sense of causing
the infant's condition to deteriorate): (a) when the child's death is likely to
occur within six months to a year, even with treatment, and (b) when the
proposed treatment cannot restore the child's consciousness. Because
treatment is infeasible in these situations, a birth-defective neonate in
either situation "does not have a recognizable interest in the treatment."
Consequently, a nontreatment decision "should be made clearly legal" in
these circumstances by legislative enactment.[23]

For Angela Holder, Counsel for Medicolegal Affairs at Yale University
School of Medicine, the distinction between ordinary and extraordinary
medical care translates in neonatal cases into a distinction between curative and noncurative treatment. Disagreeing with Robertson's analysis

that all medically recommended, even partially corrective surgery for neonates is legally required, she observes:

> It seems to be legally mandatory for treatment to be instituted if it can cure the condition for which it is performed [but] it may be possible to justify as good medical practice a determination that a child whose condition is incurable should not be subjected to surgery for that condition solely to keep him alive.[24]

As to specific cases involving treatment decisions, she argues that infants with Down's syndrome plus an intestinal obstruction (as in cases 2.2 and 4.2) and infants such as Baby Houle (case 4.1) should be treated, because the surgical procedures can successfully correct the underlying physical anomalies and "would clearly be performed by court order if necessary on an otherwise normal newborn." In contrast, neurosurgery for infants with spina bifida cystica (as in cases 2.8, 4.3, and 4.5) is not "ordinary care" and should not be legally required because the condition is incurable, the surgery is not required for normal babies, and repetitious operations may "subject the baby to more pain than he would have felt if left alone." Parental refusal to consent to "radical surgery which cannot alleviate the condition" in spina bifida cases should not therefore be construed as neglect. Rather, given the predictable pain involved in repetitious major operations and the torment of thoughtless peers in later years, parents may decide "for religious or other reasons that it is a more loving act to allow a child to die of the same condition that will prevent him from leading a normal life with the best medicine can offer. . . ."[25]

Make neonatal euthanasia a legal option

It is clear that the last three attorneys believe that the law permits—and should permit—selective nontreatment in limited situations. Although Grad, MacMillan, and Holder approach the legality of selective nontreatment in slightly different ways, they each think that the law can be interpreted or revised in ways that would permit the selective withholding of treatment judged to be extraordinary in the more severe cases of congenital anomalies.

A different approach is taken by Arval Morris, a professor of law at the University of Washington. He argues that the potential criminal liability of parents and physicians who engage in selective nontreatment is the result of statutory laws based on a defective premise: namely, "that life, whatever its form, nature, or content, is necessarily and always a good, and that death, or any event that hastens death, is always and necessarily an evil and should be illegal."[26] The defectiveness of this premise is clear, he thinks, to anyone who seriously considers the crippling disabilities and suffering confronted by infants having such extreme birth defects that they will never be able to experience life in even a "minimally ordinary sense."

According to Morris, a preferable alternative to these laws and the potential liability they impose on parents and physicians would be the enactment of laws permitting nonvoluntary euthanasia for infants with severe congenital defects. Both withholding treatment and direct killing should be made legal options in these situations—not because severely defective infants are not "persons," not because they would cause great suffering to others, and not because they would become a socioeconomic burden, but because there are cases in which such infants "would be better off dead." Such cases involve infants born with anencephaly, Lesch-Nyhan disease, Tay-Sachs disease, and severe cases of spina bifida cystica. To treat these infants is, in his judgment, "to do them harm by engaging in a useless, pain-producing act." To administer nonvoluntary euthanasia is, in contrast, to do something that is morally justified and, possibly, morally compelled. He believes that the principle of nonmaleficence calls for nonvoluntary euthanasia in any cases in which death would be better for the infant than continued suffering:

> I think there will be widespread agreement that the use of the modern arsenal of modern technology in an attempt to prolong the biological existences of defective newborns such as the ones just described is a misguided or wrongful act that results in cruelty, is contrary to the better interests of the infant, and violates the important maxim of medical ethics, *primum non nocere*, that, first and foremost, one should do no harm.[27]

In carrying out his contention that new laws are necessary, Morris has proposed a model statute that would permit nonvoluntary euthanasia for severely defective infants. The proposed law would permit either the withholding of medical treatment from or the intentional killing of an infant suffering from a severe, incurable, and irremediable medical condition. The central provision of the proposed law reads as follows:

> Section 1. Authorization of euthanasia. Subject to the provisions of this Act it shall be lawful for a qualified physician, or his professional medical agent, as authorized by a qualified physician's written statement, to ad-

minister euthanasia to a qualified child for whom the child's parent or
guardian previously has made a written declaration voluntarily requesting
euthanasia for the qualified child and which declaration is lawfully in force
at the time of administering euthanasia.[28]

Issues in the debate among attorneys

What kind of guidance do these attorneys give to parents and physicians
who have to make the difficult decisions about treatment and nontreatment? What are the major points of difference among these legal scholars
as they interpret the law and possibly shape its future direction?

Burt, Horan, and Robertson think that the present criminal liability
attached to cases of selective nontreatment should remain. They disagree,
however, about the present enforcement pattern, with Horan arguing that
most cases of selective nontreatment should be prosecuted as vigorously
as any other acts of murder. In contrast, Grad, MacMillan, and Holder
believe that the present law should be interpreted in such a manner as to
allow physicians and parents to withhold any treatment that is judged
medically useless or harmful to a birth-defective neonate; in this manner
certain cases of selective nontreatment would be legally permissible with
no threat of criminal prosecution hanging over the heads of the decision
makers. For Morris, the law can and should do more than permit carefully
circumscribed cases of selective nontreatment. He is convinced that there
are some infants whose suffering cannot be relieved by withholding
treatment from them; to relieve these infants from present and future
harmful treatment requires the legal alternative of nonvoluntary euthanasia.

Involved in this ongoing legal debate are three points that are important
in analyzing cases of selective nontreatment: the traditional distinction of
ordinary and extraordinary means of prolonging life, the question of
intentionally killing birth-defective infants who do not die when treatment
is withdrawn, and the application of the principle of nonmaleficence in
the context of neonatal medicine and law. These points will be discussed
at greater length in subsequent chapters.

The ordinary/extraordinary distinction is addressed more often in the
legal literature on selective nontreatment than it is in the medical literature,
perhaps because attorneys who write about issues in legal medicine assume
that the distinction is clearly understood and widely used by neonatologists and other pediatricians. The legal basis for the distinction derives

from the scope of the duty owed by a person (e.g., a parent, a physician) who undertakes the care of another person: "While the duty varies, each individual is required to provide only the level of care that society may reasonably expect, given the risk, available means, and the likelihood of benefit in the precise circumstances facing the actor."[29] Thus a physician's duty to provide treatment for a patient is governed by the test of reasonableness, and that test in turn is governed by customary medical practice and an analysis of the risks and benefits of treatment in a particular clinical context.

Legal scholars disagree about the relevancy of the ordinary/extraordinary distinction in cases of selective nontreatment of birth-defective newborns. Grad thinks the distinction allows for necessary discretion on the part of physicians and parents. Horan, in contrast, rejects the use of the distinction in neonatal medicine because he is convinced that it "has led consistently to the starvation deaths of defective children who, had they been normal, but for Down's syndrome, would have received life-saving treatment."[30]

For Robertson, MacMillan, and Holder, the ordinary/extraordinary distinction has relevance in neonatal medicine when it is understood as a test of usefulness for treatment in limited clinical situations. Determining that a possible treatment is extraordinary is not merely a matter of medical discretion nor is it a matter of withholding normal treatments from infants merely because they will grow up mentally retarded. Rather, a treatment is extraordinary—and thus optional—only if it is not useful in "substantially prolonging the child's life" (Robertson), or is infeasible in providing "any hope of benefit" to the child in terms of restoring consciousness or extending life for up to a year (MacMillan), or has no "reasonable hope of success" because the child's condition is incurable (Holder).

As to the issue of euthanasia, it is rarely mentioned in the legal literature on selective nontreatment. Only Horan and Morris discuss nonvoluntary euthanasia in the literature surveyed, and they arrive at different conclusions. Horan is skeptical of the legal and moral distinction between letting die and killing, and thus regards any decision to withhold surgery from an anomalous neonate as tantamount to murder. Morris believes that some birth-defective newborns would be better off dead and that directly killing these infants is preferable to harming them by either prolonging their lives or allowing them to die in an agonizingly slow manner. The other legal scholars do not discuss euthanasia as an option for neonatal medicine because, unlike withholding treatment, the legal status of intentionally killing infants is clearly that of first-degree murder. And most attorneys do not seem to regard a change in the legal status of nonvoluntary euthanasia for infants a desirable change in the law.

The third point that appears in the legal literature is the question of the proper application of the principle of nonmaleficence. Given the tragic conditions of some severely defective infants, should the law permit some carefully defined cases of selective nontreatment as an alternative to the possible harm that will come to these infants from a legally mandated policy of treating all infants regardless of their medical conditions? Should the law define some instances in which continued life would be more harmful to an infant than death?

The legal debate over these questions is represented by the positions taken by Robertson, Morris, and Holder. Although he acknowledges at one point that conditions of extreme defect may call for nontreatment, Robertson nevertheless has difficulty understanding how death could possibly be said to be less harmful than life and thus in a child's interests. Even the tragic case of a "profoundly retarded, nonambulatory, blind, deaf infant who will spend his few years in the back-ward cribs of a state institution" cannot be said by a proxy to have a life worse than death. For such a child who has never known the pleasures of "mental operation, ambulation, and social interaction," it may be that "life, and life alone, whatever its limitations, might be of sufficient worth" to endure repeated treatment.[31]

Morris and Holder disagree with this position and find such thinking to be insensitive to the plight of infants whose severe congenital defects condemn them to an existence of profound mental retardation, crippling physical handicaps, and institutionalization for as long as they live. For Morris, the position taken by Robertson simply reflects the defective premise on which the current law is based. Because the law was written with "the usual and ordinary person" in mind, it presumes that all life, regardless of its deficiencies and suffering, is necessarily better than death. The tragic result is the legally prescribed treatment of some seriously defective infants who are cruelly kept alive when they would be better off dead.

For Holder, such life-prolonging treatment for infants with incurable conditions is harmful in a manner similar to the harm that would be involved in legally mandated surgery for an adult patient with a terminal malignancy, when the surgery offers only pain and little chance of prolonging normal life for an appreciable period of time. Because of the harm she perceives in treating neonates who are incurable, she proposes the following legal standard: "If the treatment is more painful to the child than is a failure to treat, either on a short-term or a long-term basis, there is no criminal liability if treatment is omitted."[32] Thus, contrary to Robertson, she is convinced that some treatments for incurable infants can and should legally be withheld because the treatments are both useless and harmful on balance.

Should the law be changed?

In concluding this chapter, it may be helpful to put forth my views regarding the law and criminal liability for selective nontreatment. In contrast to Burt, Horan, and Robertson, I am persuaded that laws presently governing selective nontreatment not only need to be changed but will inevitably be changed as society responds through its legal institutions to the practice of selective nontreatment. The major unknown factor at this time is the form these changes will take: stricter enforcement of present state homicide laws? new state laws enacted to deal with selective nontreatment practices? stricter enforcement of federal laws concerning discrimination against handicapped persons? new federal legislation? We will discuss some recent efforts along these lines by the federal government in the next chapter.

With increased publicity of cases involving birth-defective newborns, the temptation for lawmakers is to go to one of two legal extremes: give parents and physicians virtually unlimited discretionary power in deciding which neonates live or die (by rarely enforcing existing laws), or mandate the preservation of all neonatal lives no matter how seriously handicapped (by enacting new state or federal laws). Both of these legal alternatives, in my judgment, are wrong.

Instead, what is needed at the present time is the development of a third alternative: a new, flexible legal framework for handling selective non-treatment decisions apart from blanket, often unenforceable threats of criminal liability. That framework, the specifics of which will have to be worked out by legislators and legal authorities, will need to be consistent with the fundamental legal principles of this society, reflective of the complex realities of medical practice in NICUs, flexible in allowing discretionary decisions in limited neonatal cases, and sensitive to the inherent difficulties of legislating the fundamentally moral decisions that have to be made regarding the treatment or nontreatment of severely defective newborns.

This new legal framework should include some of the views set forth by attorneys in this chapter, especially some of those developed by Robertson, MacMillan, and Holder. Sketched in general outline, this new legal approach to selective nontreatment should contain the following features:

1. legal provision for selective nontreatment in limited, carefully defined circumstances in which life-prolonging treatment is not in an infant's best interests (examples of these circumstances, in which selective nontreatment would not be criminally liable, are discussed in chap. 8);
2. procedural safeguards to ensure that selective nontreatment is done only in limited circumstances and that no birth-defective newborns are denied medical treatment merely because they are less-than-normal, unwanted by their parents, or fail to meet someone's quality-of-life standards (these procedural safeguards will sometimes require the involvement in selective nontreatment decisions of a hospital committee or some other disinterested, objective third party);
3. the continued but fairly infrequent involvement of lower courts in (a) transferring custody of some handicapped infants to other parents or to state agencies, and (b) handling criminal charges brought against parents who in especially egregious cases withhold treatment from and refuse to transfer custody of infants who should receive treatment and live; and
4. very strict procedural safeguards (more strict than Morris advocates) for rare instances in which neonatal euthanasia is morally justifiable subsequent to selective nontreatment.

Notes

1. John A. Robertson, "Involuntary Euthanasia of Defective Newborns: A Legal Analysis," *Stanford Law Review* 27 (1975): 217.
2. Angela Roddey Holder, *Legal Issues in Pediatrics and Adolescent Medicine* (New York: John Wiley & Sons, 1977), p. 118.
3. This case, usually referred to as the Baby Boy Houle case, is taken from the court record. The case is reprinted from Robert Weir, ed., *Ethical Issues in Death and Dying* (New York: Columbia University Press, 1977), pp. 185–86. A *Washington Post* story about this case in February 1974, subsequently picked up by *Obstetrical and Gynecological News* (April 1974), indicated that the Houle boy also had some unfused vertebrae. The court record makes no mention of this condition, if it existed.

4. This case is reprinted by permission from Anthony Shaw, "Dilemmas of 'Informed Consent' in Children," *The New England Journal of Medicine* 289 (October 25, 1973): 888.

5. This case is adapted from Robertson, "Involuntary Euthanasia," p. 217.

6. This case has received unusual publicity because of its unusual importance. The case was prepared from information in the *Washington Post*, June 5, 1981, p. A6; *Newsweek*, June 22 and August 31, 1981; and John A. Robertson, "Dilemma in Danville," *Hastings Center Report* 11 (October 1981): 5–8.

7. This case is adapted from *Newsweek*, July 6, 1981, p. 24.

8. Robertson, "Involuntary Euthanasia," pp. 213–69; Robert A. Burt, "Authorizing Death for Anomalous Newborns," in Aubrey Milunsky and George J. Annas, eds., *Genetics and the Law* (New York: Plenum Press, 1976), pp. 435–50; Dennis J. Horan, "Euthanasia, Medical Treatment and the Mongoloid Child: Death as a Treatment of Choice?" *Baylor Law Review* 27 (1975): 76–85; Jacqueline M. Nolan-Haley, "Defective Children, Their Parents, and the Death Decision," *Journal of Legal Medicine* 4 (January 1976): 9–14; and T. S. Ellis, "Letting Defective Babies Die: Who Decides," *American Journal of Law and Medicine* 7 (1982): 393–423.

9. Robertson, "Involuntary Euthanasia," pp. 217–22; see also idem, "Discretionary Non-Treatment of Defective Newborns," in Milunsky and Annas, *Genetics and the Law*, pp. 451–65.

10. Robertson, "Involuntary Euthanasia," pp. 222–24.

11. Ibid., p. 216.

12. Ibid., pp. 224–35. These points are updated in idem, "Legal Aspects of Withholding Treatment from Handicapped Children," in Dennis J. Horan and Melinda Delahoyde, eds., *Infanticide and the Handicapped Newborn* (Provo, Utah: Brigham Young University Press, 1982), pp. 17–32.

13. Robertson, "Involuntary Euthanasia," pp. 235–42.

14. Catherine Damme, "Infanticide: The Worth of an Infant under Law," *Medical History* 22 (1978): 22, 24.

15. Robertson, "Dilemma in Danville," p. 7.

16. Burt, "Authorizing Death for Anomalous Newborns," p. 447.

17. Ibid., p. 444. Burt repeats this point in *Taking Care of Strangers* (New York: The Free Press, 1979), p. 171, and then comments that legal immunity for physicians and parents "can too readily feed the destructive dynamic already visible in some physicians' and families' reaction even to minimally deformed children."

18. Dennis J. Horan, "Euthanasia as a Form of Medical Management," in Dennis J. Horan and David Mall, eds., *Death, Dying, and Euthanasia* (Washington, D.C.: University Publications of America, 1977), p. 219.

19. John A. Robertson, "Legal Issues in Nontreatment of Defective Newborns," in Chester Swinyard, *Decision Making and the Defective Newborn* (Springfield, Ill.: Charles C Thomas, 1978), p. 370.

20. Ibid., p. 379.

21. Frank P. Grad, "Legal Aspects of Informed Consent," in Swinyard, *Decision Making and the Defective Newborn*, p. 443.

22. Elizabeth S. MacMillan, "Birth-Defective Infants: A Standard for Nontreatment Decisions," *Stanford Law Review* 30 (February 1978): 620.
23. Ibid., pp. 632–33.
24. Holder, *Legal Issues in Pediatrics*, p. 114.
25. Ibid., pp. 118–19.
26. Arval A. Morris, "Law, Morality, and Euthanasia for the Severely Defective Child," in Marvin Kohl, ed., *Infanticide and the Value of Life* (Buffalo, N.Y.: Prometheus Books, 1978), p. 149.
27. Ibid., p. 145.
28. Arval A. Morris, "Proposed Legislation," in Kohl, *Infanticide and the Value of Life*, p. 221. The full text of the proposed law is contained on pp. 221–27.
29. Robertson, "Involuntary Euthanasia," p. 235.
30. Horan, "Euthanasia as a Form of Medical Management," p. 215.
31. Robertson, "Involuntary Euthanasia," p. 254.
32. Holder, *Legal Issues in Pediatrics*, p. 121.

5

The Law and Handicapped Infants

A cause of action brought on behalf of an infant seeking recovery for wrongful life demands a calculation of damages dependent upon a comparison between the Hobson's choice of life in an impaired state and nonexistence. This the law is incapable of doing.

BECKER V. SCHWARTZ[1]

Considering the short life span of many of these children and their frequently very limited ability to perceive or enjoy the benefits of life, we cannot assert with confidence that in every situation there would be a societal consensus that life is preferable to never having been born at all.

TURPIN V. SORTINI[2]

In addition to the issue of criminal liability in nontreatment cases, there are other areas of legal activity that have bearing on the legal implications of nontreatment decisions. Several state and federal courts, a few state legislatures, some federal agencies, the executive branch of the federal government, and the Congress have all become involved in recent years in legal issues arising out of the medical conditions of handicapped infants and young children.

To fill out the analysis of selective nontreatment and the law, it is necessary to discuss, even if somewhat briefly, these other areas of legal activity. We will begin with a discussion of two relatively recent types of tort suits and point out the implications these tort actions have for decisions regarding treatment or nontreatment. We will then discuss several recent efforts at the federal level to curtail the practice of selective nontreatment.

The legal issue of wrongful life

Supplementing the legal debate about criminal laws and their enforcement is another legal debate that has potential implications for persons making nontreatment decisions. Taking place during the same two decades in which NICUs came into existence in hospitals, this second debate concerns tort law rather than criminal law and has its focus in a series of legal actions seeking compensation for injurious existence. These tort actions are commonly known as "wrongful birth" and "wrongful life" suits. Although neither legal commentators nor courts have been consistent in using these classifications, it is possible and helpful to distinguish between the two tort actions.

A *wrongful birth* action is a suit brought by *the parents* of a child born as the result of the defendant's negligence. In some of these tort actions, occasionally called "wrongful pregnancy" or "wrongful conception" cases, the parents seek to recover damages incident to the unexpected pregnancy and birth of a healthy but unwanted child. Brought against pharmaceutical companies and physicians who perform sterilizations, these actions claim that the parents would have avoided conception but for the negligence of the defendant. Most wrongful birth suits, however, take a different form in that they involve the births of planned children who are born with serious congenital defects. Brought against obstetricians and gynecologists, these actions (such as case 5.1) claim that the parents would have decided to terminate the pregnancy had they been properly advised of the risk of birth defects to the potential child. In both forms of wrongful birth actions, damages are usually sought for emotional distress, loss of wages, medical expenses, and the costs of raising the child.

By contrast, a *wrongful life* action is a suit brought *solely by the child*, who argues that he or she would never have been born but for the defendant's negligence. A few wrongful life cases, sometimes called "dissatisfied life" or "bastard" cases, have had child plaintiffs seeking to recover damages from their fathers by claiming that they were injured or seriously disadvantaged through the illegitimate status of their births. The majority of wrongful life cases, however, have had child plaintiffs with serious mental and/or physical defects. These severely handicapped children have brought suit against physicians (and medical laboratories in case 5.2) claiming that they would never have been born or have experienced great suffering but for the negligence of the defendant in failing to inform the child's parents concerning the risks of genetic or other congenital defects. With the aid of legal guardians, these severely handicapped children have sought damages for their very existence (compared with nonexistence) calculated on the basis of their expected life span.[3] Simply put, the birth-defective child's position in these wrongful life suits can be characterized in one sentence: "I'd rather not be here suffering as I am, but since your wrongful conduct preserved my life, I am going to take advantage of my regrettable existence to sue you."[4]

Case 5.1

The year was 1972. Anna Robak was approximately one month pregnant. Because her husband, Robert, was in the army at Fort Rucker, Alabama, she visited the OB-GYN clinic at the base to get medical assistance for a rash and a fever. She was examined by Dr. Joshua Roth, who gave her a pregnancy test and two rubella tests over a period of several days. He informed her that she was pregnant and that the first rubella test was negative; he did not tell her that the second test was positive, nor did he tell her of the consequences of rubella for the embryo she was carrying.

Jennifer Robak was born in January 1973. She had all of the common symptoms of rubella syndrome: a rash, deafness, bilateral cataracts, congenital heart disease, and mental deficiency. She subsequently had two operations to remove the cataracts, but remained industrially blind. Additional operations will be required in the future, and she will need deaf-blind care and supervision for the rest of her life.

In 1977 the Robaks initiated a medical malpractice action against the United States under the Federal Tort Claims Act. Their attorney argued that Dr. Roth's negligence constituted a breach of physician's duty. Moreover, because Roth was employed by the government and could not personally be sued, the attorney argued that the government should compensate the Robaks and Jennifer for the damages ensuing from her birth and handicapped life.

The case was heard in a U.S. district court in Illinois. The court dismissed the "wrongful life" suit brought on Jennifer's behalf, but ruled in favor of the Robaks' "wrongful birth" suit. The court reasoned that the staff at the OB-GYN clinic had been negligent in failing to inform Anna of her rubella and the potential defects for her child once born. Had the staff not been negligent, Anna would have had an abortion and the Robaks would have avoided the costs of caring for a handicapped child. The Robaks were awarded $900,000 in damages—$450,000 to each plaintiff—for the purpose of establishing a reversionary trust for Jennifer's maintenance and medical care for the 71.8 years of her expected lifetime.

The government appealed the case, and it was subsequently argued before the U.S. Court of Appeals (Seventh Circuit) in 1981. The importance of the case was noted by Judge Swygert.

This appeal presents a question that has never been decided by a federal court of appeals: whether a cause of action exists for wrongful birth. We hold that it does and affirm the judgment of the district court. . . . In the absence of any direct precedent from the state involved, a federal court applying state law should consider decisions of its sister states on the same issue. Since *Roe v. Wade*, these precedents have been unanimous in recognizing a cause of action for the parents of a child born as a result of a physician's negligence. . . ."[5]

Case 5.2

The year was 1977. Phillis and Hyam Curlender retained the services of Bio-Science Laboratories in California for genetic screening tests. The Curlenders wanted to know if either of them was a carrier for Tay-Sachs disease. The tests were performed in January, and apparently inaccurate information was given to the Curlenders regarding their status as carriers of the disease. On the basis of that information, Phillis did not have amniocentesis performed during her pregnancy.

In May 1978, the Curlenders were informed that their infant daughter, Shauna, had Tay-Sachs disease and a life expectancy of approximately four years. Two years later Shauna's condition had degenerated to the point that she suffered from

mental retardation, susceptibility to other diseases, convulsions, sluggishness, apathy, failure to fix objects with her eyes, inability to take an interest in her surroundings, loss of motor reactions, inability to sit up or hold her head up, loss of weight, muscle atrophy, blindness, pseudobulbar palsy, inability to feed orally, decerebrate rigidity and gross physical deformity.[6]

Hyam Curlender, as guardian *ad litem*, initiated a "wrongful life" suit for Shauna in which she as the plaintiff sought damages from Bio-Science Laboratories, another laboratory involved in the genetic screening, and a physician running the screening program. The Court of Appeal, Second District, heard the case in June 1980. The basic question before the court was phrased as follows:

What remedy, if any, is available in this state to a severely impaired child— genetically defective—born as the result of defendant's negligence in conducting certain genetic tests of the child's parents—tests which, if properly done, would have disclosed the high probability that the actual, catastrophic result would occur?

Acknowledging that "wrongful life" suits had "almost universally been barred" in jurisdictions other than California and that a previous California case had dealt with the issue of illegitimacy rather than congenital defects, the court reasoned that the Curlender suit was justifiable because of "the serious nature of the wrong" and the fact that "the law reflects, perhaps later than sooner, basic changes in the way society views such matters." The "real crux of the problem" confronting the court was determining whether the breach of duty by the medical laboratories was the proximate cause of an injury cognizable by law. In deciding in favor of the plaintiff and granting damages to her, the court commented:

The circumstance that the birth and injury have come hand in hand has caused other courts to deal with the problem by barring recovery. The reality of the "wrongful-life" concept is that such a plaintiff both *exists* and *suffers*, due to the negligence of others. It is neither necessary nor just to retreat into meditation on the mysteries of life. We need not be concerned with the fact that had defendants not been negligent, the plaintiff might not have come into existence at all. . . . a reverent appreciation of life compels recognition that plaintiff, however impaired she may be, has come into existence as a living person with certain rights. . . . In essence, we construe the "wrong-life" cause of action by the defective child as the right of such child to recover damages for the pain and suffering to be endured during the limited life span available to such a child. . . .

These two cases are representative of numerous tort actions in which parents and/or minor children have sought redress for wrongs committed by others in connection with pregnancy and birth. The adult plaintiffs in the cases have included parents of healthy but unwanted children, parents of wanted but unhealthy children, and parents of unhealthy and unwanted children. Children in the cases have presented conditions to the courts ranging from unplanned but normal births to illegitimacy to serious congenital anomalies such as rubella syndrome, infantile polycystic kidney disease (a fatal genetic condition involving grapelike clusters of cysts throughout the kidneys), Tay-Sachs disease, cri-du-chat syndrome (a chromosome aberration resulting in profound mental deficiency, slowed growth, microcephaly, and a catlike cry in infancy), Down's syndrome, spina bifida cystica, and neurofibromatosis (an abnormal development of the nervous system, muscles, bone, and skin, with "Elephant Man" soft tumors distributed over the entire body). Defendants in the cases have included medical laboratories, pharmaceutical companies, the U.S. government, and, most frequently, physicians practicing obstetrics and gynecology.

In addition to being different in terms of the persons bringing the suits, these two types of tort actions also differ in the probability that the suits will succeed in court. There have been over 50 wrongful birth cases over the years since 1965, and the chances of additional wrongful birth cases succeeding in the near future can hardly be questioned. As Judge Swygert pointed out in the Robak case (in August 1981), all courts handling wrongful birth cases since the abortion decision in *Roe* v. *Wade* (January 1973) have decided in favor of the parents of a child born as a result of a physician's negligence.

In fact, wrongful birth suits have become widely accepted as a form of medical malpractice action. An example of this acceptance of wrongful birth suits is *Phillips* v. *United States of America*. Kathleen Phillips gave birth to a son with Down's syndrome at the Naval Regional Medical Center in Charleston, South Carolina, in 1977. Having had a previous miscarriage and having spent much of her adult life at home caring for an older sister with Down's syndrome, Kathleen had earlier told Robert Sadler, an obstetrics resident at the center, of her concern for the mental and physical well-being of the fetus she carried. Nevertheless, he failed to tell her about amniocentesis or recommend that she undergo this procedure for prenatal diagnosis. Kathleen and her husband subsequently sued the government (Sadler could not, as a government employee, personally be sued) for $5 million in January 1981, arguing that their son would never have been born had Kathleen known that she was carrying a fetus with Down's syndrome. Judge Sol Blatt granted the parents recovery of damages for their son's wrongful birth and found the case not significantly different from other malpractice actions:

> It can readily be seen that plaintiffs' claim falls within the traditional boundaries of negligence: the essential elements of duty, breach, proximate cause, and damage are undeniably present. . . . Therefore, this court does not find that plaintiffs' "wrongful birth" claim states a new and distinct cause of action, but rather that their injury can be redressed through conventional tort principles.[7]

In sharp contrast, suits for wrongful life initiated by child plaintiffs have rarely succeeded in court. Beginning with *Zepeda* v. *Zepeda*, a 1963

Illinois appellate court decision, there have been approximately two dozen wrongful life actions. All of the 11 cases prior to 1977 denied compensation to the child plaintiffs. Of these cases, the most important was *Gleitman* v. *Cosgrove*, a 1967 New Jersey Supreme Court decision that barred recovery of damages by a child with rubella syndrome. The court's decision was based on public policy considerations and the perceived impossibility of computing damages.[8]

A wrongful life action was given judicial cognizance for the first time in 1977. The *Park* v. *Chessin* decision in an intermediate New York appellate court claimed that a child has "the fundamental right . . . to be born as a whole, functional human being."[9] However, this decision was subsequently reviewed in 1978 by the New York Court of Appeals in *Becker* v. *Schwartz* and overruled. The court specifically rejected the idea that a child has a right to be born without congenital defect.[10]

Since *Becker*, the trend of judicial decisions in wrongful life cases has been somewhat mixed. In jurisdictions outside of California and Washington, infant plaintiffs have continued to be barred from recovery of damages even in cases in which their parents have been awarded damages in parallel wrongful birth actions. The leading example of these cases is *Speck* v. *Finegold*, a Pennsylvania case involving the genetic neural disease of neurofibromatosis. Alleging that an infant daughter had been born with the disease after negligent vasectomy and abortion procedures on the parents, the Specks filed parallel wrongful birth and wrongful life suits. The superior court dismissed the wrongful life action on behalf of the daughter, but granted the parents damages for the girl's wrongful birth. When the case was appealed to the Pennsylvania Supreme Court in 1981, that court upheld the parents' wrongful birth action but refused— because of a tie vote among the justices—to overturn the lower court's decision on the wrongful life action.[11]

In California the Curlender case (case 5.2), which disagreed with *Becker* by granting damages to the infant plaintiff, was partially followed by *Turpin* v. *Sortini*. The suit in behalf of Hope Turpin, a second daughter, alleged that she would never have been conceived if Adam Sortini, a speech and hearing specialist, had correctly informed her parents that their first daughter was "stone deaf" from a hereditary form of deafness. First heard in the Fresno Superior Court, the case was appealed to the California Supreme Court in 1982. That court ruled that Hope could not recover general damages for having been born impaired, but could be compensated for the extraordinary expenses necessary to treat her hereditary condition.[12]

In the state of Washington, the supreme court affirmed the validity of wrongful life actions in January 1983. In *Harbeson* v. *Parke-Davis, Inc.*, the justices unanimously held that two minor plaintiffs were to be compensated for the extraordinary expenses involved in their conditions of fetal hydantoin syndrome. Jean Harbeson, an epileptic mother of one normal child, had checked with three physicians at McChord Air Force Base regarding the risks of using Dilantin, an anticonvulsant drug, during any subsequent pregnancies. Relying on their assurances of only minor risk, she later gave birth to Elizabeth (in 1974) and Christine (in 1975). Both girls suffered from "mild to moderate growth deficiencies, mild to moderate developmental retardation, wide-set eyes, lateral ptosis (drooping eyelids), hypoplasia of the fingers, small nails, low-set hairline, broad nasal ridge, and other physical and developmental defects." Having affirmed the parents' wrongful birth suit, the justices held that, although general damages in the case were impossible to compute, the girls were to be paid the calculable expenses required for their ongoing medical care and special training. Simply put, the justices reasoned that "were it not for the negligence of the physicians, the minor plaintiffs would not have been born, and would consequently not have suffered fetal hydantoin syndrome."[13]

Although these wrongful life cases have involved some legal questions that are not germane to the issue of selective nontreatment, several of the courts have given serious attention to two kinds of questions that have bearing on the decisions about treatment or nontreatment in NICUs. First, some courts have wrestled with the evaluative issue of comparing seriously impaired existence and nonexistence. Is life in any form always to be preferred to nonexistence? Is postnatal existence ever harmful on balance to an individual born with crippling congenital defects? Would some infants with severe birth defects be better off dead than alive? Second, some courts have taken up the more practical issue of compensation for the injury of continued existence. What should be done with an infant who, possibly through another person's negligence, both exists and suffers in our midst? Should some of these infants and/or their parents be awarded damages for the physical suffering and emotional trauma involved in an unwanted, handicapped life?

Most courts to date have concluded that impaired existence is preferable to nonexistence and that devising a fair procedure for computing the damages brought about by wrongful life is an impossible task. For example, the majority of the justices of the *Gleitman* court maintained that any suggestion that nonexistence could ever be preferred to continued existence—even with serious handicaps—is simply wrong. At one point comparing "life with defects" with "the utter void of nonexistence," the justices argued that if the infant plaintiff could have been asked prior to birth whether he wanted to live or not, "our felt intuition of human nature tells us that he would almost surely choose life with defects as against no life at all."[14] The *Becker* court agreed, stating that "whether it is better never to have been born at all than to have been born with even gross deficiencies is a mystery, more properly to be left to the philosophers and the theologians." They rejected the idea that handicapped existence could be regarded as an injury and thus denied damages to the plaintiff:

> Not only is there to be found no predicate at common law or in statutory enactment for judicial recognition of the birth of a defective child as an injury to the child; the implications of any such proposition are staggering. Would claims be honored, assuming the breach of an identifiable duty, for less than a perfect birth? And by what standard or by whom would perfection be defined?[15]

Three courts, several legal commentators, and some justices in written opinions have come to a different conclusion, arguing that postnatal existence can in some instances be a legally cognizable injury that may call for damages being granted to the plaintiff. The *Curlender* court granted Shauna Curlender general damages for her shortened life expectancy of four years and permitted the plaintiffs to proceed with their $3 million claim for punitive damages, if such could be proven.[16] The *Turpin* court, dealing with a less severe medical condition, refused to grant general damages but did grant compensation for Hope Turpin's medical expenses. Stating that life may not always be preferable to nonexistence, the court observed that when a health professional negligently fails to diagnose a hereditary condition, "he harms the potential child as well as the parents by depriving the parents of information which may be necessary to determine whether it is in the child's own interest to be born with defects or not to be born at all."[17] The *Harbeson* court agreed, arguing that extraordinary expenses for medical care and special training are calculable and should be paid by "the party whose negligence was in fact a proximate cause of the child's continuing need for such special medical care and training."[18] Several legal commentators have argued that computing damages in wrongful life cases need not be regarded as impossible and have proposed ways of determining awards for injurious life.[19] And Pennsylvania Supreme Court Justice Flaherty, in the lead opinion to

Speck v. *Finegold*, argued that courts need to recognize the merit of wrongful life actions, including the claim that nonexistence may sometimes be preferable to impaired life:

> The view that we cannot calculate the value of existence as compared to nonexistence is only . . . hyper-scholastic rationale used to deny a cause of action in these cases. . . . Existence in itself can hardly be characterized as an injury, but when existence is foreseeably and inextricably coupled with a disease, such an existence, depending upon the nature of the disease, may be intolerably burdensome. To judicially foreclose consideration of whether life in a particular case is such a burden would be to tell the diseased, possibly deformed plaintiff that he can seek no remedy in the courts and to imply that his alternative remedy, in the extreme event that he finds his life unduly burdensome, is suicide.[20]

Implications for selective nontreatment decisions

What may come out of this legal debate over wrongful life actions, and what implications do these tort actions have for parents and physicians confronted with decisions about treatment or nontreatment? If wrongful life actions become accepted by jurisdictions other than California and Washington, at least three possibilities exist for using these tort actions in connection with treatment decisions in NICUs. First, should a number of courts accept the claims of plaintiffs that severely handicapped existence is worse than nonexistence, such judicial decisions might provide the legal basis for some parents and/or physicians to claim that nontreatment in cases of severe congenital defects is legally permissible because continued existence is not in the best interests of the birth-defective infants. Parents and physicians in such cases could argue that life-prolonging treatment for an infant whose impaired existence is the result of another person's negligence would be tantamount to adding a second wrongful act (the postnatal continuation of a severely handicapped life) to the first one (the negligent conception or prenatal continuation of the handicapped life). Or they might argue, where there has been no negligence, that some instances of multiple handicap (especially those involving serious neurological impairment) are so severe that they represent "wrongful lives" whose suffering should not be prolonged through medical treatment.

A second possibility is that wrongful life actions might be initiated against neonatologists, other pediatricians, or pediatric surgeons who earlier prolonged a severely handicapped life through aggressive treatment.

Child plaintiffs in such cases, which could be initiated years after leaving the NICU, might claim that they would have been released into peaceful oblivion—or God's loving care—but for the negligence of a physician who blindly continued treatment that could neither cure nor correct an anomalous condition but only prolong an unwanted, handicapped existence for an indeterminate period of time. Should such legal actions come into being, physicians practicing in NICUs might be caught in a legal bind: failure to treat a severe birth-defective infant could lead to criminal charges, whereas noncorrective treatment of the infant's anomalous condition could lead to a later wrongful life action.

A third possibility is that birth-defective infant plaintiffs might, perhaps by citing the Curlender case, file wrongful life actions against their parents. The *Curlender* court opened the judicial door to the possibility of suits against parents by suggesting that if parents were to make a conscious choice to proceed with a pregnancy involving a seriously impaired fetus, those parents might be legally liable "for the pain, suffering, and misery which they have wrought upon their offspring."[21] To cite several examples, if a pregnant woman decided to carry a genetically defective fetus to term, or damaged the fetus by withholding proper prenatal care, or exposed the fetus to mutagens and teratogens, that fetus-become-birth-defective-infant might "claim that his right to be born physically and mentally sound had been invaded."[22] And if, to borrow Angela Holder's term, this "parenting malpractice" extended into the parents' decision in the NICU to prolong a birth-defective neonate's life that the child subsequently regards as worse than death would have been, that child plaintiff might sue the parents for negligently extending an injurious existence.[23]

The trend of wrongful life actions, however, suggests that few if any of these possibilities will become reality. Given the history of trial court cases outside of California and Washington, it is doubtful that very many wrongful life suits arising out of decisions made in NICUs would succeed in court. And at least three states have taken legislative action to ensure that whatever direction wrongful life suits take in the future, it will not be possible for children in these states to sue their parents for wrongfully continuing their lives. South Dakota, in 1981, was the first state to take this legislative step.[24] The legislatures in California and Minnesota passed similar laws in 1982, with the California statute clearly being an effort to avert the possibility of parental liability suggested by *Curlender*. The first part of the California law declares: "No cause of action arises against a parent of a child based upon the claim that the child should not have been conceived or, if conceived, should not have been allowed to have been born alive."[25] Similar laws have been proposed in several other state legislatures, with the proposed legislation in Indiana extending protection for parents into the neonatal period of a birth-defective child.[26]

Legal activity at the federal level

The absence of a national infanticide law does not mean that all legal action relating to the lives and deaths of handicapped infants resides with the 50 states. In fact, there has been a crescendo of legal activity at the federal level over the past decade.

Ten years after the Johns Hopkins Hospital case (see case 2.2) and the same year that the Shaw, Duff, and Campbell articles appeared in *The New England Journal of Medicine*, the federal Rehabilitation Act became law. Section 504 of that 1973 law is the basic civil rights statute for handicapped individuals. Section 504 states: "No otherwise qualified handicapped individual . . . shall, solely by reason of his handicap, be excluded from the participation in, be denied the benefits of, or be subject to discrimination under any program or activity receiving federal financial assistance. . . ."[27]

Three years later, and two years after the publicity surrounding the Baby Boy Houle case (see case 4.1), President Ford issued an executive order intended to bring about a consistent implementation of section 504. In his executive order he gave authority to the secretary of health, education and welfare for coordinating the implementation of the 1973 law:

> The Secretary shall establish standards for determining who are handicapped individuals and guidelines for determining what are discriminatory practices, within the meaning of section 504. . . . compliance with section 504 may be effected by the suspension or termination of, or refusal to award or continue, Federal financial assistance or by other appropriate means authorized by law. . . ."[28]

Although section 504 applies to health care services funded through the renamed Department of Health and Human Services (HHS), neither section 504 nor President Ford's executive order specifically addressed the issue of health services to handicapped neonates. Nevertheless, two cases of selective nontreatment received such unprecedented press coverage in 1982 that they led HHS to attempt to apply section 504 to any similar cases arising in the future.

Case 5.3

A baby known only as "Infant Doe" was born in Bloomington, Indiana, on Friday, April 9, 1982. He had Down's syndrome, plus esophageal atresia with associated tracheoesophageal fistula. Over the course of six days, he became the focal point of an intensive medical, legal, and ethical debate.

The physicians in the case were divided regarding treatment or non-treatment. Some of them wanted to have the baby flown to Riley Children's Hospital in Indianapolis for surgery; others argued that the baby should remain in Bloomington and be given nothing more than oxygen and antibiotics. Much of the medical debate had to do with the operation's chance of success, with some of the physicians arguing that 85–90% of such surgical attempts succeed and others giving the operation only a 50-50 chance of success.

The parents, who remained anonymous throughout the highly publicized case, were presented with the two medical options. They chose to have Infant Doe remain in Bloomington without surgery and without intravenous feeding.

The administrators at Bloomington Hospital sought legal advice on the possibility of intervening in the case with court-mandated surgery. Special Circuit Judge John Baker, in an emergency hearing Saturday night, ruled that the parents had the right to withhold medical treatment in order that the baby would die.

On Monday the Monroe County Welfare Department, which Judge Baker had appointed as the baby's guardian *ad litem*, decided not to appeal the judge's ruling. The following day—the fourth day of Infant Doe's life—Monroe County Prosecutors Barry Brown and Philip Hill intervened in the case. Judge Baker encouraged an appeal of his own ruling by appointing Hill as guardian *ad litem* in place of the welfare department. Hill, in turn, filed an emergency petition with the Monroe County Circuit Court, seeking to have the court take custody of the child.

When that move failed, the prosecutors appealed to the Indiana Supreme Court to overrule the lower court judges by ordering intravenous feeding and the potentially lifesaving surgery. On Wednesday the Indiana Supreme Court gave the case an informal hearing. The justices voted three to one not to intervene in the case, apparently because they were concerned about second-guessing physicians on medical matters.

The prosecutors made one last effort. Deputy Prosecutor Larry Brodeur, who was appointed guardian *ad litem* after the Indiana Supreme Court hearing, left for Washington, D.C., early Thursday morning. He was accompanied by Pat Baude, an Indiana University law professor. They were going to appeal to Justice Paul Stevens for an emergency stay of the Indiana court orders on the grounds that Infant Doe had been denied due process.

If they had contacted Justice Stevens, Brodeur and Baude were prepared to raise several legal questions:

"Does this child have a right to continue living under the Fourteenth Amendment to the U.S. Constitution?"

"Does this child have the same rights that we all enjoy to the protections of procedural Due Process?"

"Was this child denied Equal Protection because of his handicap?"

The questions were never asked in a formal legal hearing, however, because Infant Doe died while the prosecutors were en route to Washington.

The public outcry over the case caused the prosecutors to consider bringing criminal charges against the parents and physician. They finally chose not to do so, with Prosecutor Brown giving their reasons:

> The parents and physician were proceeding under a ruling of the Monroe Circuit Court, and therefore, under the color of law. None of the traditional purposes for invoking the criminal sanction—deterrence, punishment, rehabilitation—are applicable in this case. We can find no theory of criminal law which would justify placing the parents or the physician in criminal jeopardy. We also believe that the pursuit of criminal action in this case would only compound the tragedy.[29]

Case 5.4

A baby boy was born April 25, 1982, in Lawrenceville, Illinois. He had spina bifida cystica, and for that reason was flown by helicopter to St. John's Hospital in Springfield for specialized neonatal care. A neurosurgeon at St. John's recommended surgery. On May 2 the baby was transferred to Crawford Memorial Hospital in Robinson, Illinois, a small hospital without the capacity to offer the specialized care required by the majority of infants with spina bifida.

Apart from these details, many of the facts in this case were never divulged to the public. Neither the boy's name nor the name of the parents was given to inquiring reporters who heard about the story. Carlton King, the administrator of the hospital in Robinson, refused to discuss the case for reasons of patient confidentiality. And Larry Herron, the family's physician in Lawrenceville, claimed that the case was a private matter: "I don't think this is the public's concern."

The only reason that the case became publicly known was the report of an anonymous nurse at St. John's Hospital. After the baby had been transferred to Robinson, the nurse contacted the Family Life League, a pro-life organization in Chicago, and indicated that the parents had cancelled proposed surgery on the infant prior to moving the baby to Robinson and that the baby was apparently being starved in the Robinson hospital. Members of the Family Life League, in turn, tried to secure information about the baby and reported the case to the Illinois Department of Children and Family Services (DCFS).

The DCFS investigated the case, said that the child was "doing as well as can be expected," and ruled that there had been no parental neglect. In spite of that ruling, a news story about the case was reported in the national media on May 17, and the case suddenly became a matter of public concern to numerous individuals and organizations. The Family Life League and several other pro-life groups made assertions in the media about the baby's condition in the Robinson hospital. The Spina Bifida Association of America, headquartered in Chicago, assumed an advocacy role by publicly calling for "treatment of this baby and of every infant born with spina bifida" because "ninety percent of children born with this condition today grow to live normal, healthy lives." And both the Department of Justice and the Department of Health and Human Services sent investigators to Robinson to determine if the case fell under federal jurisdiction.

State and federal investigation of the case stopped when the parents arranged for Dr. David McLone to treat the infant. The chairman of pediatric neurosurgery at the Children's Memorial Hospital in Chicago, McLone found the infant to be "viable and healthy" and in no immediate need of surgery. The boy was subsequently transferred to Children's Memorial for treatment.

On May 21 the DCFS accepted legal guardianship of the boy and began trying to locate adoptive parents. A DCFS spokesman said the legal action was taken at the parents' request: "What we really have here is a situation where the parents explored options related to the future of the child and decided to surrender the child to the state for adoptive placement."[30]

Unlike the majority of earlier selective nontreatment cases, the cases in Bloomington and Robinson received national press coverage. Also unlike most previous cases, these cases had individuals and groups attempting to go beyond local legal jurisdictions to involve the federal government. And in contrast to the minimal attention given to all previous nontreatment cases involving neonates, the government responded to these cases with a flurry of activity.

In response to the Infant Doe case, President Reagan sent a memorandum to Richard Schweiker, Secretary of HHS. Dated April 30, 1982, the memo instructed Schweiker to notify health care providers that section 504 of the Rehabilitation Act "forbids recipients of federal funds from withholding from handicapped citizens, simply because they are handicapped, any benefit or services that would ordinarily be provided to persons without handicaps."[31]

On May 18, 1982, the day after the Robinson case received national publicity, HHS issued a "Notice to Health Care Providers" that informed the administrators of the nation's 6800 hospitals that, under section 504 of the 1973 law, they risked losing federal funds if they withheld treatment or nourishment from handicapped infant patients. Written by Betty Lou Dotson, the director of the HHS Office for Civil Rights, the notice referred to the Bloomington case and stated:

> It is unlawful . . . to withhold from a handicapped infant nutritional sustenance or medical or surgical treatment required to correct a life-threatening condition, if:
> (1) the withholding is based on the fact that the infant is handicapped; and
> (2) the handicap does not render the treatment or nutritional sustenance medically contraindicated.

The HHS notice went on to inform hospital administrators that decisions made by a handicapped infant's parents or physician could cost the hospital federal funds. To ensure the continuation of federal support, administrators were encouraged to use three guidelines to avoid any practices that might be discriminatory against handicapped infants:

(1) Counseling of parents should not discriminate by encouraging parents to make decisions which, if made by the health care provider, would be discriminatory under section 504.
(2) Health care providers should not aid a decision by the infant's parents or guardian to withhold treatment or nourishment discriminatorily by allowing the infant to remain in the institution.
(3) Health care providers are responsible for the conduct of physicians with respect to cases administered through their facilities.[32]

On May 26, 1982, another effort was made to involve the federal government in selective nontreatment decisions. Congressman John Erlenborn, a Republican from Illinois, introduced a bill called the Handicapped Infants Protection Act of 1982. With bipartisan support, the Erlenborn bill was an effort to amend the Child Abuse Prevention and Treatment Act (42 U.S.C. 5101 et seq.) and grant new authority to the National Center on Child Abuse and Neglect. The bill claimed that "it is a fundamental principle of American law to affirm the value of all human life without regard to mental or physical disability," that "the value of human life must be affirmed by law and not left to the arbitrary discretion of individuals," and that "the death of handicapped infants through deliberate neglect is a matter of gravest national concern demanding immediate action by the Congress."[33]

If it had become law, the Erlenborn bill would have empowered the secretary of HHS to intercede in nontreatment decisions to save a handicapped infant's life. Defining a handicapped infant as "any infant who has any mental or physical disability or impairment which requires the provision of multiple services during an extended period of time," the bill stated that

> a resident physician or other professional staff member of a health care facility, or any other physician, health care professional, or other person using the facilities of a health care facility, shall not deprive a handicapped infant of nutrition which is necessary to sustain life, or deprive a handicapped infant of medical treatment which is necessary to remedy or ameliorate a life-threatening medical condition, if (1) any such deprivation is carried out for the purpose of causing or allowing the death of such infant; and (2) such nutrition or medical treatment generally is provided to similarly situated infants and handicapped infants.[34]

Should this bill ever become law, an act of nontreatment may be the cause for a legal action brought against the physician by "any interested person": a parent or guardian of the handicapped infant, another individual, a private nonprofit organization, or a governmental agency. The court hearing the case may, in turn, mandate any of several remedies: injunctions to restrain further violations of the law, placement of the handicapped infant in temporary foster care or custody, compensatory damages, and punitive damages. If the secretary of HHS is informed of continuing violations by the same parties, he or she may instigate civil action against the individual physician and withhold federal financial assistance from the hospital in which the physician works.[35]

On March 2, 1983, the Reagan administration added an "interim rule" to go along with the HHS notice to hospitals. Ten months after the notice to the nation's hospital administrators, HHS issued regulations requiring hospitals receiving federal funds to post warning signs in delivery rooms, pediatric wards, nurseries, and NICUs. These warning signs read: "Discriminatory failure to feed and care for handicapped infants in this facility is prohibited by federal law. Failure to feed and care for infants may also violate the criminal and civil laws of your state."[36] In conjunction with this directive, HHS also set up a toll-free hotline to facilitate the reporting of parents, physicians, and hospitals not in compliance with these federal regulations. These regulations were to become effective March 22, 1983.

An assessment of these federal moves

It is impossible at the time of this writing to know what is going to happen with these efforts at the federal level. Only the course of future events will indicate the importance hospital administrators place on the HHS notice, the lengths to which HHS is prepared to go in carrying out the threat to withhold federal funds from hospitals in which nontreatment decisions are made, the decisions of future federal administrations to continue these policies, and the legal significance of the notice itself (as well as subsequent regulations). Carlton King, the Robinson hospital administrator who was cabled a copy of the notice the day it was issued, responded to the initial HHS action with unconcern: "We take it for what it is—a non-binding opinion."[37] Richard Givan, the chief justice of the Indiana Supreme Court, thought the notice represented unnecessary government involvement in medical matters: "There's no need for any legislation. . . . We can't legislate miracles. We can't pass a law saying doctors have to save every child that's born."[38]

As to the Erlenborn bill, it is currently pending (as H.R. 808) in the House Committee on Education and Labor and the Committee on Energy and Commerce in the Ninety-eighth Congress. Having been introduced in the Ninety-seventh Congress, it failed to get out of committee. Whether the bill comes out of committee in this Congress, and in what form, remains to be seen. By the time these words are published, the bill may be part of the law of the land—or it may have died again in committee.

In the midst of this uncertainty about what the future holds, it is important to emphasize the significance of these moves at the federal level. There is no federal statutory law that explicitly pertains to cases of selective nontreatment with infants, and no case involving a decision to withhold medical treatment from a neonate has as yet reached the U.S. Supreme Court. The HHS notice, the HHS regulations, and the pending Erlenborn bill are therefore unprecedented attempts either to apply federal legislation (the 1973 Rehabilitation Act) to neonatal cases of selective nontreatment or to enact federal legislation specifically designed to curtail instances of selective nontreatment with handicapped infants.

Given the frequency of selective nontreatment decisions in NICUs and the extent to which these decisions result in the deaths of birth-defective infants, it is understandable why these federal efforts at regulation and legislation have been made. Had some of the cases prior to the Blooming-ton and Robinson cases received the same kind of national publicity, federal attempts to intervene in selective nontreatment cases would un-doubtedly have taken place years earlier. And once such cases received widespread publicity and highly emotional public debate, it was un-doubtedly difficult for federal officials and legislators to sit by idly and permit what appeared to be arbitrary decisions by parents and physicians, accommodating policies by hospital administrators, and at least one inconsistent lower court decision (the one in case 5.3) to have the combined effect of allowing some infants to die simply because they are handicapped and not clearly protected by law.

Responses to these federal moves have been fairly predictable. Many persons and organizations have found the HHS notice, the HHS regula-tions, and the Erlenborn bill to be the kind of "medicine" necessary to save the lives of an unknown number of infants who would otherwise die from selective nontreatment. Some, but not all, of these favorable re-sponses have come from representatives of pro-life groups. For instance,

J. C. Willke, a physician and the president of the National Right to Life Committee, issued this news release:

> Fatal discrimination against Down's syndrome and other handicapped infants has been increasing for years in this country. This discrimination consists of denial of medical treatment, even food and water, which would be routinely provided to non-handicapped infants. The ethic which promotes infanticide is related to the elitist "quality of life" argument used to justify abortion-on-demand. Infanticide is a form of barbarism which our nation should emphatically reject.[39]

Even the *New York Times*, not generally regarded as an instrument of the pro-life movement, suggested in an early response to the Infant Doe case that some kind of federal intervention in nontreatment cases might be warranted: "a child . . . is a part of society and entitled to its protection. Their undoubted anguish explains the decision made by Infant Doe's parents, but not the courts' refusal to intervene. The death of Infant Doe is not a 'private matter.'"[40]

By contrast, many of the professionals who bear responsibility for nontreatment decisions found the federal moves in 1982 and 1983 to be unnecessary and troublesome. Two professional organizations responded critically to the HHS notice and presumably will take similar positions regarding the pending bill before Congress. On May 18, 1982, the day of the HHS notice, the American Hospital Association issued a formal statement denying that "hospitals have in any way been guilty of discrimination" and promising to "make every effort to assure that such simplistic solutions to complex situations involving health care delivery are avoided."[41] On June 21, 1982, the American Academy of Pediatrics (AAP) issued its official position regarding the HHS notice:

> The effort of the executive branch to solve this complex problem through strict interpretation and enforcement of the letter of section 504 may have the unintended effect of requiring treatment that is *not* in the best interest of handicapped children. Handicapped persons . . . need health care providers who will carefully examine the appropriateness of specific medical intervention. . . . It will frequently be the case that the use of a specific technology or procedures will *not* be in the best interest of the handicapped person. Withholding a medical treatment will frequently be both legally and ethically justified in our efforts to do what is right for these patients. . . .[42]

On March 18, 1983, the AAP, joined by several other medical associations, brought suit in the U.S. district court against HHS and Margaret Heckler, the new HHS secretary, to prevent the HHS regulations from going into effect. Judge Gerhard Gesell denied a temporary restraining order, but agreed to hear the case on April 8. The week following the hearing he ruled that the HHS interim rule was invalid because the agency had issued the rule without granting affected parties the normal length of time to comment on it. In addition, the judge observed that HHS had not defined what "customary medical care" meant with seriously handicapped infants, that the free hotline was "ill-considered" and could be seriously misused, that civil rights investigators ("Baby Doe Squads") might jeopardize quality care in NICUs, and that the rule was "arbitrary and capricious" and "virtually without meaning beyond its intrinsic *in terrorem* effect."[43]

In response, HHS appealed Judge Gesell's decision and on July 5 issued a revised set of regulations intended to become effective after a 60-day comment period. The proposed new rules are much more specific than the earlier version. The new rules continue the use of the hotline and the posted notice in hospitals, but indicate that the notice is required only in a conspicuous place in each nurses' station having responsibility for the care of neonates. The heart of the new rules is an effort substantially to reduce parental and physician discretion in making selective nontreatment decisions, with the claim that section 504 of the 1973 Rehabilitation Act comes into effect "when non-medical considerations, such as subjective judgments that an unrelated handicap makes a person's life not worth living, are interjected in the decision-making process." In addition, the new rules emphasize that section 504 protects only those infants who are able to benefit from treatment, exempt from these regulations the care of terminally ill infants and other infants for whom treatment would be futile, call for state child-protection agencies to work in conjunction with the HHS Office for Civil Rights in enforcing the regulations in hospitals, and grant HHS investigators access to confidential hospital records to ascertain compliance with section 504.[44]

Again, public comments regarding the new rules have been fairly predictable. An attorney for the AAP, saying that the new rules are "not really that different" from the first version, provided a concise statement of the AAP position: "We have serious concern with the presence of a sign like that in hospitals." In contrast, Surgeon General Everett Koop observed that the government's plan to curtail parental and physician discretion is working: "the fact that [three hospitals] were recently under investigation caused [the hospitals] to reassess their position."[45]

There are, in my judgment, several reasons for siding with the critics of these federal moves. Although the authors of the HHS notice, the first HHS rules, and the pending legislative bill are undoubtedly well intentioned, the results of their efforts are sufficiently vague that they will be difficult to apply to the decisions made in NICUs and virtually impossible to defend in courts of law. What, for instance, does the HHS notice mean by raising the possibility that "nutritional sustenance" might be "medically contraindicated"? Even neonates who cannot be fed by mouth (e.g., because of esophageal or duodenal atresia) are regularly fed intravenously in NICUs. What does the HHS notice mean when it says that treatment is legally required unless the handicap makes such treatment "medically contraindicated"? Is it intended to be limited to specific treatments (e.g., surgery for esophageal atresia) whose usefulness would normally be determined by means of a risk–benefit calculation? Or is it intended to allow for circumstances in which a particularly severe handicap would render virtually all treatments medically contraindicated because they would prolong the life of a child who would be better off dead? And what does the proposed law mean by saying that medical treatment is legally required for handicapped infants if "such nutrition or medical treatment generally is provided to similarly situated infants and handicapped infants"? The intention of the bill's author is clear enough as long as the handicap is Down's syndrome accompanied by esophageal atresia, and the comparative case (the "similarly situated" infant) is a neonate with esophageal atresia but no accompanying mental deficiency. But what about neonates with anencephaly or hydranencephaly or trisomy 18 or exstrophy of the cloaca or severe intraventricular hemorrhage? What kind of case represents the "similarly situated" infant whose medical treatment is the standard by which treatment in these cases is to be judged?

A second problem with these regulatory and legislative efforts is that they frequently fail to distinguish between handicaps that call for curative or corrective treatment, and handicaps that do not call for treatment because they cannot be cured or corrected. The HHS notice, the first HHS rules (but not the revised ones), and the proposed statute were written largely in response to the Bloomington case of Down's syndrome. Possibly for that reason they fail to reflect the range of congenital anomalies that occur in NICUs, some of which are much less complicated than Down's syndrome with esophageal atresia and others that fail to respond to even the most aggressive treatment because of their severity.

Nevertheless, the specter of Infant Doe leads the authors of these documents (and the authors of the HHS regulations) to imply that few if any congenital handicaps could ever legally justify decisions for nontreatment. By thus blurring the significant medical differences between rather mild congenital abnormalities (e.g., cleft lip, clubfoot) and the much more severe ones (e.g., anencephaly, trisomy 18, extreme prematurity, grade 4 intraventricular hemorrhage), these documents do not acknowledge that some medical treatment in some cases of severe congenital handicap may justifiably be withheld because the treatment is not in the infant's best interests. For Norman Fost, this failure of the HHS notice to distinguish among congenital defects makes the document itself defective:

> We withhold dialysis from an anencephalic infant girl precisely because she is so handicapped that she cannot experience any benefit from the treatment. Handicap, therefore, is a morally valid reason for withholding treatment *in some cases*. The fundamental defect of Section 504 is its failure to distinguish between handicaps that justify nontreatment and those which do not.[46]

There is another, more serious problem with these federal attempts to curtail selective nontreatment. The first two difficulties might be alleviated by revising the wording in the documents so that they more accurately reflect the complexity and diversity of congenital anomalies confronted in NICUs. And in fact, the revised HHS rules are considerably less vague than the earlier documents. Such revisions do not, however, settle the issue of whether federal intervention in the decisions made about birth-defective infants in hospitals is warranted. There is little question that for persons supporting these federal moves, the HHS notice, the HHS rules, and the Erlenborn bill represent long-overdue steps to prevent further acts of criminal homicide in some of the nation's hospitals. Many persons are concerned at the prospect of any neonate dying from only moderate birth defects that can be treated—and probably would be treated if the infant had ended up in another hospital.

Nevertheless, as high as the stakes are in cases of selective nontreatment, the question that must be addressed is whether federal legal intervention is the best way of handling the problem. I do not think it is. Even though federal regulations or a federal statute would have the beneficial effect of saving the lives of some neonates like Infant Doe, they would also have numerous detrimental consequences. Should the revised HHS rules go into effect or should a law such as the Erlenborn bill become reality, such events would severely limit the discretion of parents and physicians faced with complicated decisions, force physicians in cases of severe congenital defect to be even more surreptitious in withholding treatment than they are now, and lead other physicians already anxious about the law to practice increasingly defensive neonatal medicine. Neonatologists and other pediatricians practicing defensive medicine would, to save their own careers, decide to give aggressive treatment to all handicapped neonates— regardless of the handicap, the effectiveness of the treatment, or the harm done to those relatively few neonates who would be better off without life-prolonging treatment. Because many pediatricians disagree with regulations or a law mandating treatment in all cases of congenital handicap, the government would have to establish an ongoing form of surveillance process in NICUs to make the law work effectively and then be prepared to prosecute those parents, physicians, and hospital administrators who, perhaps for reasons of conscience and compassion toward an extremely handicapped infant, decided to break the law. Moreover, because almost all criminal law (including homicide) has traditionally been a matter of state law, any effort to involve the federal government in criminal proceedings would raise significant constitutional as well as law enforcement problems.

Finally a federal law—or state law, for that matter—mandating medical treatment for all handicapped infants would obscure the fact that decisions about neonatal medical treatment are fundamentally moral decisions that often deal with complex situations.[47] Once a birth-defective neonate's medical condition has been accurately diagnosed and a prognosis carefully made about the prospects for improvement under treatment, someone has to decide whether the treatment will, on balance, be beneficial or harmful to the infant. And that moral decision can best be made in the highly complex situations of an NICU by someone (preferably a committee in really difficult cases) exercising discretion and displaying sensitivity to the human factors in such situations—not by merely obeying insufficiently designed regulations or a blanket law that may bring about greater harm than benefit for the infants in question.

Subsequent chapters will focus on the moral dimensions of nontreatment decisions. It will be my purpose to show that the interests of handicapped infants are better served by improving the moral reasoning that goes into decisions about treatment and nontreatment, rather than by looking to federal regulations or legislation to protect those interests. In situations where moral reasoning fails—and an infant who should live is instead being left to die untreated—it may still be necessary to seek court action to protect the infant's interests. Thus far, the track record of such lower court decisions indicates that the best interests of handicapped infants are generally protected in such proceedings. Moreover, by using the courts as a backup for the moral reasoning in NICUs, it is possible to have a localized response to the particular factors in cases that simply cannot be anticipated by regulations and laws attempting to cover all cases of congenital defects in the same uniform manner.

A case in Massachusetts illustrates my position and my concern about intervention by the federal administration, the Congress, or state legislatures. "Baby Billy" was born at New England Medical Center in May 1981. Abandoned by his mother at birth, Billy was diagnosed as having cyanotic heart disease. A subsequent cardiac catheterization revealed that Billy had pulmonary atresia, hypoplastic right ventricle, hypoplastic pulmonary artery, and patent ductus arteriosus. The prognosis in the case was straightforward: because there was no treatment for all of these multiple cardiac anomalies, death would occur within several months to a year even with treatment for some of the problems. Nevertheless, PDA surgery was performed and a shunt installed to permit the flow of oxygenated blood to Billy's lungs. By October Billy's condition had deteriorated: the shunt was nonfunctional, another shunt was not medically feasible, and he had a bacterial infection and was respirator-dependent. The physicians recommended a policy of "no code." In hearings initiated by the Department of Social Services before the Boston Juvenile Court, the physicians testified that resuscitation efforts were not in Billy's best interests. When the Massachusetts Supreme Judicial Court, on its own initiative, reviewed the lower court decision to support the "no code" orders, the justices upheld the ruling and commented that the previous judge had "acted promptly, carefully, and diligently in hearing all the evidence put before him."[48] Fortunately, there was no HHS notice, federal statute, or warning sign in the NICU in Billy's case. Had there been these kinds of legal interventions into decisions about selective nontreatment, the moral reasoning in the case might have been short-circuited—and Billy subjected to needless suffering as the physicians practiced defensive medicine.

Notes

1. Becker v. Schwartz, 46 N.Y. 2d 401; 413 N.Y.S. 2d 895, 900; 386 N.E. 2d 807 (1978).

2. Turpin v. Sortini, 182 Cal. Rptr. 337, 346 (1982).
3. See Marten A. Trotzig, "The Defective Child and the Actions for Wrongful Life and Wrongful Birth," *Family Law Quarterly* 14 (Spring 1980): 15–40; Wilber L. Tomlinson, "Torts—Wrongful Birth and Wrongful Life," *Missouri Law Review* 44 (Winter 1979): 167–83: and Thomas Foutz, "'Wrongful Life': The Right Not to be Born," *Tulane Law Review* 54 (February 1980): 480–99.
4. Alexander Capron, "The Continuing Wrong of 'Wrongful Life,'" in Aubrey Milunsky and George J. Annas, eds., *Genetics and the Law II* (New York: Plenum Press, 1980), p. 89.
5. Robak v. United States, 503 F. Supp. 982; 658 F. 2d 471, 473, 475 (1981).
6. This and following quotations in case 5.2 are taken from Curlender v. Bio-Science Laboratories, 106 Cal. App. 3d 811; 165 Cal. Rptr. 477, 479, 480, 488–489, (1980).
7. Phillips v. United States, 508 F. Supp. 544, 550–551 (1981).
8. Gleitman v. Cosgrove, 49 N.J. 22; 227 A. 2d 689 (1967).
9. Park v. Chessin, 400 N.Y.S. 2d 110, 114; 386 N.E. 2d 809 (1977).
10. Becker, *supra*, 386 N.E. 2d 807.
11. Speck v. Finegold, 408 A. 2d 496; 439 A. 2d 110 (1981).
12. Turpin, *supra*, 182 Cal. Rptr. 337.
13. Harbeson v. Parke-Davis, Inc., 98 Wash. 2d 460; 656 P. 2d 483, 486, 497 (1983).
14. Gleitman, *supra*, 227 A. 2d 692–693.
15. Becker, *supra*, 386 N.E. 2d 807, 812.
16. Curlender, *supra*, 165 Cal. Rptr. 477, 489–490.
17. Turpin, *supra*, 182 Cal. Rptr. 337, 345–346.
18. Harbeson, *supra*, 656 P. 2d 483, 495.
19. See Capron, p. 93; Mark Cohen, "Park v. Chessin: The Continuing Judicial Development of the Theory of 'Wrongful Life,'" *American Journal of Law and Medicine* 4 (Summer 1978): 211–32; and Marilyn Bradley, "Wrongful Life—A Tort Whose Time Has Come," *The American Journal of Trial Advocacy* 2 (Fall 1978): 107–33.
20. Speck, *supra*, 439 A. 2d 110, 115.
21. Curlender, *supra*, 165 Cal. Rptr. 477, 488.
22. Margery W. Shaw, "The Potential Plaintiff: Preconception and Prenatal Torts," in Milunsky and Annas, *Genetics and the Law II*, p. 228.
23. For her use of this term, see Angela R. Holder, "Is Existence Ever an Injury?: The Wrongful Life Cases," in Stuart Spicker, Joseph Healey, and Tristram Engelhardt, eds., *The Law-Medicine Relation: A Philosophical Exploration* (Dordrecht, Holland: D. Reidel Publishing Co., 1981), p. 233.
24. House Bill No. 1232, South Dakota Legislative Assembly (1981).
25. Part (a) of Section 43.6 of the Civil Code, California Legislative Assembly (1982); also see House Bill No. 1532, Minnesota House of Representatives (1982).
26. Proposed amendment to IC-1-1, Indiana General Assembly (1982).
27. Rehabilitation Act of 1973, as amended, P.L. 93-112. 29 U.S.C. 794.
28. President Gerald R. Ford, Executive Order 11914, April 28, 1976.
29. This case description is based on several newspaper articles: the *Bloomington (Indiana) Herald-Telephone*, April 15–20, 1982; and the *Louisville Courier-*

Journal, April 16 and 20, 1982. The articles were supplied by David H. Smith and Judith Granbois of Indiana University, Bloomington.

30. This case description is based on several newspaper articles: the *Decatur* (*Illinois*) *Herald & Review*, May 7–12, 1982; the *Washington Post*, May 17, 1982; the *Chicago Tribune*, May 18 and 21, 1982; and the *Chicago Sun-Times*, May 18–20, 1982. The articles were supplied by Kent Smith, executive director of the Spina Bifida Association of America.

31. Mary F. Smith, "Handicapped Newborns: Current Issues and Legislation," Congressional Research Service report, July 28, 1982.

32. Mary Lou Dotson, "Notice to Health Care Providers," Department of Health and Human Services letter, May 18, 1982. The limited extent to which the Rehabilitation Act of 1973 applies to handicapped neonates is analyzed by Nancy Lee Jones in "Application of Section 504 of the Rehabilitation Act of 1973 to Handicapped Infants," Congressional Research Service report, July 9, 1982.

33. H.R. 6492, Ninety-seventh Congress, sec. 2.5–2.7.

34. Ibid., sec. 202 and sec. 206.3.

35. Ibid., sec. 203.

36. *Washington Post*, March 3, 1983. The HHS "interim final rule" was published in the *Federal Register*, March 7, 1983, pp. 9630–32.

37. *Louisville Courier-Journal*, May 19, 1982.

38. *Bloomington Herald-Telephone*, May 19, 1982.

39. J. C. Willke, news release, May 26, 1982. Quoted in Smith, "Handicapped Newborns," p. 6.

40. *New York Times*, April 27, 1982.

41. American Hospital Association, news release, May 18, 1982.

42. American Academy of Pediatrics, official statement, June 21, 1982. Quoted in Smith, "Handicapped Newborns," p. 8.

43. American Academy of Pediatrics v. Heckler, No. 83-0774, U.S. District Court, D.C., April 14, 1983. See also George J. Annas, "Disconnecting the Baby Doe Hotline," *Hastings Center Report* 13 (June 1983): 14–16.

44. *Federal Register*, July 5, 1983, pp. 30846–52.

45. *Washington Post*, July 1, 1983. The position of the American Academy of Pediatrics on the new regulations was presented in *The New England Journal of Medicine* 309 (August 18, 1983): 443–44.

46. Norman Fost, "Putting Hospitals on Notice," *Hastings Center Report* 12 (August 1982): 7.

47. Louisiana was the first state to pass such a law. Act 339, entitled "Nutritional or Medical Deprivation of Infants," was approved by the Louisiana legislature in July 1982, and signed into law two months later.

48. Custody of a Minor, 385 Mass. 697; 434 N.E. 2d 601, 610 (1982).

6

Options among Ethicists

> The fact that dying patients sometimes need no more attempts to be made to save them ought not to be carelessly applied to the case of defective newborns. Sometimes the neglected infants are not born dying. They are only born defective and in need of help.
>
> PAUL RAMSEY, PH.D.[1]

> If the fetus does not have the same claim to life as a person, it appears that the newborn baby does not either, and the life of a newborn baby is of less value than the life of a pig, a dog, or a chimpanzee. . . . the implications of this position for the value of newborn life are at odds with the virtually unchallenged assumption that the life of a newborn baby is as sacrosanct as that of an adult.
>
> PETER SINGER, PH.D.[2]

Previous chapters have contained the views of several physicians and attorneys on the issue of selective nontreatment. As indicated especially in chapters 3 and 4, physicians and attorneys have serious disagreements within their professional ranks regarding the appropriate course of action to follow with birth-defective neonates. Moreover, they tend to talk past each other when they address the issue of selective nontreatment. Physicians naturally focus on the medical aspects of cases they confront in NICUs and usually have only a very general understanding of how the law may impinge on those cases. Attorneys, in turn, naturally emphasize legal principles and precedents, and often display substantial ignorance of the range of cases and treatment options in neonatal medicine.

These differences in professional training and interest do not represent an unbridgeable gap, but they sometimes lead to suspicion, antagonism, and a devaluing of another profession's work. Although some physicians and attorneys work together cooperatively in organizations such as the American College of Legal Medicine and the American Society of Law and Medicine, many physicians in this medical malpractice era tend to take an adversarial role toward attorneys who involve themselves in the legal implications of medical practice. For neonatologists and other physicians, attorneys who concern themselves with medical matters are frequently regarded as being problematic. The reasons for this judgment by physicians are several: attorneys do not understand the complexities and pressures of medical practice, they intrude into the high-risk world of medicine from the safety of their law offices, they hamper the traditional physician–patient relationship with unnecessary legal constraints and paperwork, and they represent an ongoing threat of litigation whenever physicians make mistakes.

Somewhat similar problems exist between physicians and ethicists who reflect on the moral problems in medicine. Although some physicians and ethicists work together cooperatively in health sciences centers and in interdisciplinary research centers such as the Hastings Center and the Kennedy Institute of Ethics, many physicians tend to have a critical view of these nonmedical professionals who think they have something to say about the practice of medicine. Whether they come out of philosophy or religious studies, ethicists who reflect on and write about medical matters are suspect for a number of reasons: they do not understand the complexities of medical practice or the subtle nuances of physician–patient relationships; most of them never participate in medical rounds; they reflect on the critical life-or-death decisions of medicine from the safety of their university offices (as I am now doing); they rarely if ever have to worry about the law in their professional roles; and they occasionally engage in irresponsible and irrelevant theorizing similar to that done by "Monday morning quarterbacks."

Of course, the views just described are often held by physicians who have never done academic work in either law or ethics. This lack of training in other disciplines intersecting with medicine is at least partially due to the fact that many medical schools have just in recent years begun to offer courses in legal medicine and biomedical ethics. Some medical schools still do not offer courses in either of these interdisciplinary areas. Consequently, ethicists (and attorneys, to a lesser degree) are frequently regarded by physicians as, at best, theorists whose principles and rules are often not of practical help "in the trenches" where medical decisions are made. At worst, they are regarded as meddlers who neither understand the technical aspects of clinical medicine nor the quickness with which decisions must sometimes be made when the lives of patients are at stake.

Nevertheless, as physicians and hospital administrators occasionally seek legal advice on cases involving birth-defective infants, so some physicians are concerned about the moral dimension of medicine and seek out the views of ethicists who reflect on the moral problems in medicine. Several of the physicians discussed in chapter 3 have on numerous occasions discussed the issue of selective nontreatment with ethicists.

One such occasion was a 1976 Montreal symposium on selective nontreatment in which John Freeman and John Lorber participated. The symposium was organized by the Center for Bioethics at the Clinical Research Institute of Montreal. Freeman's presentation at this meeting consisted largely of comparing his views on selective nontreatment with Lorber's position. He observed that the majority of infants with spina bifida cystica "would probably go untreated" if taken to Lorber but would be treated if brought to him. He concluded his paper with a comment and a question:

> These are just some of the dilemmas we face in this symposium and, with equal conscience and good will, Dr. Lorber and I treat widely different numbers of patients. I fail to believe that either of us is unethical. And yet, we both can't be right—or can we?[3]

Freeman's question is an open invitation for ethicists to participate actively in the ongoing debate about selective nontreatment. In this respect, he is acknowledging that nontreatment decisions are not to be left solely to the judgments of physicians, because their agreement about the medical facts in particular cases in no way leads to agreement about the treatment decisions in those cases. In other words, their medical expertise does not make them moral experts. Rather, as we have seen in chapter 3, physicians disagree significantly about the moral decisions that have to be made in neonatal medicine.

In another respect, Freeman's question represents an undeniable challenge to ethicists writing on the subject of selective nontreatment. Although he realizes intuitively that he and Lorber cannot both be right when they take opposite courses of action with similar cases, he does not press the issue (perhaps for reasons of professional courtesy or moral uncertainty). Rather, he issues a challenge to ethicists, perhaps thinking that they are moral experts in a way he is not. That challenge, as I understand it, is not necessarily to take sides in the Lorber–Freeman debate about treating infants with spina bifida, but to demonstrate with moral reasoning why some instances of selective nontreatment are justifiable and others are not. Stated another way, Freeman's challenge is for ethicists to move beyond the emotionalism, personal opinion, and ethical relativism that often characterize nontreatment decisions to put together a well-reasoned and consistent position on selective nontreatment. It may be that such a position will actually provide guidance for Freeman, Lorber, and other decision makers in the range of cases involving birth-defective neonates.

Before putting forth my own views on selective nontreatment in subsequent chapters, I will discuss the positions of several other ethicists who have written on the subject. My intention is not to be exhaustive in surveying ethical positions, but to put forth thoughtful—and thought-provoking—views that are representative of certain ways of thinking about selective nontreatment by ethicists. The major options among ethicists will be presented under five general headings, with one or two representative thinkers under each heading getting more attention than others.

1. Treat all nondying neonates

The ethicists in the first category approach the issue of selective nontreatment from different backgrounds and perspectives. Two of them are philosophers, two are religious ethicists from different religious traditions, and all of them focus on different aspects of selective nontreatment in their writings. Yet they all agree on "the bottom line": too many nondying, birth-defective newborns are being left untreated in NICUs. These anomalous infants, who would be treated if they were normal, are defenseless victims of neonatal infanticide.

Paul Ramsey, a Christian ethicist recently retired from Princeton, is the best-known representative of this position, especially through his widely read book, *Ethics at the Edges of Life*. As an active opponent of abortion, he has consistently pointed out that most arguments for abortion logically entail justification of infanticide as well. For instance, arguments for aborting a second-trimester fetus because of genetic defects discovered through amniocentesis can easily be extended into the neonatal period: "Since we should treat similar cases similarly, if x degree of defect would justify abortion, the same x degrees of defect would with equal cogency justify infanticide."[4]

Similarly, arguments justifying abortion by denying the personhood of the fetus work equally well in justifying the deaths of neonates. Because Ramsey thinks the moral status of a developing human life does not change during pregnancy or immediately afterward, the birth of a baby "is a comparatively unimportant point in the development of the life God calls into being." Rather, "birth" is primarily a point in time indicating where the child is in its development. Moreover, because any "proof of personhood" cannot be forthcoming until the child "at about one year of age enters upon the power of speech," the implications of the personhood argument are obvious:

> The view that only personhood is sacred—personhood that comes into existence through the *post*natal process of being loved and loving—would plainly justify discretionary infanticide no less than abortion.[5]

Given the widespread use of the genetic defect and the personhood arguments to justify abortions, Ramsey is convinced that the same kind of thinking has come to prevail in decisions made about treating or withholding treatment from infants. In fact, he is convinced that decisions about neonatal medical treatment that involve *a comparison of infants* rather than a comparison of possible treatments are likely to result in the unjustifiable deaths of anomalous neonates. To ensure that the standard for treating or not treating is "the same for the normal child as for the defective child," he proposes that a "medical indications policy" be operative in NICUs. Rather than comparing defective infants with normal infants in an effort to decide which neonates should be left untreated, the decision makers in NICUs should concentrate on *the medical indications* for treatment. For example, in making a decision about surgery for an infant with esophageal atresia, the parents and physicians in the case should address the central question of whether the surgery is likely to be successful—and not let the decision hang on whether the infant also has Down's syndrome. Such a policy—comparing treatments rather than patients who might receive the treatments—is the only correct way to proceed. In Ramsey's words: "We have no moral right to choose that some live and others die, when the medical indications for treatment are the same."[6]

Decisions about treatment or nontreatment should not be made on the basis of quality-of-life judgments, even though Raymond Duff, Anthony Shaw, and John Lorber make decisions about neonates in precisely this manner. When parents and physicians attempt to project an infant's future quality of life by considering the child's degree of mental deficiency, degree of physical handicap, impact on parents and siblings, possible contributions to society, and likelihood of achieving its potential, two problems occur. First, a birth-defective neonate inevitably loses out in the comparison with a normal infant who will have "a life worth living."

Second, a birth-defective neonate's life is further devalued when it becomes clear that "quality-of-expected-life . . . *entails* in principle the view that a particular human life is replaceable by another."

For Ramsey, a preferable standard for making decisions about neonates is the "equality-of-life" principle. Rather than comparing infants in the NICU in such a manner that birth-defective neonates inevitably come up short on the evaluative scale, decision makers should emphasize "the 'equal and independent' value of each and every young life" there. Granted that some infants are born with severe mental and physical defects, they are not to be judged as being inferior in some sense merely because of their defects. Instead, decisions about treatment options should be made from a perspective that emphasizes "the *equality* of particular lives regardless of their state or condition."

Given this emphasis on the equality of infant patients in the NICU, Ramsey argues that the first order of business by physicians should be the determination of which infants are dying and which are not. A few infants, such as anencephalic neonates, are "born dying." In these tragic cases, intensive care does nothing other than purposelessly prolong the dying of the infant. In the vast majority of cases, however, neonates are not born dying and can, if given vigorous treatment, have their lives prolonged. For virtually all of these nondying infants, whether defective or normal, parents and physicians have a moral duty to provide treatment.

The published views of John Freeman and R. B. Zachary convince Ramsey that many infants who are "allowed to die" in NICUs are not actually dying. The deaths of infants with spina bifida, for instance, are "not impending." Therefore, the often presented options of "to save or let die" are not an accurate representation of the medical practices in many NICUs. Rather, physicians who decide that some defective neonates cannot be "saved" often end up with infants who, although denied vigorous treatment, refuse to die. Consequently, some physicians engage in a policy of involuntary euthanasia "in the form of heavy sedation to hasten death."

Once the decision is made that nondying infants should die as a result of the absence of vigorous treatment, Ramsey believes that two of the traditional distinctions in biomedical ethics erode if not collapse. First, the distinction between letting die and killing erodes through the practice of "benign neglect of defective infants." Although the distinction remains important to Ramsey in his analysis of our obligations to other dying patients, it becomes a distinction without a difference in the context of neonatal medicine. When "letting die" actually means benign neglect, there is no morally significant distinction between "mercy-neglecting" and "mercy-killing." In fact, the "benign neglect of defective infants—who are not dying, who cannot themselves refuse treatment, who are most in need of human help—is the same as directly dispatching them: involuntary euthanasia." Second, the distinction between ordinary and extraordinary means of prolonging life "cannot be invoked in the case of very many defective newborn infants." In many instances, the distinction collapses in the midst of benign neglect. Rather than determining which treatments are useless and thus optional in the care of particular neonatal patients, some physicians merely use "the guise of refraining from instituting extraordinary treatment" to camouflage their neglecting infants to death. As for himself, Ramsey does not think that "a series of ordinary treatments —closing the open spine, antibiotics, a contraption to deal with urinary incontinence, and a shunt to prevent hydrocephalus—today adds up to extraordinary medical care" for infants with spina bifida.

Are there any exceptions to the recommended policy of vigorously treating all nondying neonates? Ramsey discusses three such possibilities: infants with Tay-Sachs disease, extremely premature infants, and infants with Lesch-Nyhan syndrome. The first medical condition is not really an exception to the policy of treating nondying infants, because a Tay-Sachs infant "is born destined to die." It is not born dying in the manner of an anencephalic neonate, but at approximately six months of age it enters into an irreversible process of dying for which there is no treatment that does not merely prolong the dying. Therefore, "from some point in the dying of Tay-Sachs children" (he does not specify when the point is), they "ought not to be stuck away in Jewish chronic disease hospitals and have their dying prolonged through tubes."

Extremely premature infants represent a different kind of situation. They cannot be said to be born dying, and thus they fall into the general category of nondying neonates who should receive vigorous treatment. Yet, for Ramsey, the treatment often given such premature infants does not seem directed at caring for them as individual patients but rather appears to be experimental in nature. He asks, "Must we use earlier and earlier neonates as experimental subjects to improve the chances of normalcy for other infants whose lives we learned to save some years ago?" He thinks not, and suggests that it may become morally necessary at some point to establish guidelines for NICUs whereby treatment will be withheld from certain premature infants not because they fail "someone's expected-social-worthiness test" but because they fall into a particular category of cases that is targeted for selective nontreatment.

The closest he comes to allowing a current exception to his recommended policy is in his discussion of Lesch-Nyhan infants. A child with Lesch-Nyhan syndrome is not a dying patient, nor generally an experimental subject. Rather, such a child has inherited an X-linked recessive condition that involves mental retardation, uncontrollable spasms, and self-mutilative behavior. There is no curative treatment for the condition, nor effective relief for the "insurmountable pain" brought on by the condition. For Ramsey, this condition—and apparently no others—represents a clinical case in which selective nontreatment may be justifiable on an individual basis because of the pain and lack of effective treatment. In his words, "When care cannot be conveyed, it need not be extended."

As to procedural matters, he does not find parents or physicians especially well equipped for the decisions regarding treatment or nontreatment. Parents are confronted with the prospect of oppressive burdens of care, and physicians are inclined to make quality-of-life judgments. To allay these difficulties, he makes two procedural recommendations: distinguish between the question of ultimate custody of the child and the question of its immediate medical care and, if possible, let the decisions regarding medical care be made by a disinterested party. To support the latter recommendation, he refers to a traditional Jewish teaching that says "only disinterested parties may, by even so innocuous a method as prayer, take any action which may lead to premature termination of life."

For Immanuel Jakobovits, who agrees that all nondying infants should be treated, the sanctity-of-life principle allows for no neonatal exceptions to treatment. As the president of the Institute of Judaism and Medicine (in Jerusalem), he points out that Jewish law makes no distinction whatever between infants and adults in their claim to life, nor between defective infants and normal infants.[7] Because "the title to life is absolute from the moment of birth," every neonate is to be given medical treatment "however serious the defects in the child concerned."[8] Even if an infant has "teeth and tail like an animal," the Jewish tradition calls for it to be treated because of its infinite value as an innocent human being. Regardless of a defective infant's projected length of life, projected health status, or projected happiness, the fact that it has "intrinsic, absolute, and infinite" value "outweighs all other values." Moreover, no arbitrary standard can justify withholding treatment from any defective neonate without placing all neonatal lives in jeopardy: "once a single brick is removed from the dam protecting the sanctity of all life, the entire dam is liable to collapse and every life is at risk."[9]

Philip Devine, a professor of philosophy at the University of Scranton, agrees with the general thrust of the arguments put forth by Ramsey and Jakobovits, but for different reasons. Rather than using the sanctity-of-life principle, he appeals to "socially current intuitions" to argue against all acts of infanticide, including those in medical settings. He thinks that such social intuitions include the "common moral belief . . . that it is wrong to kill babies."[10] In terms of content, these social intuitions include two principles that apply to treatment decisions in NICUs. First, the *species principle* rules out homicide against all members of the human species "whatever their degree of maturity or decay." On the basis of this principle, "we are prepared to regard even the most hopelessly retarded human being as a person, and the killing of such a one as murder." Second, the *potentiality principle* rules out homicide against human beings who have the capacity or potentiality for personal activity under normal conditions for development. The convergence of these two principles means that even a child so severely retarded that we might be tempted to regard it as a "mere beast" is nevertheless not a candidate for infanticide. Furthermore, a defective neonate with conditions similar to those of Baby Boy Houle (see case 4.1) should be given medical treatment because, in spite of the congenital anomalies, "it still can be affirmed that such a child's life is an intrinsic good."

Additional application of the potentiality principle is provided by Eike-Henner Kluge, a professor of philosophy at the University of Victoria (Canada). Acknowledging that a being that lacks "the constitutional capabilities for rational, symbolic thought and self-awareness is not a person," he nevertheless argues that "babies are persons in our sense of the term."[11] His reason for this judgment is his claim that infants are among the entities that can become persons without requiring a constitutive structural change. This "constitutive potential" is evidenced by neonatal neurological activity using electroencephalogram (EEG) readings. Any infant who has a neurological system "structurally similar to that of a normal adult human being" counts as a person on the basis of this potential. And because the vast majority of neonates meet this requirement for personhood, their deaths through intentional killing or neglect are "almost without exception" to be regarded as "the deliberate and inexcusable killing" of persons.[12] The only possible exceptions to this charge of murder would be nondying neonates who fall into one of two

categories. It may be that some neonates have such severe mental deficiency that they lack the potential for personhood, or it may be that the
circumstances surrounding some "seriously defective neonates" call for
death rather than continued suffering. These exceptional cases apparently
remain hypothetical ones, because Kluge admits no specific exceptions
and consistently uses ironic quotation marks when referring to seriously
defective neonates.

2. Terminate the lives of selected nonpersons

Ethicists in this second category are at the opposite end of the philosophical spectrum from the persons just discussed. In sharp contrast to
Ramsey and other ethicists calling for the treatment of all nondying
neonates, the philosophers now to be discussed find infanticide morally
justifiable in a wide range of circumstances, because newborn infants do
not count as persons. These philosophers reject the sanctity-of-life principle, the potentiality principle, and any species-limited principle that
values human lives over intelligent nonhuman animals. In advocating
selective nontreatment for many neonates with many different conditions,
they argue that it makes no moral difference whether such neonatal
nonpersons die from the withholding of medical treatment or are directly
killed.

The best-known defense of this position is that developed by Michael
Tooley in an article first published in *Philosophy and Public Affairs* and
subsequently revised and expanded.[13] Tooley, now a social science research
fellow at the Australian National University, argues (in a move anticipated
by Ramsey) that the morality of abortion and infanticide hang on the
conceptual issue of personhood. For anyone attempting to defend either
of these actions that terminate human life, the basic question does not
concern human status but rather the issue of when a member of the
species *homo sapiens* becomes a person.

Personhood, then, is a moral category that denotes the limits of justifiable termination of life. If an entity, regardless of its age or maturity, can
meet the requirements of personhood, its life is given moral protection
from arbitrary and indiscriminate destruction. If, in contrast, an entity
cannot claim the status of a person, its continued existence is tenuous
because it has no serious right to life. A moral defense of infanticide thus
demands that "one has to get very clear about what makes something a
person, what gives something a right to life."[14]

There are, Tooley thinks, two quite different ways for philosophers to approach the personhood issue. The first way, which he simply dismisses, is to try to arrive at a relational interpretation of personhood. This approach is often used by theologically oriented philosophers who argue that what makes members of the human race persons is their special relationship with God. A preferable way of interpreting personhood is, in his judgment, to use psychological concepts that do not depend on a theistic context for their validity. For philosophers choosing this alternative, the personhood of an entity depends not on its relationships but on its intrinsic properties. The central question in a nonrelational account of personhood is thus, "What properties must something have in order to be a person, i.e., to have a serious right to life?"

Tooley proposes five such properties necessary for personhood: a capacity for desires about one's future, a capacity to have a concept of a self, the actuality of being a conscious subject of experiences, a capacity for self-consciousness, and the actuality of being a continuing subject of experiences and other mental states. He argues that "in order for something to have a right to life it must either now possess, or have possessed at some time in the past" these five properties. When these properties are put together in the form of a definition, Tooley thinks that "the characterization of a person as a continuing subject of experiences and other mental states that can envisage a future for itself and have desires about the future is essentially correct."[15]

The major argument for this proposed interpretation of personhood lies in Tooley's theory regarding the relationship between rights and desires. There is, in his view, a "conceptual connection" between the rights an individual can have and the existence in that individual of corresponding desires. Stated in the opposite manner, there is a conceptual connection between violating an individual's rights (to life, to health, to the ownership of a car) and frustrating that individual's desires for that valued thing. To cite his example, "If you do not care whether I take your car, then I generally do not violate your right by doing so."[16]

Regarding the right to life, he argues that an individual must have two factors at work at the same time. The individual *must exist* (thus disallowing as yet unconceived individuals), and the individual *must now possess* —or have possessed at some time in the past—either "a desire to continue to exist as the continuing subject of experiences" or "a desire to become a continuing subject of experiences and other mental states." In this manner he distinguishes between living human beings who have a right to life, and living human beings who lack a right to life because they lack the requisite desires. Individuals who are conscious, continuing subjects of experiences and temporarily unconscious individuals both belong in the former category, because they meet conditions for personhood; fetuses and very young neonates belong in the latter category because they do not have—and have never had—the actual desire to live.

Merely having "potential desires" does not suffice, according to Tooley. No one—neither a fetus nor a very young neonate—has a serious right to life on the basis of the potentiality principle, because no one currently lacking the desire to continue to exist could plausibly claim to have such a desire "at times that he does not in fact exist, if he were to exist at those times." To support his argument against the potentiality principle, he develops the Frankenstein example. Suppose, he says, that the technology were available to construct humans from inorganic compounds, to freeze these compounds and thaw them out without damaging them, and to program "beliefs, desires, and personality traits" into these organisms. If such an adult human organism were to be constructed and thawed out, it would be a "conscious, adult human with beliefs, desires, and a distinct personality." If, however, the organism was never thawed out and instead ground up for hamburgers, no one would be guilty of having murdered an innocent person. As for the potential desires this human organism might have, Tooley comments: "If one were to consider the desires that something would have at some later time if it were to exist at that time, it would follow that it would be wrong to destroy our frozen Frankenstein." However, because the organism has never been thawed out, it cannot possibly claim to possess a desire to continue to exist in a thawed-out condition nor a desire to become thawed out.

Regarding selective nontreatment and other forms of infanticide, Tooley believes that the morality of such acts hangs on the personal status ascribed to infants and the time period in which the termination of life takes place. If neonates—whether normal or defective—are regarded as human nonpersons because they lack the requisites of personhood, then the termination of their lives is morally acceptable "within a short time after birth." Indeed, "everyday observation strongly suggests that there is no more reason for holding that a newborn baby has these capacities or enjoys these states [of personhood] than there is for holding that this is true of a newborn chimpanzee." Therefore, the infanticide of neonatal nonpersons "is morally permissible in most cases when it is otherwise desirable." As to the time period in which such acts of termination can take place, he comments:

> The practical moral problem can . . . be satisfactorily handled by choosing some short period of time, such as a week after birth, as the interval during which infanticide will be permitted. This interval could then be modified once psychologists have established the point at which a human organism comes to satisfy the appropriate requirements.

Even if one regards human infants as potential persons—but only potential persons—the termination of their lives is "a morally neutral action," and the "correct conclusion seems to me to be that infanticide is in itself morally acceptable."[17] In particular, the withholding of treatment or direct killing of infants "suffering from some very painful condition" or infants "in such a state that anyone in that state prefers death to life" is morally unproblematic.

If, however, one goes so far as to regard newborn human infants as "generally persons" or to believe that it is wrong to destroy even potential persons, there are still three situations in which the termination of the life of a neonate would be justifiable. First, there are some infants who "presumably suffer from brain defects of such a nature that they do not possess the capacity of developing into persons." Second, there are cases in which the cost of keeping an infant alive is so great that "letting him die is, regretfully, the lesser evil." Third, there are cases of infant suffering in which the termination of an infant's life is "surely justified," because it seems virtually certain that the infant "either prefers death to continued existence or will do so as soon as it becomes capable of having such a desire."

Whether quality-of-life considerations are brought to bear in termination/nontermination decisions also depends on whether neonates are regarded as persons or nonpersons. If neonates are to be regarded as persons, quality-of-life considerations are inappropriate because the decision about life or death should rest on the infant's own best interests: whether continued existence will "at least be a life that he himself will prefer to death." If, in contrast, one follows Tooley in believing that neonates are at best only potential persons, then quality-of-life judgments become prominent because one

> is merely deciding what potential persons should be allowed to become actual, and the rational approach would seem to be to decide on the basis of the quality of life which the potential person is likely to enjoy if allowed to develop into an actual person.

Mary Anne Warren, a professor of philosophy at San Francisco State University, approaches the issue of infanticide in much the same manner as Tooley. For her also, the central issue in both abortion and infanticide decisions is the personhood of the entity subject to termination. Granting that fetuses and infants count as human beings in a genetic sense, she questions whether they should be regarded as persons or "humans in a moral sense," asserting that

> the suggestion is simply that the moral community consists of all and only *people*, rather than all and only human beings; and probably the best way of demonstrating its self-evidence is by considering the concept of person-hood, to see what sorts of entity are and are not persons, and what the decision that a being is or is not a person implies about its moral rights.[18]

There are five traits that Warren believes to be central to the concept of personhood: consciousness, reasoning ability, self-motivated activity, the capacity to communicate, and the presence of self-awareness. Not all of these attributes have to be present before an entity can be considered a person, but Warren thinks that the absence of all of the traits (and possibly the absence of just the first two) is sufficient to prove that personhood is missing. Thus, in her judgment, it is clear that "some human beings are not people": fetuses, infants, human beings with serious mental deficiency, and any individual whose consciousness has been permanently obliterated.[19]

Some of these nonpersons may nevertheless be regarded as *potential* persons. Such an entity, for Warren, is not now a person but would be "capable of developing into a person, given certain biologically and/or technologically possible conditions."[20] And because "a human being does not become a person until sometime after its birth," infants fall into the category of potential persons. Does that mean they have a serious, protectable right to continued life? Warren thinks not, because "sentience is the ultimate source of all moral rights," and "a being that lacks the capacity to have experiences, and/or to prefer some experiences to others, cannot coherently be said to have moral rights."

It thus follows that "only people . . . have a full-fledged right to life" (and can be murdered), and that "killing a newborn infant isn't murder."[21] Rather than having a serious claim to life, a neonatal nonperson is generally allowed to continue its existence because it is wanted by its parents or other people willing to pay for its care. When an infant is wanted in either of these ways, the termination of its life is "wrong for reasons analogous to those which make it wrong to wantonly destroy natural resources, or great works of art." However, "it follows from my argument that when an unwanted or defective infant is born into a society which cannot afford and/ or is not willing to care for it, then its destruction is permissible."[22]

Peter Singer, a professor of philosophy at Monash University (Australia), addresses the issue of selective nontreatment in a much more direct manner than Warren does. He agrees with Tooley and Warren that the termination of medical treatment depends on the personhood of infants, but argues as well that many cases of terminating the lives of infants would be unproblematic if the medical community would get on with "unsanctifying human life." He finds the sanctity-of-life principle, while possibly having a religious origin, now to be nothing more than a misleading notion in a broadly secular ethic; as such, the principle simply claims that "human life has some very special value, a value quite distinct from the value of the lives of other living things."[23]

He disagrees with the sanctity-of-life principle, for two different reasons. First, he argues that human life is not intrinsically more valuable than nonhuman forms of life. Those who hold the opposite view are guilty of "speciesism," meaning "a prejudice or attitude of bias toward the interests of members of one's own species and against those of members of other species."[24] In reaction to this view, he calls for a rejection of the "doctrine that places the lives of members of our species above" the lives of nonhumans. Second, he argues that human life—being a member of *homo sapiens*—is less valuable than any form of personal life involving rationality, self-consciousness, and a capacity for envisioning one's future. Such personal life is, of course, possible for most humans; it is not, however, restricted to humans. Experiments have demonstrated that chimpanzees, for instance, seem to exhibit such personal characteristics in a manner that some humans do not. Thus it seems that killing a chimpanzee "is worse than the killing of a gravely defective human who is not a person."[25]

What is the status of human infants in this hierarchy of life forms? Newborn infants and "some mental defectives" fall into the category of human nonpersons: they are conscious and are capable of experiencing pleasure and pain, but they are not rational and self-conscious. Human infants are, of course, appealing to us because they are small, helpless, and often cute (as are puppies and baby seals). But a week-old baby clearly does not meet the requirements of personhood, and "there are many nonhuman animals whose rationality, self-consciousness, awareness, capacity to feel, and so on, exceed that of a human baby a week, a month, or even a year old."

Do the restrictions against killing persons have any implications for killing infants or other human nonpersons? Singer thinks not. In developing what he calls the "sanctity of personal life," he argues that the killing of persons is generally wrong because they are rational, self-conscious, autonomous, and have the capacity to envision their future and have desires related to that future. In contrast, he believes that the general reluctance to terminate the lives of infants has to do with "emotionally moving but strictly irrelevant aspects" of killing babies: their helplessness, cuteness, and innocence. Once these considerations are put aside, it becomes clear that "the grounds for not killing persons do not apply to newborn infants." There is, then, nothing intrinsically wrong in killing infants, whether defective or normal. Instead, the moral and legal restrictions on infanticide—such as granting babies a legal right to life "perhaps a month" after birth—have to do more with the effects of infanticide on other persons than with the actual killing of these human nonpersons.

As to the issue of selective nontreatment, Singer believes that terminating the lives of birth-defective infants is far less problematic than the larger issue of infanticide. Whatever claims one might make for the potentiality of normal infants to become persons at some future point are significantly more difficult to make in regard to defective neonates. Given that "no infant—defective or not—has as strong a claim to life as beings capable of seeing themselves as distinct entities, existing over time," the claim to life of defective infants is substantially weaker than that of normal neonates.

Beyond the fact that they are nonpersons, the major reason for the vulnerability of defective infants to destruction is the general recognition that defective infants—like defective fetuses—are replaceable. Whether the defect is so serious that it will make "life not worth living" (he mentions spina bifida in this regard), or will merely make the child's life prospects "less happy than those of a normal child" (he uses hemophilia as an example), the infant's life may be terminated and replaced by a normal infant born to the same parents. This "replaceability argument," set in a utilitarian context, thus allows for the lives of all defective infants to be terminated if that is the course of action desired by the parents:

> When the death of a defective infant will lead to the birth of another infant with better prospects of a happy life, the total amount of happiness will be greater if the defective infant is killed. The loss of happy life for the first infant is outweighed by the gain of a happier life for the second.

Once the decision has been made to "replace" a defective infant by terminating its life, Singer does not believe it matters morally who does the act of termination or how it is done. In a brief criticism of the distinction between letting die and killing, he simply asks, "what is the cessation of any form of life-sustaining treatment if it is not the intentional termination of the life of one human being by another?"[26] As long as the medical profession holds on to this irrelevant distinction, the only practical consequence will be the prolonged suffering of defective infants with little if any chance for meaningful lives. It would be far better, he thinks, if we simply acknowledged that "killing a defective infant is not morally equivalent to killing a person." In fact, "very often it is not wrong at all."[27]

3. Withhold treatment according to parental discretion

This third category is a distinctive departure from the two general views previously discussed. The ethicists whose views fall under this heading do not believe that all nondying neonates should be treated, nor do they believe that the lives of infants can be terminated morally on the basis of a definitional point made about personhood. Rather, they are convinced that decisions regarding treatment or nontreatment are frequently very difficult to make and that such decisions usually inflict suffering on the adults most emotionally involved in the decision process. Because parents in such cases are likely to suffer whether a birth-defective infant lives or dies, it is they who should make the decision to treat or to withhold treatment.

The ethicist who most consistently advocates this position is John Fletcher, currently an assistant to the director at the National Institutes of Health. In his writings on genetic counseling, abortion, and selective nontreatment of neonates, he regularly indicates the need for an alternative perspective in religious ethics—a moderate perspective—to the well-known views of Paul Ramsey and Joseph Fletcher. Both Ramsey and Joseph Fletcher have strongly held views on abortion and infanticide based on the moral status of the lives in question, with Ramsey defending the right to life of human beings victimized through these acts of killing and Fletcher defending the morality of many acts of abortion and infanticide by stressing the importance of quality-of-life considerations. In contrast to both of these positions, *John* Fletcher argues that the *plight of parents* making decisions about abortion and selective nontreatment is a necessary but often neglected feature of an ethical analysis of these actions.

As an example, in analyzing the decisions of couples to abort genetically defective fetuses following amniocentesis, John Fletcher points out that the couples (many of whom already have a genetically defective child)

undergo an enormous amount of "moral suffering" as they attempt to
cope with their situation. Moral suffering, in his judgment, is "a state of
being threatened by no resolution, even as we are caught between strong
forces or principles, both of which are right and good."28 Thus caught in a
moral dilemma between "a loyalty to the life" of the fetus and "a loyalty
to the norm of 'healthy' life (as expressed in children with no genetic
defects)," couples generally opt for abortion even though they suffer
"from the thought of being responsible for ending the life of their child."29
This suffering is reflected in the quoted words of a woman who followed
abortion with sterilization by hysterotomy:

> I am just crushed and disappointed. I had so hoped to give my husband a
> healthy baby, and now I know that I will not. You spend all your life looking
> at pictures of pretty babies and their mothers and growing up thinking that
> will be you. It is pretty gruesome when you are the one who is different.30

This interest in parental decision making and parental suffering dom-
inates Fletcher's analysis of abortion and selective nontreatment, even
though he believes that there are morally relevant differences between the
lives at stake in the two situations. In fact, he believes that there are three
morally relevant differences between the situations, even if the fetus and
neonate have the same genetic impairment. First, the neonate has a
separate physical existence from the mother and thus "confronts parents,
physicians and legal institutions with independent moral claims for care
and support." Second, the genetic defect in the neonate "is more available
to physicians for palliation or perhaps even cure." Third, parental acceptance of the infant "as a real person is much more developed at birth" than
in the earlier stages of pregnancy.31

Given these differences between fetuses and neonates, Fletcher's position
on selective nontreatment consists of three substantive points followed by
a major procedural one. He begins by claiming a moral status for neonates
over and beyond the status he attributes to fetuses. The moral status of a
fetus depends on its stage of development, with fetuses late in gestation
being more valuable and subject to greater protection from destruction
than younger fetuses. By balancing this developmental view of the fetus
with "the individual and social interests of the parents," he reasons that
"the fetus prior to viability is [not] yet a fellow human being." By
contrast, any newborn infant, even one with "a serious defect," is regarded
as "a fellow human being who deserves protection on both a legal and an
ethical basis."32

The status of humanness on the part of neonates—Fletcher does not address the personhood question—leads to a distinction between caring and killing. The great majority of neonates, like other "fellow human beings," are to be given care and also cure, whenever the latter option is possible. No neonates, no matter how seriously defective, are to be the victims of medical killing any more than any other patients are. To kill such children, even when motivated by compassion, would be to destroy human lives that could be offered care and parental support. Moreover, a policy of neonatal euthanasia would likely result in the "brutalization" of those who participate in the acts of killing and also lead to "destructive social consequences" by endangering the fabric of trust that normally exists between parents and their children. Therefore, acts of direct killing can never be a part of the caring relationship that should exist between parents and physicians and the defenseless lives placed in their trust. Rather than even considering killing, the emphasis in the thoughts of parents and physicians should be on care:

> If we choose to be shaped by Judeo-Christian visions of the "createdness" of life within which every creature bears the image of God, we ought to care for the defective newborn as if our relation with the Creator depended on the outcome. If we choose to be shaped by visions of the inherent dignity of each member of the human family, no matter what his or her predicament, we ought to care for this defenseless person as if the basis of our own dignity depended on the outcome.[33]

Having made these two points, Fletcher addresses situations in which cure for neonatal human beings is impossible and care is ineffective. In such situations, "terribly damaged newborns" may be allowed to die through the withdrawal of medical treatment because that treatment can do little other than "prolong the ordeal without definite ground for hope" for either the child or the parents. Assuming that every reasonable therapeutic alternative has been "evaluated negatively" and that a neonate's pain will be effectively relieved, nontreatment can be justified in a number of cases "for reasons of mercy to the infant and relief of meaningless suffering of the parents and medical team." Cases in which these reasons —mercy for the defective infant and a realistic assessment of parental needs—coalesce to call for nontreatment include Lesch-Nyhan syndrome, spina bifida cystica, and Down's syndrome with esophageal atresia or duodenal atresia.

Of these conditions, the only one he discusses at length is spina bifida. As one of the better medically informed ethicists, he knows about the variability in spina bifida cases, the selection criteria used by John Lorber, and the ongoing debate between Lorber and John Freeman. Fletcher sides with Lorber, because he thinks "the overwhelming evidence of evaluation shows negative consequences for vigorous treatment of the high-risk infant."[34] Stated another way, he argues that "it is better to accept death for a child . . . than to incur consequences that would, in most informed judgments, lead to situations in which the survival of the person is manifestly an injustice."[35]

Who should make these nontreatment decisions regarding spina bifida infants and other birth-defective neonates? This question is more important to Fletcher than to the ethicists discussed previously, and he answers the question by emphasizing the importance of parental involvement. Rather than giving physicians an exclusive right to make the decisions (thus disallowing parental participation) or turning the decisions over to a disinterested committee (thus abdicating both medical and parental responsibility), he thinks that decisions about "the injustices of prolonging life" should be made by "those most involved in the suffering." For him, this means a process of decision making modeled roughly along the lines followed by Raymond Duff and Anthony Shaw (see chap. 3).[36] The importance of this approach is that it recognizes the inherent moral suffering in making these difficult moral choices, and allows for considerable parental discretion as parents consider the limited number of alternatives available to them.

Michael Garland, a philosopher at the University of California School of Medicine in San Francisco, agrees with this emphasis on parental discretion. As an organizer of the 1974 Sonoma (California) conference on ethics and newborn intensive care, he coauthored a summary report of the conference that stresses the centrality of parental responsibility in nontreatment decisions.[37] In a subsequent article he argues that, in at least some neonatal cases, parents have the "right to avoid severe and unnecessary familial burdens" that would be brought on them should their birth-defective infants continue to live.[38]

Garland proposes that neonates in NICUs be divided into three broad categories. In one category—labeled "duty to treat"—are to be placed the vast majority of infants. In another category—called "duty not to treat"—are infants "for whom there is no hope; parents and other responsible persons have an obligation to let them die." In clinical terms, these infants would be extremely premature, or anencephalic, or have "severe and irreparable defects in vital organs such as the heart, lungs, or liver." In conceptual terms, these infants would be identified as those "who would never be able to participate in social existence, or who can be saved from death for only a brief time (up to a few months maximum), or who can live only in severe and continuous pain."

The third category—labeled "option to treat"—encompasses a small minority of infants whose treatment or nontreatment depends exclusively on parental discretion. Infants placed in the category are not definable by clinical syndromes as much as by quality-of-life parameters that generate significant familial burdens: degree of physical mobility, independence in taking nourishment and maintaining basic hygiene, socializing capacities, and "potential for intellectual and affective participation in human experience." Additional considerations regarding financial costs of treatment, effect on siblings, and psychological burden may also be a relevant part of the decision to treat or not to treat. For infants with spina bifida or other conditions that place them in this borderline category, Garland states that the "right to life" is "sometimes limited by the parental right to avoid unnecessary familial burdens." Simply put, the argument for parental discretion in these third-category cases

> rests on the perception that the good of the child's future life is proportionate to the good of avoiding the familial burden associated with that continued life, and that it is a matter of parental prudence to determine which good should be pursued.[39]

Another philosopher working in a medical center agrees that spina bifida infants, at least, should be given treatment or denied treatment on the basis of parental discretion. A philosopher at the University of Tennessee Health Sciences Center, Terrence Ackerman proposes that infants with spina bifida cystica be selected for nontreatment not according to clinical criteria (such as those used by John Lorber) but according to the nonclinical criterion of parental commitment to rear the child. There is an extensive literature describing the medical, psychological, economic, and social burdens of having a spina bifida child in a family. In the light of this literature, he argues that "the grounds of selection for treatment should be the presence of a commitment by the parents to care for and nurture this child, following their efforts to assess, as best they can, the information conveyed to them" regarding the child's future physical disability and the regimen of care required by the child's condition. The goals sought in this selection policy are the minimization of suffering for spina bifida children and their families and the enhancement of the opportunity to achieve a meaningful life by those children able to achieve it with parental support. It is therefore appropriate that parents, in consultation with a team of health care professionals, "should determine whether the child stricken with meningomyelocele is to be treated."[40]

4. Withhold treatment according to quality-of-life projections

The ethicists under this heading represent a perspective generally identifiable as utilitarianism, even though they offer different variations of this ethical theory. One of them is a rule-utilitarian, one leans toward act-utilitarianism, and another one works with a modified form of utilitarianism that also includes deontological and natural law considerations. In spite of these differences, they are in general agreement that decisions about medical treatment for birth-defective neonates should be made by projecting the *kind of life* that will be prolonged through treatment. More than simply asking if anomalous infants can be salvaged with aggressive medical management, they inquire into the potential these individuals have for *meaningful lives* in the face of the predictable mental deficiency and/or physical disability that will characterize their existence.

Richard McCormick, a moral theologian at the Kennedy Institute of Ethics, approaches the issue of selective nontreatment from a teleological perspective that often resembles utilitarianism but contains features that many utilitarians would not accept. His analysis of the issue begins with a rejection of John Fletcher's distinction between the moral status of fetuses and that of neonates. Granting Fletcher's factual claims regarding a neonate's greater independence, availability for treatment, and acceptability to parents, McCormick claims that it is "manifestly erroneous" to draw moral implications from these differences. Rather, he argues that "a position advocating or justifying abortion after prenatal diagnosis of severe impairment is one that, in moral consistency, ought to advocate or justify neonatal euthanasia."[41]

McCormick therefore agrees with Ramsey, Tooley, and many other ethicists regarding the logical connection between justifying acts of abortion for genetic reasons and justifying acts of infanticide for the same genetic reasons. The crux of the matter in both instances, he thinks, is the moral status granted the life that may be terminated. That status, for him, is best defined with the concept "protectable humanity," and included under this category are virtually all fetuses and neonates.[42] Whether neonates (and late-term fetuses) should be assessed under some sort of personhood concept is quite unimportant to him. It is enough that fetuses and neonates are regarded as members of the human community, subject to the same protective instincts, rules, and laws according to which other humans are normally protected from destruction. He occasionally refers to neonates as "persons," but it is clear that he does not attach the moral implications to this terminology that Tooley, Warren, and Singer do. In fact, he believes that "anyone who would attempt an even tentative personhood inventory is trying to catch, bottle, and display what most men have regarded as ultimately a mystery."[43]

With the concept of protectable humanity, however, it is important to distinguish between two interpretations of the "life" human beings may have at birth or afterward. Some human beings have "life" in a vitalist sense: "vital and metabolic processes with no human functioning or capacity." When parents and physicians have this understanding of "life," they attempt to preserve that life in a neonate "no matter what the condition of the patient." Other human beings—most human beings—have "life" in a quite different sense: "a state of *human* functioning (or capacity thereof), of well-being." When parents and physicians have this understanding, they realize that there are times in which it is wrong to preserve "the life of one with no capacity for those aspects of life that we regard as *human*."[44]

In explaining what he means by "those aspects of life that we regard as human," McCormick finds it necessary to make quality-of-life judgments. In so doing, he claims that he is merely extending a sanctity-of-life ethic into the practical arena of decision making, not proposing an alternative to the sanctity-of-life principle:

> Actually, the two approaches ought not to be set against each other. . . . Quality-of-life assessments ought to be made within an overall reverence for life, as an extension of one's respect for the sanctity of life . . . to separate the two approaches and call one *sanctity* of life, the other *quality* of life is a false conceptual split. . . ."[45]

McCormick is, of course, moving against the stream of ethical consensus when he makes this claim. Most ethicists accept the distinction between a sanctity-of-life principle and a quality-of-life principle. And McCormick, though on one occasion stating that "every human being, regardless of age or condition, is of incalculable worth," generally functions within a context in which it is not only necessary to make evaluative distinctions between human beings but appropriate to do so. To do otherwise, to claim that "every life is of equal value," he thinks is simply false, because humans differ both in the kinds of lives they presently experience and in the kinds of lives they can be projected to have in the future.

This difference in both present and potential quality has obvious implications for the decisions made about preserving lives in clinical settings. In particular, this quality differential means that "life is a relative good, and the duty to preserve it a limited one."[46] For McCormick, such a statement does *not* mean that the value of an individual's life is relative to income, education, gender, marital status, profession, or any other test of one's "utility" in society. Rather, he argues that in the context of a Judeo-Christian perspective, the value of an individual's life is relative to the pursuit and attainment of the "spiritual goods" of love of God and neighbor. Life itself—especially when represented only in metabolic processes—is not a good that must always be preserved. Instead, because in "Judeo-Christian perspective, the meaning, substance, and consummation of life is found in human relationships," life is a value "to be preserved only insofar as it contains some potentiality for human relationships."

McCormick believes that this *relational potential* on the part of neonates can and should be used as a guideline for nontreatment decisions in NICUs. He recognizes that the guideline cannot be translated into specific rules and that mistakes in applying the guideline will be made. Such problems are inherent in making decisions about neonates, he argues, because "relational capacity is not subject to mathematical analysis but to human judgment." Nevertheless, he thinks this ethical criterion can be used to identify two classes of infants for whom treatment may justifiably be withheld: neonates in whom "this potentiality is totally absent" and infants so severely defective that this potentiality for relationships would be "totally subordinated to the mere effort for survival." To indicate how the guideline can apply to neonatal cases, he observes that anencephalic infants would not be given treatment and infants with Down's syndrome would receive treatment under this approach. In commenting on some of the cases presented earlier in this book, he indicates that the guideline would have called for treatment for the infant at Johns Hopkins (case 2.2) and "Infant Doe" in Bloomington (case 5.3) but not for Baby Boy Houle (case 4.1), which is precisely the opposite from the way decisions in these cases were actually made.[47]

The appropriate persons to use this guideline are "parents in consultation with physicians." The focal point of their decisions should be "the child's good, this alone." The method to be used in determining the child's good is the collective judgment of reasonable people, even though McCormick acknowledges the virtual impossibility for healthy adults to "extrapolate backwards on what kind of life will be acceptable to the infant."[48] Yet, that is exactly the kind of decision that has to be made in deciding whether to treat birth-defective infants. And where there is little if any potentiality for human relationships because of severe congenital defects, reasonable persons will usually judge that "mere life" need not be prolonged with medical treatment.

Joseph Fletcher, retired but active as a visiting professor of biomedical ethics at the University of Virginia School of Medicine, agrees that quality-of-life judgments must be made in neonatal cases. However, he differs significantly from McCormick in his interpretation of what these judgments entail and how they apply to specific cases of congenital anomaly. He also disagrees with McCormick regarding the intellectual context in which quality-of-life judgments are most appropriately made, because he thinks such judgments best meet human need when they are informed by act-utilitarian and humanistic considerations instead of theological claims.

In a manner somewhat similar to Tooley and Warren, Fletcher thinks that an ethical analysis of selective nontreatment and other forms of infanticide requires, as its first order of business, an inquiry into the "nature" of the infant lives to be prolonged or terminated. He observes that "synthetic concepts" such as "human," "man," and "person" call for "operational terms, spelling out the which and what and when." Only in this manner, he thinks, can we "get down to cases—to normative decisions."[49]

He therefore proposes certain "indicators" of personhood, even though he reflects his own inconsistent use of terminology by calling them "indicators of humanhood." His original list of these features includes 15 "positive human criteria" and 5 "negative human criteria." The list ranges from fairly common items (e.g., minimal intelligence, self-awareness, relational capacity) to more exotic features (e.g., a sense of time, concern for others, idiosyncrasy.)[50] A revised list of personhood criteria mentions but four features that comprise persons: neocortical function, self-consciousness, relational ability, and happiness. Of these, he argues that there is actually only one "cardinal or hominizing trait" on which all other personal traits hinge, and that trait is neocortical function. Not only is neocortical function "the key to humanness, the essential trait, the human *sine qua non*," but it is also "*medically* determinable" in a manner most other traits are not.[51]

Using this scheme, Fletcher grants that "defective fetuses, defective newborns, [and] moribund patients" are all human lives. The important question, however, is whether they are *personal* lives. He thinks not. Declaring that "what is critical is personal status, not merely human status," he says that many "human lives are subpersonal." As an example of what he has in mind, he states: "Any individual of the species *homo sapiens* who falls below the I.Q. 40-mark in a standard Stanford-Binet test, amplified if you like by other tests, is questionably a person; below the 20-mark, not a person."[52]

Having argued in this manner for a neocortical definition of person-hood, he goes on to point out that the conceptual issue of personhood does not settle the ethical issue of infanticide. This issue hangs on the question whether, in some situations, the life of a defective neonate may be terminated *even if* the infant is classified as a person.[53] There are, he thinks, only two alternative answers to the question. For "vitalists" and "absolutists," who use a sanctity-of-life ethic to claim an absolute right to life for all neonates, the answer to the question is negative. For himself and other ethicists who embrace a quality-of-life perspective, the prece-dence of human needs over human rights means that the answer to the question is, depending on situational factors, sometimes positive.

This, then, is the context in which Fletcher interprets selective nontreat-ment. The decision to treat or to withhold treatment from a birth-defective neonate depends on neither the infant's "right to life" nor the ability of physicians to provide treatment for the child's medical condition, but on quality-of-life projections regarding the child's future. For Fletcher, such quality-of-life judgments necessarily mean that decisions about se-lective nontreatment are teleological, based on the principle of "propor-tionate good."[54] For instance, parents and physicians need to try to determine if the proposed treatment will promote human well-being and reduce suffering for all individuals involved, or simply prolong the life of an infant who will end up in an institutional "warehouse" for the mentally and/or physically handicapped.[55]

In contrast to McCormick's call for quality-of-life judgments to be made exclusively in terms of the child's good, Fletcher opens up a much broader range of considerations in his contextual and teleological approach to decisions about neonates. Because he thinks that parents and physicians should have only a "*qualified* respect for human life," he goes on to suggest that the continuing existence of a defective neonate is qualified not only by the quality of its projected future but also by the quality of its projected impact on the lives of persons who will be affected by it. Thus he indicates a number of "practical elements" that should go into decisions about treatment or nontreatment:

> first, the extent to which the parents are counseled; second, the parents' attitude toward defects; third, the size or proportion of the risk in terms of a projected distribution of chances; fourth, the severity of the risk; fifth, the economic resources of the family; sixth, the welfare of other children involved, as well as the parents' physical and emotional capacity to cope.[56]

Once the decision has been made that an infant's projected quality of life is insufficient to prolong its life through medical treatment, Fletcher thinks the means chosen to terminate the child's life do not really matter. There are, he suggests, four possible options in the care of defective neonates: to kill them, to starve them, to withhold all medical treatment from them, or to give them aggressive treatment. For him, there is no moral difference among the first three options: "A decision not to open an imperforate anus in a trisomy-18 newborn is 'mercy killing' as surely as if they used a poison pellet."[57] Thus, regarding the case at Johns Hopkins (case 2.2), he thinks that "some form of direct termination would have been far more merciful as far as the infant, nurses, parents, and some of the physicians were concerned."[58]

Another ethicist who agrees about the necessity for quality-of-life judgments is Jonathan Glover, a philosopher at Oxford. He argues that in cases of infanticide, as in other types of killing, the sanctity-of-life principle simply does not work. If interpreted to mean that "taking human life is *intrinsically* wrong," the principle is unacceptable, because killing is sometimes permissible to avoid greater evils. As an alternative to this principle, Glover suggests that there are two different kinds of reasons for the wrongness of killing. Killing is *directly* wrong whenever it "reduces the length of a worth-while life" or overrides an autonomous person's desire to go on living. Killing is also *indirectly* wrong because of its harmful side effects on other people.[59]

Because these reasons can provide the basis for utilitarian rules against killing, it is important to see how they apply to decisions about prolonging or terminating the lives of anomalous infants. For Glover, who finds the killing/letting die distinction morally irrelevant, the obvious inapplicability of the principle of autonomy to cases involving neonates means that the issue of terminating the lives of defective infants hangs on either of two questions: can such infants be said to have "lives worth living," and will their lives (or deaths) produce beneficial or harmful side effects on other persons?

Regarding the question of "lives worth living," Glover responds in two ways. When he considers the question in an "impersonal" manner, he reasons that "a defective baby is better replaced by a later, normal one, as a more worth-while life is the result." However, given the difficulty of "deciding the point at which someone's life is not worth living," he thinks the best way to personalize the question of worthwhile life is to "substitute" ourselves for the defective infant. In this hypothetical manner we need to ask ourselves whether, if we were born with a particular congenital anomaly, we would prefer to go through life with the condition or have our lives terminated. He concludes, in a manner similar to McCormick, that many reasonable adults positioned in this hypothetical situation would prefer death to severely handicapped existence. And "those of us who think that we would opt for death rather than some kinds of lives have a good reason for holding that some lives are not worth living."

In contrast to McCormick, Glover thinks that a second way of making decisions about defective neonates is to consider the side effects of their lives (or deaths) on other persons. Even if there is no indisputable test for determining whether a life will be worthwhile, there are instances (e.g., infants with spina bifida) in which death is the beneficial alternative for all parties involved. He comments: "Where the handicap is sufficiently serious, the killing of a baby may benefit the family to an extent that is sufficient to outweigh the unpleasantness of the killing (or the slower process of 'not striving to keep alive')."

5. Withhold treatment judged not in the child's best interests

The disagreements among McCormick, Glover, and Joseph Fletcher regarding the confining limit of quality-of-life projections reflects a dual ambiguity inherent to the fourth position. Are quality-of-life judgments to be restricted to the current and future interests of the birth-defective infant, or are these judgments to include the current and future interests of other persons (parents, siblings, society) as well? Are quality-of-life judgments in neonatal cases to determine the circumstances in which severely handicapped life (as compared with death) is not in a particular infant's interests, or are these judgments to determine the circumstances in which an abnormal infant (as compared with normal infants) is unlikely to attain certain standards of acceptability for personal human life?

For the ethicists now to be discussed, these ambiguous aspects of quality-of-life judgments are removed by focusing on the infant whose life hangs in the balance in nontreatment decisions. Rather than emphasizing the desires of parents or the interests of other parties in neonatal cases, these ethicists concentrate on the best interests of the infant in question. Moreover, the comparative alternative for these ethicists differs from the alternative posed by advocates of the quality-of-life position. Instead of comparing abnormal infants with normal infants and then proposing that some members of the first group not be treated because they lack the potential for "meaningful" lives or "lives worth living," these ethicists argue that anomalous infants should not be treated only when the severity of their conditions makes the alternative of death preferable to continued life.

For these ethicists, the projected burden of continued existence, rather than the projected lack of quality, is the point at issue. The central question in the quality-of-life position can be phrased in this manner: does a handicapped infant (mentally deficient, paralyzed, blind, or whatever) have the likelihood of a meaningful life? In contrast, the central question in the best interests position is this one: given the possibility that a handicapped infant will not have a meaningful life by normal (non-handicapped) standards, is that life likely to represent a fate worse than death or a life worth experiencing even with the handicaps? Thus ethicists advocating the best interests position find selective nontreatment justifiable only when death appears to be in the best interests of a nondying infant, and do not think as many cases of congenital anomaly call for nontreatment as the ethicists in categories 2 through 4 permit.

Tristram Engelhardt, a philosopher at Baylor College of Medicine in Houston, is one of the representatives of this position. For him, an inescapable aspect of the issue of selective nontreatment is the moral status of the infant whose life is either to be prolonged or terminated. The question of moral status is implicit in two claims he makes about human life: that human existence from the zygote stage to "sometime after birth"

is a "spectrum manifesting only gradual, quantitative changes," and that
only persons have a right to life because only they (as self-conscious,
rational beings) can make the claim on which this right depends.[60]

These claims would seem to indicate that neither fetuses nor infants (at
least until they acquire minimal language skills) have a right to life that
should be recognized. Engelhardt, however, thinks that viability, when
interpreted as a social category, allows "one to draw a line in the quantitative growth of the fetus that can be understood as a qualitative change, as
the emergence of a new measure of worth."[61] In this manner he agrees
with John Fletcher's claim that a justification of abortion (of pre-viable
fetuses) need not entail a justification of infanticide as well.

In explaining what he means by calling viability a "social category,"
Engelhardt suggests that a viable fetus is distinctive in two ways from a
pre-viable fetus. In addition to having the biological capacity to survive
outside the uterus, a viable fetus also has a socializing potential that needs
only the event of birth to become actualized. Once born, a neonate "plays
a part in an already developed social schema and is, as such, construed as
a human person."[62]

It is precisely because of a neonate's social role as "child" within a
family that Engelhardt thinks the personhood concepts developed by
Tooley are too restrictive. In fact, he argues that it is "a false pre-
supposition" that we can have only one concept of "person." For him, at
least two concepts of "person" are required if we want to be intellectually
consistent in the use of language and also in touch with the social
significance of language. Used in a *strict* sense, the concept of "person"
identifies entities who possess certain mental and psychological characteristics: self-consciousness, rationality, and so forth. Persons in this strict
sense are also moral agents, by which Engelhardt means "individual,
living bearers of rights and duties." Most clearly applicable to "normal
adult humans," this concept of personhood recognizes the possiblity of
nonhumans who should nevertheless be regarded as persons because they
are self-conscious, rational agents.

However, because the concept rules out human infants and possibly
other humans who are non-self-conscious or not yet self-conscious, it
needs to be supplemented by a less restrictive concept. That concept
identifies "person" in a *social* sense and includes all forms of human
biological life that "are treated as if they were persons strictly, even
though they are not."[63] This second—or "as if"—concept of personhood
builds on social practices or customs rather than inherent qualities pos-

sessed by a human being. In addition, this social sense of personhood involves the imputing of personlike rights to human beings because of their special roles, even though in a strict sense they cannot make rational claims on us nor do we have duties to them. They nevertheless are capable of engaging "in at least a minimum of interaction" not usually found in other forms of nonpersonal life.[64]

Infants provide the clearest example of this second concept of personhood. Although "humans do not become persons strictly until sometime after birth," there is a long-standing social practice of ascribing personhood to human infants and acting toward them as though they were persons. For instance, when an infant cries we respond to that cry as though it were a self-conscious, rational expression of a desire for food, dry clothing, or attention. In this manner the social role of the infant as "child" gives this nonpersonal human being the imputed status of "person," with the same kind of rights normally held by older human beings who are persons in the more formal sense.

For Engelhardt, this dual concept of personhood is preferable to making distinctions between nonpersons, potential persons, and actual persons. He agrees with Tooley in defining pre-viable fetuses as nonpersons and in rejecting the applicability of the potentiality principle to fetuses and neonates: "the potentiality of X's to become Y's may cause us to value X's very highly because Y's are valued very highly, but until X's are Y's they do not have the value of Y's."[65] Nevertheless, he finds a number of benefits in imputing social personhood to infants rather than placing them in the category of nonpersons. By regarding them as persons, we attribute a certain sort of dignity to them, nurture the virtue in parents of caring for dependent persons, accentuate the obligations of adults to minimize the suffering of small children, and enhance the possibility that the great majority of infants will in time become persons in the strict sense.

Neonates with imputed personhood, then, are the lives at stake in nontreatment decisions. Whether they will grow into persons in the strict sense depends, in an increasing number of cases, on whether they are given medical treatment for congenital anomalies. Similarly, whether parents consent to proposed medical treatment for birth-defective neonates often depends on whether they think the treatment-prolonged lives will be in the best interests of the affected children.

Engelhardt occasionally uses a quality-of-life perspective in describing neonatal lives (e.g., those of anencephalic infants) that are "not worth living" because they will never be able to achieve personhood in the strict sense. However, he emphasizes that an alternative perspective—that of the child's best interests—is a preferable way of making nontreatment decisions. When this perspective is adopted, there is a moral framework for withholding treatment or intentionally killing in cases where, in the parents' judgment, the child's existence after treatment will primarily "be characterized by severe pain and deprivation." Even though the cost of the proposed treatment is not high—thus not making the treatment "extraordinary"—the treatment may still be withheld when it is judged not to be in the child's best interests.[66]

For Engelhardt, this perspective of occasionally withholding even ordinary medical treatment from a severely defective neonate is a moral analog to tort suits for "wrongful life." These legal suits, as we observed in chapter 5, involve infant plaintiffs arguing in court (through their legal guardians) that they have been wronged by life to the extent that they would prefer death to continued existence. An analogous moral perspective involves the claim that any life-prolonging treatment for a severely defective neonate may be withheld if it appears that such treatment will only result in the *injury of continued existence*. Or, equally acceptable to Engelhardt, the avoidance of an ongoing injurious existence—or "wrongful life"—may call for intentionally killing an infant as the most appropriate means of aiding its death. Once the decision has been made by parents that death is in the child's best interests, the only reason for not engaging in direct killing is a prudential one: directly killing a defective neonate could lessen "one's duty to protect children in general."[67]

The concept of injury of continued existence has two implications for parents making decisions about the treatment or nontreatment of birth-defective neonates. First, the concept means that in instances of severe birth defect, life can be regarded as an injury rather than a gift. Even though the birth of normal infants is often interpreted by religious persons as "a gift from God," the birth of severely abnormal infants may force even religious parents to conclude that such injurious existence cannot be interpreted with gift language. Rather, the birth of infants with Tay-Sachs disease or Lesch-Nyhan syndrome or spina bifida cystica leads to such "painfully compromised" types of existence that the only appropriately descriptive language is that of injury.

Second, such injurious existence imparts to parents a duty not to prolong the lives of the infants involved. It is possible, Engelhardt suggests, to perceive from the injured child's perspective that life not only need not be prolonged but *should not* be prolonged through treatment that can neither cure nor correct the anomalous condition. In such instances, morally responsible parents should follow the principle of nonmaleficence and conclude that the avoidance of harm requires nontreatment, if not intentional killing.

According to David H. Smith, a professor of religious studies at Indiana University, the determination by parents that treatment is not in the best interests of a child is the only way of justifying nontreatment. Assuming that the vast majority of human infants (excluding only anencephalic infants) count as persons and are thus generally protected against being killed, he argues that there are but two plausible ways of constructing moral arguments about nontreatment—and one of them does not work. Sometimes the argument is advanced that nontreatment is necessary "for the sake of others: the family, community, or even the human race." This argument fails, in Smith's judgment, because it is unlikely that anyone can demonstrate that the continuing existence of a defective infant represents a clear threat to "the personal life of at least one specifiable other person" (in which case the infant could be classified as an "unjust aggressor"), or that the infant's death is the only way (a "last resort") of removing that threat of harm to the other person.[68]

The second kind of moral argument for selective nontreatment says that nontreatment is sometimes necessary for the sake of the infant. This argument occasionally works, but is more problematic and less inclusive than Engelhardt seems to suggest. Smith thinks that in rare instances (e.g., the prenatal diagnosis of Tay-Sachs disease), a consideration of best interests also justifies abortion.[69] In most late-term abortion cases and neonatal cases, however, a serious consideration of the best interests of the life at stake leads to the conclusion that the life should be prolonged. For instance, Smith believes that parents who decide not to treat infants with Down's syndrome plus duodenal atresia (perhaps following Anthony Shaw's advice) or infants with spina bifida cystica (using John Lorber's selection criteria) are making the wrong decision.

The best interests test is therefore a test that errs in favor of prolonging life. The test means that "we can decide for the death of some newborns [only] insofar as we can plausibly say that the choice is in the best interest of that child—the best option open to him."[70] Acknowledging that there could be rare instances (e.g., an infant with permanent unconsciousness or intractable pain) in which nontreatment would be in the interests of the child, Smith believes that the best interests test "amounts to a prohibition of active or passive infanticide on most newborns."[71]

For Philippa Foot, a philosopher at Oxford and U.C.L.A., the crucial question in cases of selective nontreatment concerns the child's best interests: "Is it for the sake of the child himself that the doctors and parents choose his death?"[72] Or is it not usually for the sake of the parents, siblings, or society that handicapped infants are denied life-prolonging treatment? In most cases of selective nontreatment, she judges that the interests being served are not the defective infant's but those of other parties. Furthermore, if she is right in this assessment, she argues that such decisions are wrong because no one (neither adult nor infant) should be allowed to die or be intentionally killed merely "to avoid trouble to others."

She therefore argues that medical treatment is in the best interests of infants with Down's syndrome (even when complicated by esophageal or duodenal atresia) and many other infants with "severe mental defects." She observes that "not even severe mental handicap automatically brings a child within the scope even of a possible act of euthanasia."[73]

Nevertheless, she acknowledges that when "the medical prognosis is wretchedly bad, as it may be for some spina bifida children," it is possible that someone deciding about treatment for the sake of the child would be morally justified in choosing not to provide treatment. Her reason for this judgment is her belief that continued life can, for some severely afflicted adults or infants, be correctly viewed as "a misery" rather than "a good." When this judgment is made by adult patients, she argues that voluntary euthanasia is acceptable. Even though she finds allowing patients to die and directly killing them "contrary to the distinct virtues" of love and justice and thus morally distinguishable, she thinks "no right is infringed" when a patient is killed on his or her own request.

With infants, however, there is a serious moral problem in bringing about death for the infant's sake. Because an infant cannot request to be killed even if that infant's life represents misery for the child, the only justifiable alternative is to withhold treatment, which may, unfortunately, lead to death from dehydration and starvation. Should the law ever allow for voluntary euthanasia, it might at that time be possible to appoint a legal guardian "to act on the infant's behalf" in requesting a lethal injection.

Robert Coburn, a philosopher at the University of Washington, provides another perspective on determining whether treatment is in the best interests of a birth-defective child. He suggests that the only way to ensure impartiality in a situation of choice, assuming that impartiality is an important element in moral decisions, is to follow the hypothetical choice approach advocated by John Rawls. According to this approach, one attempts to arrive at correct ethical principles by construing a hypothetical situation in which an "ideal moral legislator" has to "will" or choose a course of action from behind a "veil of ignorance": not knowing one's gender, race, intelligence level, personality type, social circumstances, and so forth. This ignorance, coupled with the legislator's desire to make himself or herself as well off as possible in future situations, basically precludes the choice of principles or courses of action that would be biased toward any particular individuals, groups, or alternatives.[74]

When applied to cases involving defective neonates, this hypothetical choice approach is an attempt to determine the best interests of such infants by having rational adults assume the role of the ideal moral legislator and thus "position" themselves in the situation of birth-defective infants. What principles would be chosen by these impartial adults as serving the best interests of infants with severe congenital anomalies? Coburn thinks this hypothetical approach would result in several principles, which can be summarized in the following manner. Withholding treatment or directly killing defective neonates *would not* be regarded as justifiable in cases where "it cannot be concluded beyond any reasonable doubt that the infant would be better off dead," where the infant "will not undergo significant amounts of suffering," or where the infant's life can "be saved by practicable medical procedures." By contrast, withholding treatment and/or directly killing defective neonates *would* be regarded as justifiable in cases where the infant is not likely to survive "the first several years of life," where its experiences "will either be of no value to it or mainly negative," and where it will undergo significant amounts of suffering.[75]

Assessment

What can be made of these five different positions and the variations within them? It is clear, at the very least, that ethicists disagree as much among themselves on the issue of selective nontreatment as physicians and attorneys do. I do not plan to unpack all the reasons for the disagreements among ethicists, nor do I plan to do an exhaustive analysis and comparison of the positions just presented. What I do want to do, as a transitional step to the remaining chapters, is to comment briefly on some of the general problems common to the ethical literature on selective nontreatment and to assess in slightly more detail each of the five typological views we have discussed.

One of the problems common to the ethical literature is the minimal attention given to the medical realities and range of cases that actually characterize NICUs. Fully one-third of the ethicists just discussed refer to no specific congenital anomalies and analyze no actual cases in their comments about selective nontreatment. Some other ethicists only set up polar opposites—usually anencephaly and Down's syndrome—to suggest the types of conditions that need not and should be treated, but say nothing about the other anomalous conditions that require decisions about treatment or nontreatment. Only Ramsey, McCormick, both Fletchers, Garland, and Engelhardt even begin to suggest the range of birth defects that actually occur in NICUs.

A second common problem is the vagueness of terminology used by ethicists. Of course, some of the terminology used in ethical analysis is inherently vague, but it is nevertheless perplexing to observe the number of times many ethicists hang an entire argument on an ethical principle or evaluative concept that remains undefined and insufficiently explained in the context of selective nontreatment. What is meant, for instance, by appeals to the "sanctity of life" or "quality of life" or "harm" or "meaningful life" that, depending on how these concepts are used, may call for treatment or justify nontreatment in selected instances? A related terminological problem is the inconsistent use of "human" and "person." With some exceptions (Tooley, Warren, Singer, Kluge, and Ramsey), most of the ethicists surveyed either do not distinguish between these concepts or simply use them in such an inconsistent and overlapping manner as to blunt whatever distinctive meaning they have.

Another problem is especially difficult to avoid and is shared by many physicians, attorneys, and ethicists writing about selective nontreatment. That problem, as already indicated in chapter 3, is the general lack of clear, consistent ethical criteria that may be used in nontreatment cases. Some ethicists do not even try to develop specific, coherent ethical criteria for selective nontreatment. Those who do put forth ethical criteria often gain clarity by using criteria that are too inclusive (e.g., Tooley or Singer) or too exclusive (e.g., Ramsey or Jakobovits), or they sacrifice clarity by using inherently vague criteria (e.g., McCormick or Glover). And few of these ethicists take the additional step of showing how their ethical criteria relate to the clinical criteria that are often used in NICUs in nontreatment cases.

Procedural questions are also problematic for ethicists, in two quite different ways. Some ethicists (e.g., Kluge, Tooley, Joseph Fletcher, Foot) virtually ignore the issue of who should bear the responsibility for making nontreatment decisions, perhaps assuming that if substantive issues are handled correctly it really does not matter who makes the decisions. Other ethicists (notably John Fletcher) place considerable emphasis on procedural matters, to the point that it sometimes seems that there is no "right" decision to be made but only "right" persons to make it. Either way, there is a serious mishandling of important questions pertaining to procedure.

A final problem to be mentioned at this point is the tendency of many ethicists to write about selective nontreatment as though such cases occur in a legal vacuum. Of course the legal status of nontreatment decisions in NICUs does not determine the issue of the morality of such decisions, but it is nevertheless striking to notice the number of ethicists who apparently think the law is not even a factor in these decisions. Of the ethicists discussed above, only McCormick makes a consistent effort to relate his ethical analysis to cases that have been handled in courts of law. And only Foot clearly indicates that legality and morality are related in such a way that if euthanasia were a legal option, she would change her opinion about the moral alternatives available to parents and physicians in nontreatment cases.

In concluding this chapter on ethical options, it may be helpful to point out certain strengths and weaknesses in each of the five typological positions discussed above. The strengths of the first position are several. Especially as represented in the writings of Ramsey, the position stresses the moral necessity of protecting defenseless lives, allows for religious and philosophical claims regarding the intrinsic value of human life, recognizes that nontreatment decisions do not automatically result in the deaths of infants left untreated, and emphasizes the distinction between the obligation to cure nondying individuals and the obligation only to care for individuals who are dying. In addition, as most clearly pointed out by Devine, the position is consistent with the commonly held intuition that it is wrong to kill babies.

The position also has several weaknesses. For one, in their emphasis on the basic equality of infants and refusal to allow birth-defective neonates to be compared with normal neonates, the advocates of this position draw an unbending egalitarian line that claims that all infants on the nondying side of the line have an equal right to all the life-prolonging treatment physicians can give them. In this manner, they assert that pediatricians and pediatric surgeons have a virtually exceptionless duty to give maximum treatment to all nondying neonates—even if the physician in a particular case believes that such treatment will do more harm to the infant than good. A second weakness connects with this first one. The advocates of position 1, although surely as compassionate as the representatives of the other positions, often seem to have a blind spot in relation to infant suffering. When Ramsey calls for treatment for all nondying infants "regardless of their state or condition," and Jakobovits writes about the obligation to save the lives of infants having "teeth and tail like an animal," and Devine opts to require treatment for tragically handicapped neonates who are "mere beasts," there is an implication that *no amount of suffering or handicap* could ever justify nontreatment for a nondying infant. This implication is partially due to a third weakness in this position, namely the scarcity of congenital anomalies actually discussed and the few conditions seriously considered as exceptions. Jakobovits, Devine, and Kluge allow no specifiable exceptions. Ramsey allows for Lesch-Nyhan syndrome as an exception, but he also fails to address the number of other severe congenital defects (e.g., hydranencephaly, trisomy 18, trisomy 13) that cannot effectively be treated and that raise the issue of whether death in some instances (even for nondying infants) may not be preferable to life with unmitigated suffering.

The strengths and weaknesses of position 2 are more narrowly focused, given the emphasis placed on the issue of personhood. Tooley, Warren, and Singer make important contributions to the ethical literature on selective nontreatment in their call for greater conceptual clarity and greater terminological consistency whenever ethicists address the ontological and moral status of infants. Moreover, they contribute to the ongoing ethical analysis of selective nontreatment by recognizing that birth is no magic moral moment and that arguments about the personhood of late-term fetuses and neonates are logically connected.

There are, however, several problems with the handling of the personhood issue by these philosophers. First, they consistently reject the potentiality principle by arguing that there is no middle ground between being a nonperson and being a person. In advocating this all-or-nothing position on personhood, they are forced to defend a perspective that is counterintuitive. We will return to the potentiality principle in chapter 7. For the moment it is sufficient simply to point out that we typically—and I think correctly—attribute *some value* to individuals on the basis of their potentiality to achieve a status they do not presently possess. Second, because these philosophers argue that nonrelational personhood is a status one either has or does not have (like pregnancy, there are apparently no gradations of personhood), they have to choose an arbitrary time at which a developing human being attains personhood. Because birth is not the time at which personhood occurs, they arbitrarily choose a "magic moment" of either one week after birth (for Tooley) or one month after birth (for Singer). Third, and much more seriously, they open the door to the *unlimited, indiscriminate termination* of an indeterminate number of neonatal lives. Without regard to a neonate's medical condition, it is permissible under this perspective to withhold treatment or intentionally kill any unwanted neonate who has not lived long enough to attain personhood.

The third position is significantly different from either of the first two perspectives. Representatives of this position correctly recognize that selective nontreatment is a complex issue that includes moral considerations other than whether a birth-defective neonate is dying or has achieved personhood. John Fletcher, Garland, and Ackerman also correctly point out that parental acceptance of a less-than-perfect infant is vitally important to cut down on the prospects of subsequent child abuse, to maximize whatever chance the child has to realize its mental and physical potential, and to make parental sacrifices (in terms of money, time, energy, and life-style) for the child tolerable.

Problems arise, however, in the amount of emphasis given to parental discretion in neonatal cases. To justify selective nontreatment on the basis of "meaningless parental suffering" (John Fletcher) or "unnecessary familial burdens" (Garland) or the absence of "parental commitment" to care for the child (Ackerman) is tantamount to giving parents a blank check to engage in infanticidal practices *whenever they feel like it*. Do we really want to allow anomalous infants to live or die depending on their parents' desires? I think not. To do so would be to place the fate of birth-defective neonates entirely in the hands of persons who may be emotionally overwhelmed by the prospect of rearing a child who varies (a little? a lot?) from the "perfect" child they had anticipated. To do so would also be to encourage physicians to acquiesce (as some of them already do) in the face of parental death-causing decisions that are illegal and that might generally be regarded as immoral. To do so would additionally be to collapse the distinction between immediate care and long-term custody, and to permit a birth-defective infant to die who might well be adopted if the parents not wanting it would give up custody to someone else.

For ethicists holding position 4, the central moral consideration in neonatal cases is the kind of lives birth-defective neonates will have beyond infancy. In arguing for the necessity of quality-of-life judgments, they make the obvious point that there is some correlation between the quality of one's life (at least in terms of self-perception) and the enjoyment or satisfaction with which one lives. Moreover, they are correct in pointing out that whereas mere biological function in a neonate is sufficient to indicate the presence of a human life, it is insufficient to denote a "life worth living."

Nevertheless, there are problems with a quality-of-life perspective, and these problems are only accentuated when a quality-of-life perspective is introduced into neonatal medicine. One of the problems is the inherent vagueness of the concepts central to this perspective on life. What, specifically, is built into the notion "quality of life" when this concept is applied to infants who have no "track record," no accomplishments, no failures, no education, no income, no life-style, or any other ingredients that normally comprise quality-of-life judgments? And what, specifically, is meant by the standards of "relational capacity" (McCormick) or "well-being" (Joseph Fletcher) or "worth-while life" (Glover), according to which, if projected as lacking in an infant, life need not be prolonged?

A second problem is that quality-of-life assessments vary according to the persons making them. Rather obviously, the quality an individual's life is judged to have differs significantly depending on the age, educational level, socioeconomic status, cultural background, and health of the person making the assessment. It is for this reason (among others) that quality-of-life projections made about birth-defective infants are to be suspected whenever they are made by adults who have never experienced physical disability, serious illness, or educational limitations.

A third problem in the quality-of-life perspectives of Joseph Fletcher and Jonathan Glover (but not Richard McCormick) is that they project an infant's "quality" not only in terms of that particular infant but also in terms of that particular infant's impact on other people. Instead of focusing on projections of the "child's good, this alone" (McCormick), Fletcher and Glover expand their projections of an infant's worth to include the infant's future contributions or "detributions" in relation to parents, siblings, and society. In these utilitarian positions, therefore, the quality control standard that is often used in neonatal cases is the quality-of-other-lives principle, depending on whether a defective neonate lives or dies.

A fourth problem, especially in Glover's position, is that infants whose projected quality is quite minimal may be "replaced" by another child born to the same parents who may be normal and thus projected to have "a worth-while life." The implication of this replaceability argument (as well as Singer's similar argument) is that it is morally preferable to kill a defective infant and replace it with a "better" one, than not to kill the infant in the first place.

Position 5, in my judgment, is the best of the ethical options on selective nontreatment. Its strengths, which I hope to build on in subsequent chapters, are several. Especially as represented in the writings of Engelhardt, Foot, and Smith, the position focuses the issue of nontreatment where it belongs: on the birth-defective neonate. The questions it raises reflect the same focal point: are the available medical treatments in this child's best interests? Will treatment be done—or be withheld—for the child's sake? Is the child's medical condition such that, even with treatment, death will be preferable to a torturous existence? Or, stated in another manner, the position emphasizes that decisions about treatment or nontreatment should focus on the neonate's medical condition, that such decisions concern suffering and irremediable handicap rather than projected social worth, that comparative judgments involve contrasts between injurious existence and nonexistence (rather than between abnormal infants and normal ones), and that in some neonatal cases it is justifiable to conclude that treatment should be withheld because life, on balance, will be harmful rather than beneficial to the child.

This position, of course, is not without problems. In subsequent chapters I will be aware of two inherent difficulties with this perspective. First, this ethical option shares the conceptual and evaluative difficulties of some of the legal arguments discussed in chapter 5; namely, it involves contrasting severely handicapped existence with nonexistence and argues that in some cases death may be judged preferable to continued life.

Second, this ethical option has its own share of vague concepts. Given the importance of the principle of nonmaleficence to this position, an explanation of what is meant by "harm" in neonatal medicine will be particularly important.

Notes

1. Paul Ramsey, *Ethics at the Edges of Life* (New Haven and London: Yale University Press, 1978), p. 194.
2. Peter Singer, *Practical Ethics* (Cambridge and New York: Cambridge University Press, 1979), p. 123.
3. John Freeman, "Ethics and the Decision Making Process for Defective Children," in David J. Roy, ed., *Medical Wisdom and Ethics in the Treatment of Severely Defective Newborn and Young Children* (Montreal: Eden Press, 1978), p. 37.
4. Ramsey, *Ethics*, p. 190.
5. Paul Ramsey, "Feticide/Infanticide upon Request," *Religion in Life* 39 (Summer 1970): 174–75.
6. Ramsey, *Ethics*, p. 192. The unfootnoted quotations that follow come from chaps. 5 and 6 of this book.
7. Immanuel Jakobovits, *Jewish Medical Ethics*, rev. ed. (New York: Bloch Publishing Co., 1975), pp. 123–25, 275–76.
8. Immanuel Jakobovits, "Jewish Views on Infanticide," in Marvin Kohl, ed., *Infanticide and the Value of Life* (Buffalo, N.Y.: Prometheus Books, 1978), pp. 24–25.
9. Ibid., p. 28.
10. Philip E. Devine, *The Ethics of Homicide* (Ithaca and London: Cornell University Press, 1978), p. 62. The unfootnoted quotations that follow come from this book.
11. Eike-Henner W. Kluge, *The Practice of Death* (New Haven and London: Yale University Press, 1975), p. 209. For the legal implications of his views on neonatal euthanasia, see Eike-Henner W. Kluge, "The Euthanasia of Radically Defective Neonates: Some Statutory Considerations," *Dalhousie Law Journal* 6 (November 1980): 229–57.
12. Eike-Henner W. Kluge, "Infanticide as the Murder of Persons," in Kohl, *Infanticide and the Value of Life*, p. 33.
13. Michael Tooley, "Abortion and Infanticide," *Philosophy and Public Affairs* 2 (Fall 1972): 37–65. The revised version of the article is entitled "A Defense of Abortion and Infanticide" and is in Joel Feinberg, ed., *The Problem of Abortion* (Belmont, Calif.: Wadsworth Publishing Co., 1973), pp. 51–91.
14. Tooley, "A Defense of Abortion and Infanticide," p. 53. The unfootnoted quotations that follow come from this article.
15. Michael Tooley, "Decisions to Terminate Life and the Concept of Person," in John Ladd, ed., *Ethical Issues Relating to Life and Death* (New York and Oxford: Oxford University Press, 1979), p. 91.

16. Tooley, "A Defense of Abortion and Infanticide," p. 60.
17. Tooley, "Decisions to Terminate Life and the Concept of Person," pp. 80–81. The unfootnoted quotations that follow come from this article.
18. Mary Anne Warren, "On the Moral and Legal Status of Abortion," *The Monist* 57 (January 1973): 43–61. An expanded version of the article, with a "Postscript on Infanticide," was published in Richard Wasserstrom, ed., *Today's Moral Problems* (New York: Macmillan Publishing Co., 1975), pp. 120–36.
19. Warren, "On the Moral and Legal Status of Abortion," in Wasserstrom, *Today's Moral Problems*, pp. 130–31.
20. Mary Anne Warren, "Do Potential People Have Moral Rights?" *Canadian Journal of Philosophy* 7 (June 1977): 275. The unfootnoted quotations that follow come from this article.
21. Warren, "On the Moral and Legal Status of Abortion," p. 135.
22. Ibid., pp. 135–36.
23. Singer, *Practical Ethics*, p. 73.
24. Peter Singer, *Animal Liberation* (New York: Avon Books, 1975), p. 7.
25. Singer, *Practical Ethics*, p. 97. The unfootnoted quotations that follow come from chaps. 6 and 7 of this book.
26. Peter Singer, "Unsanctifying Human Life," in Ladd, *Ethical Issues Relating to Life and Death*, p. 55.
27. Singer, *Practical Ethics*, p. 138.
28. John C. Fletcher, "Choices of Life or Death in the Care of Defective Newborns," in Louis W. Hodges, ed., *Social Responsibility: Journalism, Law, and Medicine* (Lexington, Va.: Washington and Lee University Press, 1975), p. 72.
29. John C. Fletcher, "Parents in Genetic Counseling: The Moral Shape of Decision-Making," in Bruce Hilton et al., eds., *Ethical Issues in Human Genetics* (New York and London: Plenum Press, 1973), p. 310.
30. Ibid., p. 319; see also idem, *Coping with Genetic Disorders: A Guide for Clergy Counseling and for Parents* (New York: Harper and Row, 1982), pp. 102–25.
31. John C. Fletcher, "Abortion, Euthanasia, and Care of Defective Newborns," *The New England Journal of Medicine* 292 (January 9, 1975): 76.
32. Ibid.; see also idem, "Prenatal Diagnosis, Selective Abortion, and the Ethics of Withholding Treatment from the Defective Newborn," in Alexander M. Capron et al., eds., *Genetic Counseling: Facts, Values, and Norms* (New York: Alan R. Liss, 1979), p. 249.
33. John C. Fletcher, "Abortion, Euthanasia, and Care of Defective Newborns," p. 78.
34. John C. Fletcher, "Spina Bifida with Myelomeningocele: A Case Study in Attitudes towards Defective Newborns," in Chester Swinyard, *Decision Making and the Defective Newborn* (Springfield, Ill.: Charles C Thomas, 1978), p. 295.
35. Ibid., p. 296.
36. John C. Fletcher, "Choices of Life or Death in the Care of Defective Newborns," p. 77.

37. Albert R. Jonsen and Michael J. Garland, "A Moral Policy for Life/Death Decisions in the Intensive Care Nursery," in Albert R. Jonsen and Michael J. Garland, eds., *Ethics of Newborn Intensive Care* (Berkeley: University of California, Institute of Government Studies, 1976), pp. 142-55. A revised version of this chapter appears as A. R. Jonsen et al., "Critical Issues in Newborn Intensive Care: A Conference Report and Policy Proposal," *Pediatrics* 55 (June 1975): 756-65.
38. Michael J. Garland, "Care of the Newborn: The Decision Not to Treat," *Perinatology/Neonatology* 1 (September-October 1977): 15.
39. Ibid., p. 17.
40. Terrence F. Ackerman, "Meningomyelocele and Parental Commitment: A Policy Proposal Regarding Selection for Treatment," *Man and Medicine* 5 (Fall 1980): 298, 300.
41. Richard A. McCormick, S. J., "Life-Saving and Life-Taking: A Comment," *The Linacre Quarterly* 42 (May 1975): 112.
42. Richard A. McCormick, S. J., *Notes on Moral Theology, 1965 through 1980* (Washington, D.C.: University Press of America, 1981), pp. 445-46.
43. Ibid., p. 445.
44. Richard A. McCormick, S. J., "The Quality of Life, the Sanctity of Life," *Hastings Center Report* 8 (February 1978): 34-35.
45. Ibid., p. 35.
46. Richard A. McCormick, S. J., "To Save or Let Die: The Dilemma of Modern Medicine," *Journal of the American Medical Association* 229 (July 8, 1974): 174. The unfootnoted quotations that follow come from this article.
47. Ibid., pp. 172-75. Also see Richard A. McCormick and Laurence H. Tribe, "Infant Doe: Where to Draw the Line," *The Washington Post*, July 27, 1982.
48. McCormick, "The Quality of Life, the Sanctity of Life," p. 36.
49. Joseph Fletcher, "Medicine and the Nature of Man," in Robert M. Veatch, Willard Gaylin, and Councilman Morgan, eds., *The Teaching of Medical Ethics* (New York: Institute of Society, Ethics, and the Life Sciences, 1973), p. 52. A shortened version of this article appeared as idem, "Indicators of Humanhood: A Tentative Profile of Man," *Hastings Center Report* 2 (November 1972): 1-4. For applications of this theory, see idem, *Humanhood: Essays in Biomedical Ethics* (Buffalo, N.Y.: Prometheus Books, 1979).
50. Joseph Fletcher, "Medicine and the Nature of Man," pp. 52-57.
51. Joseph Fletcher, "Four Indicators of Humanhood—The Enquiry Matures," *Hastings Center Report* 4 (December 1974): 6-7.
52. Joseph Fletcher, "Medicine and the Nature of Man," p. 52.
53. Joseph Fletcher, "Infanticide and the Ethics of Loving Care," in Kohl, *Infanticide and the Value of Life*, p. 19.
54. Joseph Fletcher, "Ethics and Euthanasia," in Robert H. Williams, ed., *To Live and To Die* (New York: Springer-Verlag, 1974), p. 119. A shortened version of this article appeared in the *American Journal of Nursing* 73 (April 1973): 670-75.
55. Joseph Fletcher, *The Ethics of Genetic Control* (Garden City, N.Y.: Anchor Press, 1974), p. 153.

56. Joseph Fletcher, "Moral Aspects of Decision-Making," in Tom D. Moore, ed., *Report of the Sixty-Fifth Ross Conference on Pediatric Research: Ethical Dilemmas in Current Obstetric and Newborn Care* (Columbus, Ohio: Ross Laboratories, 1976), p. 70.
57. Joseph Fletcher, "Infanticide and the Ethics of Loving Care," p. 16.
58. Ibid., p. 15.
59. Jonathan Glover, *Causing Death and Saving Lives* (Harmondsworth, England, and New York: Penguin Books, 1977), pp. 113–14. The unfootnoted quotations that follow come from chap. 12 of this book.
60. H. Tristram Engelhardt, "Viability, Abortion, and the Difference between a Fetus and an Infant," *American Journal of Obstetrics and Gynecology* 116 (June 1, 1973): 430; idem, "Bioethics and the Process of Embodiment," *Perspectives in Biology and Medicine* 18 (Summer 1975): 495.
61. Engelhardt, "Viability, Abortion, and the Difference," p. 432.
62. Ibid.
63. H. Tristram Engelhardt, "Medicine and the Concept of Person," in Tom Beauchamp and Seymour Perlin, eds., *Ethical Issues in Death and Dying* (Englewood Cliffs, N.J.: Prentice-Hall, 1978), p. 277.
64. H. Tristram Engelhardt, "On the Bounds of Freedom: From the Treatment of Fetuses to Euthanasia," *Connecticut Medicine* 40 (January 1976): 52.
65. Engelhardt, "Medicine and the Concept of Person," p. 276.
66. H. Tristram Engelhardt, "Ethical Issues in Aiding the Death of Young Children," in Marvin Kohl, ed., *Beneficent Euthanasia* (Buffalo, N.Y.: Prometheus Books, 1975), p. 185.
67. Ibid., p. 188.
68. David H. Smith, "On Letting Some Babies Die," *Hastings Center Studies* 2 (May 1974): 40–42.
69. David H. Smith, "The Abortion of Defective Fetuses: Some Moral Considerations," in David H. Smith and Linda Bernstein, eds., *No Rush to Judgment: Essays on Medical Ethics* (Bloomington, Ind.: The Poynter Center, 1978), p. 141.
70. David H. Smith, "Death, Ethics and Social Control," in Roy, *Medical Wisdom and Ethics*, p. 74.
71. Smith, "On Letting Some Babies Die," p. 45.
72. Philippa Foot, "Euthanasia," *Philosophy and Public Affairs* 6 (Winter 1977): 109.
73. Ibid., p. 111.
74. Robert C. Coburn, "Morality and the Defective Newborn," *The Journal of Medicine and Philosophy* 5 (December 1980): 340–45. For John Rawls' position, see his *A Theory of Justice* (Cambridge, Mass.: Harvard University Press, 1971).
75. Coburn, "Morality and the Defective Newborn," pp. 346–48, 354.

7
Ethical Criteria

The final lesson of the Danville case [case 4.4] is that substantive and procedural criteria consistent with current law should be developed forthwith for nontreatment decisions. If they are not, the current haphazard, arbitrary pattern of selection for nontreatment is likely to continue.

JOHN A. ROBERTSON[1]

Unless those who favor selective nontreatment for defective infants can develop more precise guidelines and rationales, the fundamental weakness of their position will remain: it will commit us to courses of action and to social policies that are at odds with one of the oldest and most basic moral principles in the medical profession—to provide life-saving therapy to all of those who need it.

RICHARD SHERLOCK, PH.D.[2]

At least three things are clear from the foregoing chapters. First, there is agreement among most pediatricians, attorneys, and ethicists that some neonates with severe congenital anomalies should not be given life-prolonging medical treatment. Second, there is widespread disagreement among pediatricians, attorneys, and ethicists regarding *which* birth-defective infants should not be treated, and *why* they should be denied treatment. Third, among the reasons for this disagreement are the inherent complexity of some NICU cases, the ambiguity of the law, and the vagueness of many of the views put forward regarding the ethics of selective nontreatment.

As indicated by the statements above by John Robertson and Richard Sherlock, the time has come to move beyond generality and vagueness to increased specificity and clarity regarding the ethics of selective nontreatment. With the lives of numerous birth-defective infants at stake, it is necessary to move beyond the ad hoc, whenever-the-physician-or-parents-think-best approach that currently characterizes selective nontreatment decisions in the nation's hospitals. These arbitrary, stress-laden decisions often result in withholding treatment from or intentionally killing some infants who should live (and would live in other hospitals), or needlessly using aggressive treatment to prolong the lives of some infants who should die (and would die in other hospitals).

A much better approach to selective nontreatment decisions is to develop a reasonable, consistent policy that is applicable from one hospital to another. In general terms, such a policy should (1) focus on the child's best interests (the fifth option presented in the previous chapter), (2) be based on substantive and procedural criteria that are clear, related to one another, and defensible on both medical and moral grounds, and (3) provide guidelines for decision making that are consistent with the informed moral and legal reasoning used in the public forum.

The remaining chapters present and defend such a policy. This chapter presents the ethical criteria necessary for justifying decisions to deny certain birth-defective newborns life-prolonging treatment. Chapter 8 contains a discussion of the clinical applications of these criteria. Chapter 9 focuses on procedural matters regarding selective nontreatment.

Earlier chapters contain a variety of ethical criteria put forth by professionals in medicine, law, and ethics. Sometimes these criteria simply surface as physicians or legal scholars discuss selective nontreatment, with limited effort to support or defend the criteria with argumentation. Other times—especially in the positions discussed in chapter 6—ethical criteria function as an integral part of philosophical positions on selective nontreatment and other forms of infanticide. In many of these instances, as we observed, the ethical criteria used are insufficiently developed, quite vague, or have wide-ranging and undesirable implications beyond NICUs.

The ethical criteria now to be presented are an improvement over the criteria previously discussed. Adequate and defensible criteria are necessary if one is interested in justifying nontreatment in some neonatal cases but not others, and if one wants the distinction between neonates to be treated and those not to be treated to be one of principle rather than happenstance. Six ethical criteria are required, the first three of which are conceptual in nature and the last three operational. Along with the clinical criteria to be discussed in the following chapter, these ethical criteria comprise the substantive basis for a reasonable, consistent position on selective nontreatment.

The first three ethical criteria provide a conceptual framework with which to approach selective nontreatment decisions. The two clinical requirements to be presented in chapter 8 constitute the foundation on which morally responsible medicine is practiced with anomalous new-borns. In the context established by these ethical and clinical considerations, it is possible to present a reasoned argument for three operational criteria that are ethical in nature and clinical in application. The arrangement of the various criteria can be depicted in the following manner:

Conceptual ethical criteria	*General clinical criteria*
Neonates as potential persons	Correct diagnosis
The best interests of the neonate	Careful prognosis
The principle of nonmaleficence	

                          ↘   ↙

Operational criteria
Select by diagnostic categories
Select by withholding optional
means of treatment
The morality and practice of
intentional killing

Neonates as potential persons

The first substantive issue regarding selective nontreatment is the legal and moral status of the life being prolonged with treatment or shortened in the absence of treatment. Because we have already discussed the legal status of neonates (in chaps. 1 and 3), it will suffice at this point simply to repeat that the U.S. Constitution defines personhood as beginning at birth. However, as previously mentioned, the manner in which criminal laws are enforced in cases of neonatal deaths (especially those occurring in hospitals) suggests that neonates do not in actuality have the same legal status as older children, teenagers, and adults. Neonates clearly have a greater legal status than fetuses, but a less frequently enforced legal status than older persons in society.

When turning to the moral status of neonates, some ontological considerations must be considered first. What kind of entity is it whose life is at stake in nontreatment decisions? Is a neonate, in terms of its ontological status, the same as a late-term fetus? Is a neonate, in terms of its ontological status, the same as an older child, a teenager, or an adult?

There can be little doubt, in my judgment, that a normal neonate is more similar to a late-term fetus than to an older infant. To state the same point more specifically, a neonate is more similar to a fetus in the twenty-fourth week of gestation than to a three-month-old infant. Granted that there are important differences between third-trimester fetuses and neonates (e.g., the change from an aquatic to a gaseous environment), the similarities between these two forms of life in terms of neurological and physiological development make it very difficult to argue persuasively for an ontological (or moral) difference between the lives at stake in late-term abortions and those at stake in acts of infanticide. Most of the differences between the late fetal and neonatal stages of life are differences in degree, not differences in kind. Thus physicians typically refer to spontaneous abortions occurring before the third trimester as miscarriages, but those after that point as premature deliveries.

By contrast, neonates are significantly different from older infants and children. They differ in nutritional needs, metabolism, major and minor motor skills, mobility, tolerance for medication, and so forth. Additionally, they differ in terms of self-consciousness, rationality, and most of the other properties that Tooley, Warren, and Singer believe necessary for an entity to possess personhood. Moreover, if one builds certain language skills into the concept of personhood, as Ramsey does, it is surely clear that neonates cannot correctly be regarded as having the ontological status of persons. The point remains the same even if one has a minimal concept of personhood that does not require the acquisition of language skills or all of the other properties discussed in the philosophical literature on personhood. Therefore, even if neonates are persons in the sense of constitutional law, they are not persons in the nonlegal and nonrelational sense of personhood used by most psychologists and philosophers.

If newborn infants cannot correctly be regarded as persons, what kind of ontological status do they have? Obviously the term "human being" is a correct description of neonates, given their genetic code and membership in the species *homo sapiens.* For some ethicists (e.g., McCormick, Ramsey, John Fletcher), the designation of neonates as human beings is sufficient to give newborn infants protection from having their lives indiscriminately terminated. However, given the ease with which abnormal young human beings were for centuries redefined as "changelings" and then killed, it is obvious that membership in the human community does not provide infants sufficient protection from arbitrary acts of killing. Moreover, given the importance of the personhood argument in philosophical discussions of infanticide, it is obvious that young human beings who do not yet possess the requisite properties of personhood can be categorized as "nonpersons" and then have no more moral protection from being killed than if they were nonpersons belonging to another species.

An alternative regarding ontological status is advocated by Engelhardt. Granting that neonates are not persons in a strict sense, he argues that their ontological status is something more than membership in the human community. For him, as discussed in the previous chapter, neonates are best understood as having the imputed status of person. They are persons in a social sense, as best illustrated in the bonding that takes place in the mother–child relationship. As attractive as this theory is, it has a serious weakness when applied to neonates with serious congenital anomalies. In assuming a traditional family context characterized by love, Engelhardt's theory fails to allow for infants born into a social setting in which they are not wanted. The result is that in cases of unwanted births, and especially when a neonate has one or more serious birth defects, there often is no imputation of social worth by parents (the father of the child may not even be known) and certainly no mother–child bonding. Such unwanted and defective infants are often abandoned by their parent(s) in the hope that the neonates will die in the NICU.

A preferable alternative is to regard neonates as potential persons. This alternative also grants that neonates lack the sufficient properties for personhood, however philosophers may define those properties. In contrast to the theory of social personhood, however, this interpretation of ontological status emphasizes the potential a neonate has to become a person in the normal course of his or her development, rather than relying on the choice of other persons (typically, parents) to ascribe a conjectural status of personhood to a neonate who does not actually possess it. Rather than depending on members of the personhood club to bend the rules of membership for an individual who does not really qualify for membership, this alternative suggests that neonates will at some future point naturally meet the requirements for membership in the personhood club as long as the rules for membership do not change between now and then.

Of course the potentiality principle is a topic of considerable debate among philosophers. The major point of contention in the debate about potentiality is clear enough: advocates of the potentiality principle believe that personhood is a condition that develops gradually over a period of time, whereas critics of the principle are convinced that personhood is an all-or-nothing condition that allows for no degrees of possession. The sharpness of the potentiality/actuality distinction drawn by critics of the potentiality principle is best illustrated by Tooley's Frankenstein example: this laboratory-constructed human has the status either of hamburger meat or a person, with no other options available.

I believe there are several reasons for siding with the proponents of the potentiality principle, and in particular for using it to interpret the ontological and moral status of neonates. Before doing that, however, it is necessary to clear up some of the conceptual confusion that often surfaces in discussions of the principle. Clarity can be gained by distinguishing between persons, potential persons, and possible persons. *Persons* are beings (usually human beings) who meet or have met the sufficient condition(s) for personhood and thereby possess the rights and obligations normally held by beings such as adult humans. *Potential persons* are nonpersonal beings who will become persons in the normal course of their development. *Possible persons* are, in contrast, entities who will become persons only as a consequence of a causal event or constitutive structural change (e.g., a human sperm or ovum).[3]

There are three reasons for classifying most neonates as potential persons. First, neonates without severe central nervous system dysfunction have a neurological system that is structurally similar to that of a normal adult human being. Having had detectable brain activity since the eighth week of gestation, a neurologically normal neonate produces brain waves that are easily picked up by an EEG. In fact, EEG readings can be used to determine the gestational age of a neonate, with full-term infants producing irregular, low-voltage electrical activity that can be recorded whether they are awake or asleep. More regular, higher voltage readings appear with further development of the brain and intellectual stimulation.[4]

Second, researchers who work with neonates are discovering that newborn infants are not passive creatures waiting for the world to imprint its wisdom on them; rather they exhibit a considerable amount of alertness and responsiveness. The use of closed-circuit television, videotape, and clinical observation is making it increasingly obvious that infants during the neonatal period are capable of distinguishing between female and male voices, turning in the direction of a voice, discerning faces, integrating sight and touch, and distinguishing between a toy block and other objects.[5] With the child's additional growth, development, and stimulation during infancy, these neonatal skills will improve in an exponential manner.

Third, neonates without severe central nervous system dysfunction do not require any causal event, constitutive structural change in their makeup, act of God, or any other sort of "magic moment" to become persons.

They do not need to be activated in some manner or "thawed out" as Tooley's Frankenstein. Instead, all that they need is to have a normal period of growth and development extending into the later periods of infancy.

The moral implications of this view are obvious. If most neonates are potential persons, and if potential persons in the normal course of their development become actual persons and thus protectable members of society, the deaths of neonates cannot simply be dismissed as "morally neutral" acts (Tooley) or "not wrong at all" (Singer). Rather, the deaths of neonates are the deaths of individuals who "already [have] some claim to life" by virtue of the fact that they will later "acquire a person's claim to life."[6] Consequently, when decisions are made to terminate a birth-defective infant's life, such decisions should be made with sadness, reluctance, and regret.

Lest I be misunderstood, let me emphasize that I am not claiming that potential persons have the same moral status that persons do. Rather, I am claiming against the critics of the potentiality principle that neonates have value—and generally deserve to be protected from harm—precisely because they possess the potentiality to become persons later. To make this claim about the moral status of neonates is not to mistake potentiality for actuality, nor to get into the philosophical debate regarding the rights that potential persons may or may not have. It is instead simply to point out that we often attribute value to individuals on the basis of the potential they possess to become something they presently are not: physicians, professors, major league baseball players, corporation presidents, and so forth. We also buy stocks precisely because we judge them to have growth potential. To deny the role that potentiality plays in making such value judgments—or to suggest that medical students, associate professors, class AAA baseball players, and corporation vice-presidents have no value because they have not reached a higher level of achievement—is clearly to take a position that is counter to intuition and common practice. The same kind of reasoning applies to the potentiality neonates have to become persons.

The best interests of the neonate

As potential persons, neonates have prima facie claims to life and the medical treatment necessary to prolong life. Although there are some instances in which these prima facie claims are justifiably overridden by other considerations, such considerations should have only one focal point: the best interests of the anomalous child. No potential or actual person should be deprived of life without good reason, and in neonatal cases sufficiently good reasons for bringing about death are limited to detriment–benefit judgments made for the infant's sake.

This second criterion for selective nontreatment differs from the sorts of reasons that often comprise decisions to terminate the lives of birth-defective neonates. On the basis of available evidence, it appears that a significant number of infants with congenital anomalies are frequently denied treatment—by some pediatricians, in some hospitals—for reasons other than the condition of abnormality or the availability of treatment for the abnormality. A careful reading of the cases presented earlier (in chaps. 2–5) and some of the pediatric views discussed in chapter 3 indicates that in many instances of congenital anomaly, such infants die not because death has been determined to be in their best interests, but because their deaths advance the interests of other persons.

Of course the interests of other persons are involved in neonatal cases. Whenever a neonate is born with severe congenital anomalies, the presence of that damaged infant in the NICU unquestionably affects other persons: parents, physicians, nurses, and taxpayers. All of these parties have interests in whether such a child lives or dies. Parents, having anticipated a normal, healthy baby, are often caught in a dilemma: withholding treatment will likely lead to the child's death, whereas providing treatment will merely prolong the life of a mentally and/or physically handicapped child who may damage the family unit or have to be placed in a custodial ward of a state institution. Physicians in pediatric specialities, often aware of past successes and failures with similar cases, are torn between the alternative possibilities of treatment: treatment may be successful to the point that the child will be invited back to the NICU in three or four years for a group "birthday party," or treatment may be ineffective and only prolong life that will seem intolerably handicapped to a guilt-perceiving physician. Nurses, obligated to care for high-risk neonates and provide emotional support for parents, have their own professional interests at stake: they may have the satisfaction of seeing another anomalous infant "graduate" from the NICU, or they may have the emotionally draining task of watching another high-risk neonate suffer for a long period of time and/or slowly die in the absence of effective treatment. And taxpayers, oblivious to the details of particular neonatal cases, are caught (often unknowingly) in another sort of dilemma: to place severely handicapped children in inadequately funded crippled children's hospitals or state mental hospitals is often to doom them to a wretched existence unfit for persons, whereas to increase the funding of such institutions is to require tax increases that few people would easily accept.

Three of the ethical options discussed in chapter 6 provide philosophical support for weighting treatment/nontreatment decisions in terms of these interests external to the birth-defective neonate. For ethicists advocating the second option (terminate the lives of selected nonpersons), the third option (withhold treatment according to parental discretion), or the fourth option (withhold treatment according to quality-of-life projections), it is not necessary to consider the best interests of the neonate. In each of these alternative positions, the decision regarding life-prolonging treatment may be made in such a manner that it advances the interests of other parties to the case in question: parents of the affected infant, other persons, or society. When decisions are made in this way, the interests of the primary party—the birth-defective infant—are subordinated to the interests of other individuals or groups whose lives are not at stake in the case. The result is that some birth-defective neonates die so that other persons may avoid burdens they prefer not to assume.

A more defensible approach to selective nontreatment is to give primacy to the interests of the neonate whose life hangs in the balance. By emphasizing the interests of the birth-defective infant, one need not ignore or minimize the very real problems that such a child presents to parents, the medical team, and society. In fact, it is very easy to empathize with the parents and other persons who have the burden of caring for a mentally deficient and/or physically handicapped child. It is also easy to deplore the meager resources our society provides for the care of handicapped children. However, in wishing that life were more fair, that burdens were more evenly distributed, and that problematic cases of handicap were less problematic, it is not justifiable to override a potential person's claim to life merely to save other persons trouble.

To use the best interests of the neonate as a criterion for selective nontreatment requires that one address three interrelated questions. What is the best method of determining the interests of individuals who are incompetent now but have the potential (depending on subsequent mental ability) for competency in the future? What is the standard or principle to be used in defining the best interests of these individuals? What individual, group, authoritative body, or procedure is most likely to be impartial in determining the best interests of neonates in borderline cases? We will turn to the first question now; the second question will be addressed in the next section, and the third question will be taken up in chapter 9.

Neonatal cases obviously involve a class of incompetent patients who do not presently possess the ability to make decisions about their lives. Decisions to intervene medically to prolong their lives therefore require proxy consent before being carried out. Especially in cases calling for surgical intervention (e.g., cases of esophageal or duodenal atresia), it is necessary to secure the consent of parents or legal guardians before surgery can legally be performed.

There are times, however, in which obtaining proxy consent in neonatal cases is difficult, especially when a neonate has a severe congenital anomaly, is unwanted by the parents, and is abandoned as the parents absent themselves from the NICU. Obtaining proxy consent for invasive medical treatment is also difficult when the parents themselves disagree about whether the child should live or die. More important for our purposes, there is a fundamental moral and legal problem inherent to proxy consent in neonatal cases. Given the incompetency of these patients and the conflicting interests frequently present in such cases, it is morally necessary—when consent is given, and especially when it is denied—to try to ensure that the proxy consent is valid. Whose interests are being served in the consent given or denied, those of the defective newborn or those of other persons in the case?

When cases concerning incompetent persons (including neonates) end up in court, there are two primary standards of review used to determine the validity of proxy consent. In some cases involving young children (e.g., *Gleitman* v. *Cosgrove*) or other incompetent persons (e.g., *Jones* v. *Saikewicz*), courts rely on the "substituted judgment" test to decide whether the incompetent person would have consented to the medical procedure if competent. This test requires courts to "don the mental mantle of the incompetent," as judges focus on the inferred desires and wishes of an incompetent individual.[7] The ethical justification for using this test is that in cases involving incompetent individuals, as in cases involving competent persons, the principle of autonomy requires that we ask what that individual would have chosen in a given situation of choice.

The alternative standard of review in legal cases involving incompetent persons is the "best interests" test. In several of the cases presented in earlier chapters (see cases 4.1, 4.4, 4.5, and 5.2), the judicial decision hangs on the question whether the medical procedure will on balance benefit or harm the incompetent person, not on whether that incompetent individual would have chosen the procedure had he or she been capable of doing so. Rather than in a hypothetical manner taking on the mental perspective of the incompetent individual, this test involves an appeal to what most reasonable persons would choose in a particular situation of moral choice. Although sometimes subject to utilitarian calculations, the test has its major ethical justification in the combined use of the principles of beneficence and nonmaleficence. Instead of trying to apply the principle of autonomy to nonautonomous individuals, this method of determining the best interests of incompetent individuals relies on the consensus of reasonable persons regarding the anticipated benefits or likely detriments of a medical procedure.[8]

Of course neither of these tests is restricted to courts of law. As parents, physicians, or other persons make decisions about the treatment or selective nontreatment of neonates, either of these legal standards of review may be applicable as a moral test of the validity of proxy consent. The question is, which of the two standards provides the best method of determining the interests of anomalous neonates who may, should they live, be competent in the future?

If the substituted judgment test is applied to cases in the NICU, it takes the form of asking, "What would infant A choose if infant A could choose?" Given that an infant has no history of choices, or even of desires and preferences, this attempt at determining the validity of proxy consent or denial of consent for infants is seriously limited if not impossible. At best, adult decision makers might use a version of the test specifically geared to the situation of newborn infants. This version of the test, representing a revision and reversal of John Rawls' concept of the veil of ignorance imposed on persons in the original position, suggests that a birth-defective neonate could be given, for only a brief moment, the light of omniscience in the infant's "original position" at the beginning of life. According to Judson Randolph, the surgeon-in-chief at Children's Hospital in Washington, D.C., the result conceivably could be a choice for death by the briefly competent child:

> If a severely handicapped child were suddenly given one moment of omniscience and total awareness of his or her outlook for the future, would that child necessarily opt for life? No one has yet been able to demonstrate that the answer would always be "yes."[9]

Such an approach is fatally flawed for the simple reason that no one— especially normal, healthy adults—can "place" themselves in a defective newborn's position and view life from that perspective. A much better approach, in my judgment, is to use the best interests test. This test, when applied to the moral decisions made in the NICU, involves asking, "Would an indefinite prolongation of life through medical treatment be in the best interests of infant B?" This second method, specifically geared to determining whether available treatment would on balance be beneficial or harmful to the anomalous neonate, requires utmost care in the diagnosis and prognosis of the infant's condition, informed judgments regarding treatment possibilities, and consultation with other persons in order to arrive at a consensus decision. Although open to vacuous concepts of what constitutes "best interests" and to a proxy's own idiosyncratic notions of what would be beneficial or harmful for the infant, the test is much less hypothetical and subjective than the substituted judgment test. The possibility of error is unavoidable, but the same is true for many of the judgments made in clinical medicine. In short, determining whether treatment is in a handicapped newborn's best interests is the best way adults have of making informed decisions for the sake of neonatal patients who cannot make the decisions themselves.

The principle of nonmaleficence

With the best interests of the neonate as the focal point for decision making, it is necessary to have a reasonable standard according to which the proxy can determine what those best interests are. Such a standard is provided through the combined use of the principles of beneficence and nonmaleficence in making detriment–benefit judgments regarding treatment. The principle of beneficence requires that moral agents further the important interests of other persons whenever their proximity and efficient alternatives allow them to do so with only minimal risk to themselves. The principle of nonmaleficence (*primum non nocere*) is the more stringent of the two principles and requires that moral agents avoid intentionally or negligently harming other persons.

Taken together, the two principles represent the polar ends of a continuum ranging from the production of benefit for others to the noninfliction of harm to others.[10] As expressed in the Hippocratic Oath, the principles are placed alongside each other in the same sentence: "I will use treatment to help the sick according to my ability and judgment, but never with a view to injury and wrong-doing."[11] Along with the principle of justice (to be discussed later), these concepts provide the ethical basis for distinguishing between neonatal patients who should receive medical treatment and those who should not.

Of course in the great majority of neonatal cases the principle of beneficence has primacy. For most neonates—including most of the 6% with birth defects—continued living is unquestionably in their best interests. There are few cases in which a proxy can reasonably conclude that continued living represents a fate worse than death for the neonate in question. It is for this reason—the priority given to life as compared with death—that physicians in the majority of neonatal cases provide treatment for neonates who need it to survive. It is also for this reason that parents, physicians, or any other proxy should err on the side of life in making decisions about selective nontreatment.

Yet, the unprecedented advances in neonatal medicine and the severity of some congenital anomalies force parents, physicians, and other persons to consider an increasing number of neonatal cases in the light of the principle of nomaleficence. Are there instances in which neonates with severe congenital anomalies would be better off dead than alive? Can the proxy in some neonatal cases reasonably conclude that death—as compared with ineffective treatment and injurious life—is the lesser of two harms and thus in the best interests of the neonate? From earlier chapters, it is clear that a number of pediatricians, attorneys, and ethicists think both of these questions are to be answered in the affirmative. The majority of physicians we discussed point to cases where they believe medical treatment is actually a form of cruelty by which an anomalous neonate is condemned to a life of suffering, severe mental retardation, crippling physical disabilities, repetitious surgery, and minimal survival in an institutional setting. A comment by Gordon Avery, chief of neonatology at Children's Hospital in Washington, D.C., is illustrative of this view:

> We sometimes unnecessarily prolong the misery of both baby and family when a hopeless situation could be terminated by withdrawing extraordinary therapy. We operate, ill-advisedly at times, on babies whose prognoses for meaningful life is nil. In my opinion, we would serve our patients better if we stopped to consider the consequences more carefully before using our new techniques.[12]

This kind of reasoning represents a significant departure from traditional thinking about nonmaleficence in medical settings. From its original appearance in the Hippocratic literature to its prevalent usage in contemporary medical literature, *primum non nocere* has been understood to involve an informal ranking or cataloging of harmful actions that should not be a part of the physician–patient relationship. Chief among those harmful actions has been any act done with the intention of causing a patient's death, as illustrated by the portion of the Hippocratic Oath in which a physician pledges neither to "give a deadly drug to anybody if asked for it" nor to "make a suggestion to this effect."[13]

Indicative of this traditional understanding of death as the ultimate harm to befall a patient are two rules of medical practice that have been derived from the principle of nonmaleficence: "do not kill" and "do not assist another person's death." Given the weight of these rules in medical practice, a physician has limited options in trying to show that a particular patient's death was justified on moral grounds: (1) claim that the individual now dead was not yet a person (e.g., a fetus) or was no longer a person (e.g., an adult in permanent coma); (2) contend that the patient was not innocent but rather an "unjust aggressor" whose continuing life was not protected by the principle of nonmaleficence (e.g., a fetus in an ectopic pregnancy); (3) establish that the patient's death was through unpreventable natural causes; (4) argue that the patient's death was unintended but foreseen as a possible secondary effect of the pain medication administered, and that such a "double effect" death would not be prohibited by the duty of nonmaleficence; (5) claim that the patient was merely allowed to die, not killed, when medical treatments were withheld or withdrawn because they were judged to be medically useless for this patient; (6) establish that the patient was killed only after he or she made a voluntary, informed decision that death was preferable to a continuing existence of intractable pain, and that the death-causing action was motivated by compassion; or (7) contend that death was in the best interests of the incompetent patient in that it represented a lesser harm than sustaining a life of prolonged and unpreventable suffering.[14]

With these restrictions inherent to the principle of nonmaleficence in medical settings, it is important to be as precise as possible regarding the applicability of *primum non nocere* to neonatal medicine. More specifically, if the principle of nonmaleficence is to be used as an ethical criterion for selective nontreatment, two problems must be confronted. First, given the vagueness of the term "harm" and its loose usage in much of the literature on selective nontreatment, it is necessary to explicate its meaning and application to neonatal medicine. Second, given the traditional inter-

pretation of death as the ultimate form of harm in medicine, it is necessary
to suggest a different way of evaluating death in a ranking of harms that
might befall a newborn infant.

There are, of course, multiple definitions of harm, ranging from very
broad definitions that include injuries to one's important interests to more
narrow definitions that focus on injuries to one's physical well-being.
Instead of opting for any one of these definitions, it is more helpful to
interpret the concept of harm in terms of its three dimensions. The first
dimension is the broadest one and involves the interference with or the
invasion of one's interests. Commonly used as an interpretation of harm
in legal literature, this dimension of harm pertains to "the violation of one
of a person's interests, an injury to something in which he has a genuine
stake."[15] To harm another person—or oneself—in this manner can involve
any number of interests violated: health, property, reputation, domestic
relations, privacy, or life itself. Within this broad range of interests, some
interests are clearly more important than others. And for most persons, a
ranking of these interests in terms of importance normally ends up with
life at the top, with health following as a close second.

The second dimension of harm pertains to the impairment of one's
mental and psychological welfare. Having its roots in the Old English
term "hearm," this dimension of harm includes any psychologically defined
experience that causes a person mental anguish, emotional disruption, or
psychological trauma.[16] To harm another person—or oneself—in this
sense is to do something that causes a normal mental and psychological
condition to deteriorate. Actions that are harmful under this dimension
are deception, harassment, intimidation, "brainwashing," verbal abuse,
and any physical affront or invasion of one's "person" resulting in severe
anxiety, emotional distress, or depression. The importance of this dimension of harm is evident to anyone familiar with the psychological factors
behind many suicides: at least some persons feel sufficiently harmed by
life that they regard death preferable to continued living.

The third, and most narrowly focused, dimension of harm includes
only physical injury and the physiological effects of such injury. To harm
another person—or oneself—in this way requires actual physical damage
and the pain and suffering that accompany it. In this sense, harm-causing
actions include bruising the skin, rupturing the flesh, breaking a bone,
subjecting the body to invasive techniques it cannot tolerate (e.g., through
the use of radiation, electricity, or chemicals), or invading the body with
a foreign object (e.g., a needle, a knife, a bullet) that impairs or paralyzes

the normal functioning of one or more organs. The ultimate injury, when harm is interpreted in this manner, is any action that completely disables the heart and/or brain so that death ensues.

It should be clear that harm, understood in this three-dimensional manner, regularly occurs in the clinical practice of medicine, with at least the third dimension applying to the medical treatment of infants as well as older patients. All competent patients have some of their interests (e.g., privacy) interfered with through the normal routines of clinical medicine. With the obvious exceptions of iatrogenic conditions and death, however, there is usually the compensatory benefit of improved health that justifies the short-term interference and harm done to the patient.

Many patients are harmed, not through the intentional actions of any other person, but simply through the anxiety-raising and depression-causing circumstances of illness. Other patients are harmed in a more serious and longer lasting manner by being intentionally deceived as to the cause and severity of their illness by physicians they trusted to give them accurate information and honest counsel. Infants, because of their lack of psychological development, cannot be harmed in this second way as long as they remain infants; actions taken while they are infants, such as life-prolonging treatment, may nevertheless end up causing them psychological harm, especially if they later conclude that their "wrongful lives" offer them nothing more than the endurance of endless suffering.

The third dimension of harm is applicable to virtually all patients in a clinical setting. The great majority of infants, adolescents, and adults experience some form of physical injury as a part of their medical treatment. The injury may be so mild (e.g., a finger prick to secure a blood sample) that the patient fails to notice or remember it; or the injury may involve such major damage that it leaves a permanent wound or scar. Examples of severe physical harm occasionally inflicted on neonatal patients are numerous: neonates with hyaline membrane disease can, if too much oxygen is administered, develop retrolental fibroplasia or bronchopulmonary dysplasia; neonates with severe intraventricular hemorrhage can, as a consequence of surgery, end up with spastic diplegia and blindness; and neonates with severe cardiac problems can, as a consequence of surgery, suffer permanent central nervous system damage.

Without question, patients are harmed through these acts of physical intrusion and through any pain and suffering that accompany the intrusive acts. Whether such transient or permanent harm is justifiable on moral grounds depends, in large part, on the presence of compensatory benefit to the patient. One of the complicating features of neonatal medicine, of course, is the difficulty of determining whether there will be sufficient compensatory benefits to justify submitting some seriously defective infants to the physical injury often involved in treatment.

We now turn to the second problem mentioned earlier. Can death represent something other than the ultimate form of harm? Can life consist of such harmful conditions that continued living would be more harmful than death to an infant-turned-child? Is the principle of nonmaleficence applicable to severe cases of congenital anomaly in a manner that occasionally allows death as a justifiable option in proxy decision making?

I think so. The principle of nonmaleficence is an inherent feature of the practice of medicine. As Albert Jonsen has demonstrated, the requirement of nonmaleficence—"above all, do no harm"—influences the practice of medicine in four ways: (1) it makes medicine a moral enterprise and obligates physicians to use their medical skills not in abusive or mischievous ways but toward the end of serving the well-being of their patients; (2) physicians are required to use due care in treating patients, thereby avoiding the harmful consequences brought about by carelessness; (3) most medical procedures involve a risk–benefit assessment in which physicians and patients attempt to determine whether the anticipated benefits of a procedure are worth the risk of possible harm; and (4) many medical procedures also involve a detriment–benefit equation in assessing the "double effect" of the procedure, because the procedure will necessarily bring about a detriment at the same time that it produces the intended benefit.[17]

Each of these uses of *primum non nocere* sometimes applies to decisions regarding the medical treatment of neonates. For instance, decisions about treatment for normal infants or infants with relatively minor defects largely have to do with a risk–benefit calculation: will the benefits of a particular treatment be worth the risk of injuring the child? With infants with severe birth defects, however, the detriment–benefit aspect of nonmaleficence is much more important for decision making. Decisions regarding the treatment of these infants are made in the context of a very different question: given the ongoing detriment of the congenital defect(s) even after treatment, does the proposed treatment offer the promise of sufficient benefit to compensate for the detriment? To phrase it in another way, is the proposed treatment in the best interests of the already harmed child?

Even to raise these questions may seem odd or possibly illogical to some persons. For them, life-prolonging treatment for nondying infants is always to the benefit of the infants. According to this ethical perspective (treat all nondying infants), death is the irreplaceable ultimate harm to happen to anyone: no other harmful condition, no matter how damaging or tragic, can outweigh death as a harm. I disagree. It is logical—and morally imperative—to raise the question whether life-prolonging medical treatment is in the best interests of an infant with severe congenital anomalies for the simple reason that there are some infants who have such serious congenital conditions that they cannot receive the benefits normally accompanying treatment. They can be provided with an array of neonatal medicines and procedures, but they cannot be cured; in some instances they cannot be relieved of ongoing pain; in other instances they cannot be rescued from an irreversibly deteriorating medical condition; and in other instances they cannot have their lives prolonged apart from severe neurophysiological disabilities. For at least some of these severely affected, but nondying infants, the detriment–benefit aspect of the principle of nonmaleficence is tipped toward detriment. To offer such infants ineffective treatment is, on balance, to harm them rather than help them.

The question remains whether the combined harms of the congenital condition(s) and ineffective treatment can reasonably be said to represent a fate worse than death. An affirmative answer to the question requires two interrelated points. First, competent persons inevitably have some sort of informal ranking or cataloging of harmful events that might come into their lives. Although few persons have gone to the trouble of giving such events (some of which would only be hypothetical possibilities) a formal ranking in terms of a priority list, all of us nevertheless have some sense of more-or-less harmful things that could—or will—happen to us. A fairly typical listing of harmful events or experiences would include items such as the following: intractable pain, death to spouse or children, loss of own life, severe mental deficiency, loss of two or more limbs, permanent paralysis of two or more limbs, involuntary institutionalization or imprisonment, divorce initiated by spouse, loss of employment in chosen field, irremediable damage to personal reputation, permanent dependence on repetitious medical treatment, deception by a friend or other trusted person, and loss of valuable personal property.

The ordering or ranking of these items varies, of course, depending on personal preferences and value systems. An event or experience that might be perceived as extremely harmful to one person might be regarded in a much less serious manner by another person. However, there are two features of these varying lists that would, I think, be common: (1) one's own death would be listed quite near the top in terms of severe harm, but (2) another experience—or combination of experiences—would be judged *more harmful* than death. It is for precisely this reason that some competent persons fill out "living will" documents, that other competent but terminally ill persons decline certain life-prolonging treatments, and that other competent persons occasionally decide to commit suicide. My point is a simple one: most if not all competent persons can conceive of circumstances that would represent, for them, a fate worse than death.

Second, a similar kind of reasoning can and must be a part of the proxy's attempt to determine the best interests of a neonate with severe congenital anomalies. Although one should not (as Paul Ramsey has pointed out) regard infants and children merely as "little adults" and should (as Norman Fost has observed) be mindful of the problem of "adult elitism" in ascribing adult perceptions of harm to infants, it is nevertheless necessary to have some informal ranking of harms for infants if there is to be any logical basis to the statement that some seriously handicapped neonates would be "better off" dead than alive and thus should not be given medical treatment. The importance of such a ranking is that it provides a general framework for trying to determine when, in a neonatal medical setting, one or more of the lesser harms can outweigh death as a harm and thus justify terminating the lives of some neonates with severe defects.

The medical literature on congenital anomalies clearly indicates that there are several harmful conditions awaiting some seriously defective neonates if their lives are extended through medical treatment. It may be helpful, therefore, to suggest an informal ranking of these harms in terms of their severity. The harmful events or experiences are listed in certain general categories, even though many of these harmful conditions are inseparable from one another when they cluster together as multiple aspects of a given disease or syndrome. In descending order of severity, the list includes death, severe mental deficiency, permanent institutionalization in a state mental hospital, severe physical handicaps, abandonment by parents, an indefinite consignment to a state facility for handicapped children, physical and psychological abuse by parents, moderate mental deficiency, moderate physical handicaps, and repeated surgical procedures.

Can any of the harms ranked below death sometimes be regarded as more harmful for an anomalous neonate than death? In a traditional ranking of harms in medicine, the answer would be negative. In the context of modern neonatal medicine, however, increasingly sophisticated procedures and technology present parents, physicians, and any other proxy with infant patients who can have their lives prolonged with severe congenital anomalies that traditionally would have been incompatible with life. Infants with multiple severe anomalies affecting the central nervous system, for example, would not usually have lived before the advent of neonatal medicine, and their conditions would not have been listed in a traditional ranking of harms.

The very nature of neonatal medicine therefore compels physicians, parents, and other reflective persons to reassess the traditional ordering of harms in medical practice. When this reassessment is done, it becomes clear that in extreme, relatively rare circumstances an extension of a seriously defective infant's life can represent a greater harm than does nontreatment resulting in death. In such cases, to be specified later, to withhold treatment in order to bring about the infant's death is to do something *less harmful* to the infant than would treatment resulting in an extension of the infant's life for an indeterminate period of time. Infants in these extreme circumstances can rightfully be said to be better off dead precisely because death represents a lesser harm for them than enduring an injurious, torturous existence.

Perhaps an analogy will be helpful at this point. Rather than picturing a neonate suffering from one or more severe congenital anomalies, imagine instead that a group of sadistic terrorists has kidnapped an infant and plans to torture the child for as many months or years as possible before finally killing the child. Given the group's low profile and secretive operations, there is virtually no possibililty that the child will be rescued by anyone. In addition, imagine that you are a physician also held by the group. You have the job of administering medical treatment to the child. Should the torturers ever go to excess and inflict a physical injury on the child that will be fatal unless treated, you will be responsible for administering the treatment. Could you or any rational person reasonably claim that it is in the child's best interests to receive the life-prolonging treatment and thus be saved from imminent death to endure more torture for an indeterminate period of time? Is is not true that in such a situation, the infant's death would be less harmful to the infant than the alternative would be?

One final point about nonmaleficence. If the proxy in a particular case determines that treatment is not in the best interests of the neonate because continued life represents a greater harm than death, the principle of nonmaleficence imposes *a duty not to treat* the child. In such a case, as pointed out by Engelhardt, treatment not only may be withheld, but should be withheld on moral grounds. The recognition of this duty is not new, but actually antedates neonatal medicine by more than 2000 years. The Hippocratic Corpus contains a treatise entitled "The Art" that defines medicine as having three roles, the last of which is relevant to the issue of selective nontreatment:

> I will define what I conceive medicine to be. In general terms, it is to do away with the sufferings of the sick, to lessen the violence of their diseases, and *to refuse to treat those who are overmastered by their diseases*, realizing that in such cases medicine is powerless. . . .[18]

Select by diagnostic categories

If decisions regarding life-prolonging treatment should be made in terms of the best interests of neonatal potential persons, and if there are relatively rare instances in which continued life is not in an anomalous neonate's best interests, it is still necessary to take these ethical criteria out of the conceptual realm and put them into practice in NICUs. For this reason, we now turn to three additional ethical criteria that are operational in nature.

The first of these operational, or practical, ethical criteria calls for selective nontreatment according to standard diagnostic categories. This *primary method of selection* is grounded in the principles of nonmaleficence and justice. Given the detriment–benefit aspect of the principle of nonmaleficence, it is important to point out that there are certain kinds of congenital anomalies that are so severe that they automatically make efforts at treatment detrimental rather than beneficial for the infant. Regardless of the particular infant in question, the parents' desire that the infant live, or the physician's medical skill, there are some birth defects that are simply inaccessible to effective medical treatment by any physician in any hospital.

More specific details regarding these diagnostic categories will be given later. At present it is sufficient to indicate in general terms that neonates with some specific inheritable diseases, certain neurological defects, chromosomal disorders, or extremely low birthweight present physicians with medical conditions that they are powerless to cure or correct. At best, an aggressive use of medical procedures and technology will prolong some of these seriously defective lives for a marginal length of time; at worst, these efforts to prolong even the most damaged neonatal lives will subject some of the infants to iatrogenic conditions that merely exacerbate their underlying medical problems. Rather than helping them, the medical procedures will harm them by inflicting additional physical injury on them. Moreover, because of the severity of these extreme neonatal conditions, physicians who opt for aggressive treatment—when the consensus of pediatric medical opinion indicates there is no effective treatment—can correctly be described as merely using these seriously birth-defective neonates as experimental subjects for nontherapeutic medical research.

The principle of justice also applies to this method of selection. This principle, in terms of its formal structure, requires that similar cases be given similar treatment (with "treatment" here referring to moral activity in nonmedical as well as medical settings). Exactly what that similar (nonmedical) treatment is, depends on which conception of social justice one adopts. Any conception of social justice involves the distribution of burdens and benefits in some manner, but theories of justice differ as to whether these burdens and benefits are to be distributed equally, on the basis of merit, on the basis of need, on the basis of societal contribution, or according to some other formula.

Of these theories, the only ones that apply to birth-defective newborns in NICUs are those calling for the equal distribution of burdens and benefits to all persons (or potential persons) in need. The prima facie need of anomalous neonates, of course, is for medical treatment that will effectively prolong their lives and enhance their continued living. All neonates with serious congenital anomalies have an equal need for that medical treatment, in that each of them will sooner or later die in the absence of such treatment. Only in rare instances, to be discussed later, is this prima facie need for treatment overridden by a recognition that the treatment will actually be futile or harmful to the infant in question.

Given this equal need, birth-defective neonates should be given equal access to medical treatment (but, of course, not identical treatment). They should not be compared with one another or with normal newborns, for there is no fair basis for comparison other than disease categories and need for treatment. Neonates do not differ in merit or societal contribution, and the differences among their parents (in terms of merit, societal contribution, wealth, etc.) are irrelevant to their medical conditions and need for treatment. Attempts to project future qualitative differences among them are also to be rejected, because such quality-of-life judgments typically reflect the biases of the persons making them and usually include the projected quality of lives other than the one of the neonate in need of medical attention.

Therefore, when neonates are compared for the purpose of determining which ones shall receive medical treatment, the principle of justice requires that such comparisons be done in terms of disease categories. Newborns with serious birth defects are similar in their need for medical treatment; they are dissimilar in the particular birth defects they have, and in the ability of physicians to provide effective medical treatment for those differing birth defects. Thus to treat similar cases in similar ways *does not mean* comparing trisomic 18 infants with normal infants, anencephalic infants, or infants with Down's syndrome. To treat similar cases in similar ways *does mean* handling all neonates with the same congenital anomaly similarly: if the diagnostic condition can be effectively treated, all infants having that particular defect should generally be given medical treatment; if the condition cannot be effectively treated, then all infants having the condition should generally have aggressive treatment withheld, because such efforts at treatment will be in the best interests of none of them. As Paul Ramsey observes, "Selection for treatment (or allocation of medical care) must be by categories and not by drawing distinctions between individual patients if these fundamental norms [of justice] are not to be violated."[19] As Gene Outka correctly states:

> Illness is the proper ground for the *receipt* of medical care. However, the *distribution* of medical care in less-than-optimal circumstances requires us to face the collisions. I would argue that in such circumstances the formula of similar treatment for similar cases may be construed so as to guide actual choices in the way most compatible with the goal of equal access. The formula's allowance of no positive [or preferential] treatment whatever may justify exclusion of entire classes of cases from a priority list. Yet it forbids doing so for irrelevant or arbitrary reasons. So (1) if we accept the case for equal access, but (2) if we simply cannot, physically cannot, treat all who are in need, it seems more just to discriminate by virtue of categories of illness than, for example, between the rich ill and poor ill.[20]

Selecting for nontreatment in this manner has three advantages over the ad hoc, haphazard ways in which nontreatment decisions are currently made in NICUs. First, selection by diagnostic categories has the objectivity provided by pediatric medical consensus, rather than the subjectivity of quality-of-life projections made under the stressful conditions of an NICU.

Although neonatologists and other physicians with pediatric specialities are far from unanimity on the severity of all the disease categories (as was obvious in chap. 3), they nevertheless are in general agreement on several of the more severe ones. Second, selection by disease categories provides the basis for greater consistency in nontreatment decisions from one pediatrician to another, from one hospital to another, from one legal jurisdiction to another, and from one country to another. At present such consistency is sadly lacking, as many birth-defective neonates live or die depending not on the severity of their medical condition, but on where they happen to be located at birth and shortly afterwards. Third, selection by categories of congenital defect affirms the basic equality of neonates. When decisions are made to withhold treatment in this manner, it is because a particular neonate has a medical condition for which there is no beneficial treatment—not because the infant is judged to be of little value or to have a life not worth living.

Select by withholding optional means of treatment

Selection by diagnostic categories is not the only operational criterion in selective nontreatment. As the primary method of selection, it is the fairest and most consistent way we have of distinguishing between birth-defective neonates who should and who should not be given life-prolonging treatment. By itself, however, this method of selection does not provide the flexibility necessary to make treatment/nontreatment decisions regarding (a) the range of cases that occur *within* some diagnostic categories or (b) complex cases involving multiple anomalies that fall *outside* the parameters of established diagnostic categories. A secondary, more flexible method of selection is therefore required to address the relative differences among some of these neonatal cases.

The distinction between "ordinary" and "extraordinary" means of life-prolonging treatment provides the necessary *secondary method of selection*, once its traditionally vague terminology is replaced and the distinction is applied to the incompetent patients whose lives are at stake in NICUs. This traditional distinction, as we have observed, is often used in the medical and legal literature on selective nontreatment. The inherent ambiguity and relativity of the distinction, however, means that it is understood in different ways and its applicability to neonatal cases is in some dispute among physicians and attorneys. The same kinds of disagreements occur when ethicists discuss the distinction.[21] Some ethicists (including several of those surveyed in chap. 6) do not find the distinction helpful; others (such as Paul Ramsey) apply the distinction to cases involving competent patients but think it has little applicability to neo-natal cases; and others think that some version of the distinction is important in writing on the ethics of selective nontreatment.[22]

The ordinary/extraordinary distinction was originally developed by Roman Catholic moral theologians to determine, prior to the discovery of antisepsis and anesthesia, whether the refusal of surgery by a competent patient was tantamount to suicide. Subsequently the distinction was used to assess the morality of treatment refusal by competent patients in a variety of medical settings. With the development of modern drugs, surgical procedures, and technological ways of prolonging life, the dis-tinction has been updated by Pope Pius XII, Pope John Paul II, and numerous ethicists.[23] The widely quoted definition of what the distinction means in the modern period is that of Gerald Kelly:

> *Ordinary* means of preserving life are all medicines, treatments, and opera-tions, which offer a reasonable hope of benefit for the patient and which can be obtained and used without excessive expense, pain, or other incon-venience. . . . *Extraordinary* means of preserving life . . . mean all medi-cines, treatments, and operations, which cannot be obtained without excessive expense, pain or other inconvenience, or which, if used, would not offer a reasonable hope of benefit.[24]

This distinction has become increasingly prominent in medical practice and in judicial decisions in recent years. For instance, the A.M.A. House of Delegates used the distinction in its 1973 statement on euthanasia. The A.M.A. indicated that a dying patient—or the patient's immediate family —can decide about the "cessation of extraordinary means to prolong the life of the body when there is irrefutable evidence that biological death is imminent."[25] The distinction was also used in the 1980 statement on euthanasia by the British Medical Association.[26] As to judicial decisions, the most important one involving an appeal to this distinction was the New Jersey Supreme Court's decision regarding Karen Ann Quinlan. In overturning a lower court decision, the justices observed that in this case involving an incompetent patient,

> one would have to think that the use of the same respirator or like support could be considered "ordinary" in the context of the possibly curable patient but "extraordinary" in the context of the forced sustaining by cardio-respiratory processes of an irreversibly doomed patient.[27]

We now turn to the question regarding how this distinction can be used as a secondary method of selection in neonatal cases. First, it is necessary to point out that in its traditional formulation, the ordinary/extraordinary distinction served as one of the ways of expressing the relationship between the principles of beneficence and nonmaleficence. Whether a specific case concerned a competent patient's decision about surgery or a proxy's decision regarding life-prolonging treatment for an incompetent patient, the distinction helped to formulate the balancing between probable benefit and detriment that is central to many moral decisions concerning proposed medical treatment. Kelly's definition makes this traditional understanding of the distinction especially clear. For according to his definition, a life-prolonging treatment can be judged ordinary (and thus morally obligatory) only if it does two things at once: (1) provides a reasonable prospect of benefit and (2) does not, on balance, inflict harm on the patient.

Second, it is clear that the traditional language of the distinction needs to be replaced if the distinction is to have relevance in neonatal cases. Most ethicists agree that "ordinary" and "extraordinary" are not only hopelessly vague, but also tend to be misunderstood by many physicians who think the terms connote "usual" or "customary" treatment as opposed to "unusual" or "heroic" or "bizarre" treatment. Even the recent papal proclamation on euthanasia replaces the traditional language with "proportionate" and "disproportionate" means of treatment.

Among the proposals for replacement terms, Paul Ramsey's objective language of "medically indicated/not medically indicated" and Robert Veatch's more subjective language of "reasonable/unreasonable" have received considerable attention.[28] However, it seems much simpler and clearer to replace the traditional language with the moral language of "obligatory" and "optional"—thereby bringing the traditional meaning of the distinction into the language itself. For whatever language is used, the traditional purpose of the distinction remains basically the same in the age of ICUs and NICUs as before: to emphasize that some life-prolonging treatments are morally expendable for some patients, no matter how customary the treatments are in medical practice, because the treatments are judged to be nonbeneficial and possibly harmful on balance to the patient whose life is at stake.

Third, the obligatory/optional distinction is a relative one whose applicability in particular neonatal cases (as well as in other cases) depends on the specific factors in the cases. Perhaps most clearly, the distinction between obligatory and optional treatment aimed at prolonging life is *relative to the status of the medical technology* available at a particular time and place. The newer and more experimental a medical procedure is, the more likely it is to be judged optional on moral grounds. Thus treatment options that not long ago would usually have been judged as optional in neonatal cases—exchange transfusions, shunting for hydrocephalus, surgical correction of tracheoesophageal atresia, cardiopulmonary resuscitation, ventilatory assistance for premature infants—are now increasingly judged to be obligatory by physicians and parents. Additionally, the obligatory/optional distinction is *relative to the severity of a neonate's medical condition.* The more severe a neonatal patient's condition is, the more optional certain kinds of treatment become. Treatments become optional in this manner not because neonates with severe conditions have less "quality" than other neonates, but because there are some conditions that may be so severe that efforts at treatment are ineffective and harmful. It is for this reason that even pediatric neurosurgeons who generally favor aggressive treatment sometimes advise against treatment in unusually severe cases of intraventricular hemorrhage (stage 4 cases) and spina bifida (cases with the cystic cavity at T-12 or above, plus other complicating conditions).

Finally, it is possible to put forth guidelines that may help to indicate when life-prolonging treatment can be judged to be optional rather than obligatory. With the best interests of the birth-defective neonate foremost in one's considerations, treatment may be judged optional whenever (1) it is nonbeneficial on balance to the neonate, (2) it is harmful on balance to the neonate, or (3) it is harmful on balance to the family as a functioning unit.[29] The first two guidelines are, I think, clear enough and consistent with the criteria previously discussed. If a neonate's anomalous condition is such that treatment cannot reasonably be expected to restore the child to consciousness or extend the child's life beyond six months to a year, the treatment should be withheld because it will be futile. Treatment in such cases represents nontherapeutic experimentation on neonates, which cannot correctly be said to be in their best interests. Likewise, if a neonate's medical condition is such that medical treatment is likely to exacerbate rather than alleviate the birth defect(s), the treatment should be withheld because it may be more harmful to the neonate than nontreatment resulting in death. Treatment in such cases inflicts excessive pain and/or repetitious surgery and/or prolonged dependence on ventilatory assistance on the child without the realistic prospect of compensatory benefit that would justify this physical harm.

The third guideline is an exception to the criterion regarding the neonate's best interests, at least in cases involving a conflict of interest between the neonate and other family members. It is, however, tragically necessary in rare cases. To regard treatment as optional on the grounds that it represents excessive harm to a family unit is not to say that treatment becomes optional any time a family does not want an anomalous newborn, or wishes to avoid a drastic change in lifestyle, or prefers to spend its financial resources for things other than the medical care required by a handicapped child. Rather, to regard treatment as optional in this manner is to acknowledge that some cases of congenital anomaly are so complicated medically and require such unusual expense and emotional involvement on the part of parents that the continued existence of the family unit is itself placed in serious jeopardy.

In such cases parents should, before withholding treatment, explore the possibility of giving up custody to another family or to a state agency. If parents choose to protect their family unit but refuse to give up custody of the child, physicians, nurses, hospital administrators, or social workers should seek legal action to take custody away from the parents in order to provide necessary medical care for the child. If immediate care and long-term custody cannot be separated in this manner in a given case, and if the provision of care in the form of ongoing medical treatment is likely to decimate the family unit, then such treatment may regrettably but justifiably be regarded as optional and be withheld.

The morality of intentional killing

When the principle of nonmaleficence is applied to the more extreme diagnostic categories for infants, it is clear that a few congenital anomalies are so severe that treatment may generally be withheld from infants diagnosed as having these conditions. When the principle of nonmaleficence is applied to particular cases, it is clear from the facts of a few of these cases that continuing treatment will be detrimental on balance to the infants and should thus be withheld or withdrawn because of its optional nature. In most instances where either of these methods of selection is used, the selective nonuse of treatment results in the neonate's death.

However, as John Freeman and R. B. Zachary point out (see chap. 3), selective nontreatment does not always result in the death of the neonate.

Parents and physicians are consequently faced with the problem of what to do with untreated infants who do not die quickly or painlessly. The resolution of this problem represents the last of the operational criteria in an ethics of selective nontreatment. Simply put, the criterion states that under certain conditions it is justifiable to kill birth-defective infants who have previously been denied treatment on sound moral grounds.

Several steps are required to explicate the limited, but necessary ethical role that intentional killing has as an extension of selective nontreatment. At the outset it is important to note that "nontreatment" is a term whose meaning and connection with life termination is understood in different ways by different physicians. Suppose, for instance, that a physician recommends nontreatment in a case involving an infant with spina bifida cystica. If that physician is John Lorber, he means by "nontreatment" ordinary feeding and nothing else (no surgery, no oxygen, no intravenous fluids, and no antibiotics). If, in contrast, the physician in the case is R. B. Zachary, he means by "nontreatment" only the withholding of surgery, but the provision of virtually all other forms of treatment (including antibiotics for infection). To take another example, suppose that a physician recommends nontreatment in a case involving an infant with an intestinal obstruction plus another major anomaly such as Down's syndrome. Depending on the physician in the case, medical management described as "nontreatment" could mean (a) withhold surgery and feeding (the infant will die from starvation and dehydration within one to three weeks); (b) withhold surgery and feeding, but provide intravenous fluids (the infant's death from starvation will only be postponed); (c) withhold surgery and feeding, but provide intravenous fats and proteins (hyperalimentation will provide the infant with sufficient nutrition to live for an indefinite period of time); (d) withhold surgery but provide feeding (the infant will likely aspirate and die); or (e) administer intravenous potassium to terminate the child's life quickly and avoid the period of starvation.[30] Given these varied meanings of "nontreatment," it is hardly surprising to note that selective nontreatment does not always lead to an infant's death.

In addition, much of the literature compounds the terminological and conceptual difficulties involved in discussing selective nontreatment by using expansive interpretations of the ethical category known as "allowing to die." Some infants who are denied treatment die in a relatively short period of time; others remain alive for relatively long periods (e.g., perhaps 10% of spina bifida infants survive without surgery for more than a year); and others actually have their deaths caused by certain practices of their physicians. The category "allowing to die" simply cannot cover all of these cases.

Yet when an anomalous newborn is denied treatment, physicians and other persons often suggest that *whatever is done* to the infant prior to death counts as "allowing" the child to die. For instance, two quite different scenarios resulting in the death of a child are frequently described as "allowing to die." Scenario one involves (a) limited, sustaining treatment of an infant (with food and fluids, and possibly oxygen and antibiotics); (b) an indefinite, prolonged period of deterioration and possible suffering by the infant; and (c) an indefinite, prolonged period of psychological harm experienced by physicians, nurses, and parents as these persons wait for—and wish for—the infant to die. Scenario two, in contrast, involves (a) withholding virtually all treatment (no oxygen or antibiotics, and reduced nutritional support); (b) overdoses of sedatives, feeding only on demand, and other intentional efforts to hasten the infant's death; and (c) an abbreviated period of waiting for the infant to die. Can both of these scenarios correctly be described as allowing-to-die cases? I think not.

Then why do some writers—and clinicians—use the same ethical category to describe both of these courses of action? At least three factors contribute to this practice. First, there is the long cross-cultural history of infanticide in which members of various societies have judged that there are more and less acceptable ways of terminating infants' lives. Whereas intentionally killing infants (by beating, drowning, strangulation, etc.) has for centuries been regarded as morally reprehensible and legally punishable, terminating the lives of infants by leaving them exposed to the elements (and animals) has often been morally and legally acceptable because of the possibility that such infants would be rescued from death by someone else (see chap. 1). Second, there is a widely held belief that killing and allowing to die are morally distinguishable. Persons accepting the killing/letting die distinction, including some of the physicians discussed in chapter 3, believe that intentionally killing patients (whether neonates or not) is rarely if ever justifiable, whereas allowing patients to die is more easily justifiable in certain circumstances. Third, there is a probable difference in legal liability for the physician in charge of an infant's medical care, depending on whether that neonatal patient is killed through an act of neonatal euthanasia or is merely allowed to die. The potential criminal charge against any physician who intentionally kills an infant is first-degree murder. However, in the unlikely event that legal

charges are brought against a physician who allows an infant to die by
withholding treatment, those charges (as discussed in chap. 4) are likely to
be less serious ones than murder.

The conceptual confusion that seems to surround the category "allowing to die"—coupled with a general reluctance to address the ethical issue
of intentionally killing birth-defective infants—has a number of unfortunate consequences in NICUs. One of these consequences is that some
anomalous neonates, having been denied corrective and life-prolonging
treatment, are put through needless suffering as the medical staff allows
them to die over an agonizingly long period of time (see case 2.2). Of
course the nursing staff also suffers as they watch untreated infants slowly
dehydrate and starve to death. Another consequence is that some physicians in pediatric specialities, having decided that a birth-defective infant
would be better off dead, engage in surreptitious actions to hasten the
"allowed" death (see case 4.4). Still another consequence is at the level of
moral discourse among the adults involved in these relatively rare cases.
Having decided that certain kinds of treatment should be withheld from
an infant, physicians and parents simply do not discuss the moral option
of intentionally killing the child. "Euthanasia," it seems, is an inappropriate term to use in such discussions. Instead, even if they are in agreement that death is in the untreated child's best interests, the threat of the
law (among other factors) leads them to use the expansive label "allowing
to die" to cover all efforts at hastening the child's death.

Given these terminological and conceptual difficulties, it is important
to distinguish among three ethical categories that can be used to describe
actions in NICUs that justifiably often result in neonatal deaths: desisting
unsuccessful rescue, allowing to die, and intentional killing. *Desisting
unsuccessful rescue* is a necessary ethical category for analyzing some
death-resulting actions in neonatal medicine, because some neonatal
deaths simply do not fit either of the two conventional categories. Developed by Robert Baker, this category applies to neonatal cases in which
physicians and nurses would prolong life if they could. Determining that
they cannot prolong life in certain cases, no matter how hard they try,
they cease their futile efforts. Neonates who are born dying (e.g., anencephalic newborns) and numerous cases involving seemingly futile resuscitative efforts fit this pattern of neonatal medicine. Illustrative of this
category is the comment made by two physicians when they were asked
why they had not resuscitated (for the second time) a two-week-old infant
with prune-belly syndrome, an imperforate anus, one absent kidney,

hydronephrosis of the remaining kidney, and congestive heart failure. They asked, "What would be the sense?"[31]

Allowing to die is, of course, the ethical category that is most closely related to selective nontreatment. In spite of its frequent misinterpretation, this category remains the appropriate one to use in describing any of three decisions and actions that will probably result in a patient's death: the refusal of life-sustaining treatment by a competent patient, the withholding of treatment judged to be optional for a competent or incompetent patient, or the withholding of treatment judged not to be in an incompetent patient's best interests. In the context of neonatal medicine, this category is not to be confused with desisting unsuccessful rescue. The first category applies to cases in which further medical treatment is stopped because it is a futile waste of time, money, and effort, whereas the category "allowing to die" applies to cases in which treatment could be continued but is withheld or withdrawn by someone's choice. Rather than being unable to prevent a neonatal patient's death, physicians decide (or accede to parents' decisions) not to try to prevent a neonate's death. That some neonates who are "allowed" to die through selective nontreatment do not in fact die, should not be surprising. All of us from time to time are allowed or permitted to do things (by parents, teachers, physicians, and others in authority) that we do not or cannot do, for a variety of reasons.

The point is a simple one: neonates cannot correctly be said to have died because someone "allowed" them to do so, if that someone was powerless to prevent death from occurring. The category "allowing to die" thus applies only to neonatal (and other) cases in which physicians have the power—in terms of professional skill and available technological procedures—to prevent death from occurring for an indeterminate period of time but choose not to do so.

In contrast, the category of *intentional killing* (or euthanasia) applies to neonatal and other cases in which physicians do not merely permit death to occur in one of the situations mentioned under category two, but deliberately cause death to occur. This category is useful in describing death-causing decisions and actions in three kinds of clinical situations. When competent, dying patients decide that death is preferable to a continually painful existence and request that they be killed, the subsequent intentional killing of the patient for reasons of mercy by the physician (or someone else) is *voluntary euthanasia*. When competent patients express a desire to continue living, any subsequent killing of the patient by someone else is *involuntary euthanasia* (in moral terms) or murder (in legal terms). When neonatal patients or other incompetent patients are intentionally killed for reasons of mercy, the causation of their deaths is correctly described as *nonvoluntary euthanasia*, because they were unable to express a desire or preference regarding the continuation or termination of their lives. Given the current status of the law, nonvoluntary euthanasia also falls under the category of homicide.

The intentional killing of handicapped newborns can be done in two kinds of ways. The paradigm case of nonvoluntary euthanasia with neonates involves some kind of direct action that quickly kills the child. Perhaps the clearest example of such direct killing is the use of intravenous potassium: the quick, undeniable causation of death precludes any prolonged period of starvation by the child. The second way of engaging in nonvoluntary euthanasia is more common and, as previously noted, often misinterpreted as "allowing" a newborn to die. However, rather than permitting death as a possible (and even desirable) outcome, physicians in some neonatal cases clearly *intend to cause* infants to die through planned inaction. Perhaps the clearest example of this type of intentional killing is the decision not to perform surgery or provide nutritional support for an anomalous neonate with an intestinal obstruction that is known to be lethal in the absence of surgery.

Again, my point is a simple one: the absence of a single, direct action that kills a neonate (the NICU analogy to a "smoking gun") does not necessarily mean that a physician has merely allowed the child to die. Rather, when a life-prolonging medical procedure that is (a) in the child's best interests and (b) ethically obligatory is withheld from a neonate, the child's death has been intentionally caused by the responsible parties in the case.

Two questions remain: Is the killing/allowing to die distinction morally relevant? Under what circumstances is it morally justifiable to kill an infant who has been denied treatment? The first question is, of course, seriously debated by ethicists to the point that it appears on the verge of being one of the perennial issues for philosophical debate.[32] Much of the debate centers around whether there is an intrinsic moral difference between killing and allowing to die and, if so, what that intrinsic difference may be. As is already evident, I do not think the distinction hangs on the difference between acts and omissions, but do believe that there is at least limited intrinsic difference (the limit having to do with different kinds of situations) between killing and allowing to die in terms of (a) causation and (b) the intention of the moral agent. Perhaps more clearly, there are often two extrinsic moral differences between killing patients and allowing them to die. First, there is the obvious fact that some neonatal patients (and other patients, such as Karen Ann Quinlan) do not die if allowed to do so, but clearly would die if someone killed them. Second, there is the fact based on clinical observation that neonatal patients who are allowed to die by withholding treatment from them often endure long periods of suffering from dehydration and starvation, whereas infants who are intentionally killed—especially those killed quickly—do not presumably suffer.[33]

As to the second question, the intentional killing of birth-defective newborns is necessary in rare circumstances as a moral option of last resort in neonatal medicine. Nonvoluntary euthanasia in NICUs is justifiable under three necessary and jointly sufficient conditions. First, the withholding of treatment shall have been done on the basis of one of the two selection methods presented earlier, with the proxies determining that *life-prolonging treatment is not in the best interests of the child*. Second, having made the decision to allow the child to die, it becomes clear to the decision makers that the child is not going to die quickly and is going to *endure prolonged suffering* in the absence of treatment. Third, the decision to cause the child's death is carried out in a manner that will *quickly and painlessly* end the child's life.

The upshot of these statements is that intentionally killing anomalous neonates can be justified, but in rare instances. Moreover, if the killing meets the conditions above, it will more than likely be motivated by compassion for a potential person who will otherwise endure needless suffering. Depending on the case, nonvoluntary euthanasia may only be an act of killing done for reasons of mercy, or it may also be intended as an act of conscientious objection to laws that proscribe intentionally killing neonates even for humane reasons.

Notes

1. John A. Robertson, "Dilemma in Danville," *Hastings Center Report* 11 (October 1981): 8.
2. Richard Sherlock, "Selective Non-Treatment of Newborns," *Journal of Medical Ethics* 6 (September 1979): 140.
3. For further development of these distinctions, see Edward A. Langerak, "Abortion: Listening to the Middle," *Hastings Center Report* 9 (October 1979): 24–28.

4. See Mary Coleman, ed., *Neonatal Neurology* (Baltimore: University Park Press, 1981), pp. 155–57.
5. Richard M. Restak, "Newborn Knowledge," *Science 82* (January–February 1982): 58–65.
6. Langerak, "Abortion: Listening to the Middle," p. 25.
7. John A. Robertson, "Organ Donations by Incompetents and the Substituted Judgment Doctrine," *Columbia Law Review* 76 (January 1976): 57–58.
8. For a helpful analysis of these tests and their applicability to a range of cases, see Richard A. O'Neil, "Determining Proxy Consent," *The Journal of Medicine and Philosophy* 8 (November 1983): 389–403.
9. Quoted in Richard A. McCormick, S. J., "The Quality of Life, the Sanctity of Life," *Hastings Center Report* 8 (February 1978): 36.
10. For a discussion of these principles, see Tom L. Beauchamp and James F. Childress, *Principles of Biomedical Ethics*, (New York: Oxford University Press, 1979), pp. 97–167.
11. Quoted in Stanley Joel Reiser, Arthur J. Dyck, and William J. Curran, eds., *Ethics in Medicine* (Cambridge, Mass.: The MIT Press, 1977), p. 5.
12. Gordon B. Avery, "The Morality of Drastic Intervention," in Gordon B. Avery, ed., *Neonatology: Pathophysiology and Management of the Newborn*, 2nd ed. (Philadelphia: J. B. Lippincott Co., 1981), p. 14.
13. Quoted in Reiser, Dyck, and Curran, *Ethics in Medicine*, p. 5.
14. See a similar listing in Beauchamp and Childress, *Principles of Biomedical Ethics*, pp. 101–102.
15. Joel Feinberg, *Social Philosophy* (Englewood Cliffs, N.J.: Prentice-Hall, 1973), p. 26.
16. John Kleining, "Crime and the Concept of Harm," *American Philosophical Quarterly* 15 (January 1978): 27.
17. Albert R. Jonsen, "Do No Harm: Axiom of Medical Ethics," in Stuart F. Spicker and H. Tristram Engelhardt, eds., *Philosophical Medical Ethics: Its Nature and Significance* (Dordrecht, Holland: D. Reidel Publishing Co., 1977), pp. 27–41. A revision of the article appeared in *Annals of Internal Medicine* 88 (June 1978): 827–32.
18. Quoted in Reiser, Dyck, and Curran, *Ethics in Medicine*, p. 6 (emphasis added).
19. Paul Ramsey, *Ethics at the Edges of Life*, (New Haven and London: Yale University Press, 1978), p. 264.
20. Gene Outka, "Social Justice and Equal Access to Health Care," *The Journal of Religious Ethics* 2 (Spring 1974): 24.
21. For recent interpretations and criticisms of the ordinary/extraordinary distinction by philosophers, see Richard O'Neil, "In Defense of the 'Ordinary'/'Extraordinary' Distinction," *The Linacre Quarterly* 45 (February 1978): 37–40; Bonnie Steinbock, "The Intentional Termination of Life," *Ethics in Science and Medicine* 6 (1979): 59–64; and Helga Kuhse, "Extraordinary Means and the Intentional Termination of Life," *Social Science and Medicine* 15F (September 1981): 117–21.

22. See James M. Gustafson, "Mongolism, Parental Desires, and the Right to Life," *Perspectives in Biology and Medicine* 16 (Summer 1973): 529–57; Warren T. Reich, "Quality of Life and Defective Newborn Children: An Ethical Analysis," in Chester Swinyard, ed., *Decision Making and the Defective Newborn* (Springfield, Ill.: Charles C Thomas, 1978), pp. 489–511; Robert M. Veatch, *Death, Dying, and the Biological Revolution* (New Haven: Yale University Press, 1976), pp. 105–14; Leonard J. Weber, *Who Shall Live?* (New York: Paulist Press, 1976), pp. 73–103; and Beauchamp and Childress, *Principles of Biomedical Ethics*, pp. 117–26.

23. See Pius XII, "The Prolongation of Life," *The Pope Speaks* 4 (1958): 395–97; and the Sacred Congregation for the Doctrine of the Faith, *Declaration on Euthanasia* (Vatican City: Polyglot Press, 1980), pp. 11–12.

24. Gerald Kelly, S. J., *Medico-Moral Problems* (St. Louis: The Catholic Hospital Association, 1958), p. 129.

25. The House of Delegates of the American Medical Association, official statement, December 4, 1973.

26. *Handbook of Medical Ethics* (London: British Medical Association, 1980), pp. 30–31.

27. *In re Quinlan*, 70 N.J. 10 (1976).

28. Ramsey, *Ethics at the Edges of Life*, pp. 145–227; and Veatch, *Death, Dying, and the Biological Revolution*, pp. 105–14.

29. For somewhat different guidelines, see Weber, *Who Shall Live?*, pp. 80–98; and Warren T. Reich and David E. Ost, "Ethical Perspectives on the Care of Infants," in Warren T. Reich, editor-in-chief, *Encyclopedia of Bioethics* (New York: The Free Press, 1978), pp. 727–29.

30. See John Michael Hemphill and John M. Freeman, "Medical Aspects and Ethical Dilemmas," in Reich, *Encyclopedia of Bioethics*, p. 721.

31. Robert Baker, *Ceasing to Save: An Analysis of the Moral Methodology of One Neonatal Intensive Care Unit with Special Reference to the Killing/Allowing Death Controversy* (Philadelphia: The Society for Health and Human Values, 1979), p. 151.

32. A number of articles on this subject are in Bonnie Steinbock, ed., *Killing and Letting Die* (Englewood Cliffs, N.J.: Prentice-Hall, 1980). Notable articles not included in the Steinbock book are Gilbert Meilaender, "The Distinction between Killing and Allowing to Die," *Theological Studies* 37 (September 1976): 467–70; K. Danner Clouser, "Allowing or Causing: Another Look," *Annals of Internal Medicine* 87 (1977): 622–24; and James Rachels, "Killing and Starving to Death," *Philosophy* 54 (April 1979): 159–71.

33. See Richard A. O'Neil, "The Moral Relevance of the Active/Passive Euthanasia Distinction," in David H. Smith and Linda Bernstein, eds., *No Rush to Judgment: Essays on Medical Ethics* (Bloomington, Ind.: The Poynter Center, 1978), pp. 177–202; and Robert Reid, "Spina Bifida: The Fate of the Untreated," *Hastings Center Report* 7 (August 1977): 16–19.

8

Clinical Applications

> Now we shoot for a meaningful life rather than how long we can maintain a heart beat. You always have to be helpful, not harmful. And there are times when to do everything you can is harmful rather than helpful.
>
> GORDON B. AVERY, M.D., PH.D.[1]

> As new operative procedures, medications, and ancillary care develop, the natural history of a disease can be progressively altered. The impact of the cerebrospinal fluid shunting on hydrocephalus and the even more recent utilization of computed tomography to diagnose and assess treatment of hydrocephalus are good examples of this type of progress.
>
> DAVID G. McLONE, M.D., PH.D.[2]

Neonatal medicine is moving ahead rapidly. As indicated by David McLone's statement above, new technology, new medications, new surgical procedures, and new therapeutic programs make older approaches to neonatal medicine outmoded. And as implied by Gordon Avery's statement, these technological changes also bring about changes in the moral perspectives of neonatologists as they attempt to decide when treatment is beneficial to anomalous neonates and when it is, on balance, detrimental to these handicapped newborns.

Such detriment–benefit calculations lie at the center of decisions regarding selective nontreatment. The rationale behind these assessments of relative benefit and harm to newborns was presented in the preceding chapter, along with a discussion of three operational criteria that follow from an emphasis on treating or denying treatment to birth-defective neonates in terms of their best interests. In this manner the ethical principles of beneficence, nonmaleficence, and justice were shown to be of crucial importance to selective nontreatment decisions.

It is now necessary to be more specific regarding the applicability of the ethical principles and criteria discussed in chapter 7. As we "get down to cases" in this chapter, we will apply substantive criteria to neonatal medicine in two interrelated ways. First, the framework of the chapter will consist of a discussion of clinical requirements and ethical criteria that are generally applicable to cases arising in NICUs. Second, throughout the chapter we will discuss specific cases to indicate how these substantive considerations (both ethical and clinical) relate to the decisions that sometimes have to be made in neonatal medicine.

Accurate diagnosis

As is true with all medical specializations, physicians engaged in neonatal medicine have accurate diagnosis as the sine qua non of responsible medical care of patients with serious medical problems. In fact, there are two reasons for thinking that the need for accurate diagnosis is even greater in neonatal medicine than in other specializations: newborns present neonatologists and other pediatricians with a much greater variety of medical problems than do most patients seeing other physicians, and neonatal patients with severe congenital anomalies are much more vulnerable to life-threatening complications and death than are older patients who are less susceptible to apneic spells, cyanosis, and infection.

Accurate diagnosis of congenital medical problems is not always easy for even the most skilled neonatologists. Every neonate has the possibility of one or more congenital anomalies, and many newborns have multiple anomalies. Even diagnosing the general type of anomaly or isolating the organ system that is affected does not settle the more complicated diagnostic dilemmas. For example, if a pediatrician suspects a chromosomal abnormality in a newborn, there is still the diagnostic question of whether it is trisomy 21, trisomy 18, trisomy 13, or one of the rarer translocation combinations. If a pediatrician diagnoses a newborn as having congenital heart disease, there is still the question of diagnosing which of the 100 different cardiac anomalies a particular neonate has. If a newborn has some sort of neurological dysfunction, there is still the diagnostic task of determining if there is hydrocephalus, some degree of intraventricular hemorrhage, intracerebellar hemorrhage, one of the leukodystrophies, or something else.

It is, of course, because of the difficulties involved in providing accurate diagnosis in the more complicated cases that neonatologists regularly call in medical colleagues for consultation. Thus geneticists, neurologists, cardiologists, urologists, neurosurgeons, and other medical specialists pool their combined diagnostic skills in trying to solve some of the medical mysteries that appear in NICUs. At their command are numerous diagnostic procedures: physical examination, dermatoglyphics, biochemical analysis of blood and urine, chromosome studies, cardiac catheterization, roentgenographic examination, ultrasound, CT scans, and so forth.

The importance of careful, accurate diagnosis in neonatal cases is obvious. As an application of the principles of beneficence and nonmaleficence, accurate diagnosis of congenital anomalies means that most birth-defective neonates can benefit medically from effective treatment specifically geared to their anomalous condition(s). In a few instances, accurate diagnosis of congenital anomalies means that parents, physicians, or some other proxy can determine that life-prolonging treatment will be futile or, on balance, harmful to a particular infant. Either way, an accurate diagnosis is indispensable to making informed decisions regarding treatment or nontreatment, as illustrated by the following case.

Case 8.1

> A 950-gram premature infant was born to a young married couple. The infant appeared stable and the father returned home to care for his older daughter. Several hours later he received a telephone call, informing him that his wife was bleeding severely and his infant was deteriorating. He rushed back to the hospital in his car, striking a teenage bicycle rider who subsequently died.
>
> His wife recovered and was discharged, but the infant experienced continuous difficulties in four major areas: (1) congestive heart failure, apparently due to a heart defect; (2) renal insufficiency, apparently due to infantile-type polycystic kidney disease, a condition incompatible with long life; (3) breathing difficulties, requiring a respirator, apparently due to the combined effects of the heart disease and oxygen toxicity; and (4) neurological deterioration, apparently due to intraventricular hemorrhage. The infant was maintained with intensive care, during which time many critical decisions had to be made. The parents visited regularly, and were closely consulted about all major decisions, including decisions about continuing the respirator and whether or not to resuscitate the infant if he experienced cardiac arrest.
>
> The parents experienced increasing anxiety and depression throughout this period. The father suffered recurrent nightmares relating to the death of the teenager, and one night put his fist through a window while sleep-walking. Their newborn child's apparent

suffering increased their suffering, and the nursery staff felt conflict over their duty to their infant patient and to the parents as patients. It sometimes seemed that the child's continued existence was harmful to the parents' health, and the parents began requesting that medical care be discontinued in the hope that the infant would die.[3]

Given the tentative diagnosis in this unusual case, it is not surprising that the parents decided to discontinue treatment. After all, if an infant has an inoperable form of congenital heart disease, infantile-type polycystic kidneys, intractable bronchopulmonary dysplasia, and neurological dysfunction, life-prolonging treatment is contrary to the child's best interests. However, in this case the initial diagnosis proved inaccurate. The "inoperable" heart disease turned out to be patent ductus arteriosus, which was surgically closed; the polycystic kidney disease turned out to be an adult form of the disease, compatible with long life; the "intractable" bronchopulmonary dysplasia improved, allowing the infant to be successfully weaned from the respirator; and the neurological condition was treated with a ventriculoperitoneal shunt. Although the child subsequently died after experiencing an overwhelming infection, it is clear that the revised diagnosis of the multiple anomalies resulted in quite different thinking on the part of both parents and physicians regarding the merits of treatment.[4]

Other cases presented in earlier chapters also illustrate the importance of correct diagnosis. In case 2.1 a pediatric surgeon was called in as a consultant in a case involving a two-day-old male neonate who was vomiting feedings and large amounts of green fluid. Given the infant's inability to handle feedings and several physical signs suggesting Down's syndrome, a tentative diagnosis indicated trisomy 21 complicated by an intestinal obstruction. Two diagnostic procedures confirmed this interpretation: chromosome karyotyping proved that the infant had trisomy 21, and roentgenographic examination confirmed that duodenal atresia was also present. On the basis of this diagnostic information, the infant's intestinal obstruction was surgically corrected. He lived, even though his parents decided to institutionalize him because of his mental deficiency. Without the correct diagnosis and subsequent surgery, he would have died within approximately two weeks.

Case 3.2 also involved a male infant with duodenal atresia and physical signs of Down's syndrome. The parents' willingness to consent to a surgical correction of the intestinal obstruction depended on whether Down's syndrome was present. A geneticist provided the necessary diagnostic information, having done an analysis of chromosomes present in a bone marrow sample. With that information, the parents deliberated for three days before refusing to permit surgery. Supportive therapy was subsequently withdrawn, and the infant died three days later.

Case 4.1 illustrates some of the problems that arise when the physicians in a case disagree about diagnosis. Baby Boy Houle was born with multiple anomalies, including a tracheoesophageal fistula. The recommended medical treatment was surgical repair of the fistula. However, the infant's parents, influenced by one physician's suspicion that the child had suffered brain damage, decided to refuse the surgery and to cease the intravenous feeding of their son. Other physicians in the case disagreed with the parents' decision, took the case to court, and succeeded in having court-ordered surgery performed on the child. Unfortunately the limited accounts of the case (including the court record) give no indication of why one physician suspected brain damage, why additional diagnostic tests were not performed to try to detect neurological damage prior to going to court, or why the Houles chose to go with what was clearly a minority view regarding diagnosis.

Careful prognosis

In contrast to the accuracy and precision that are often possible in clinical diagnosis, the related task of prognosis is characterized by subjective appraisals, educated guesses, and predictions that may or may not prove true. Having studied the available clinical data on a case, reviewed the literature and previous experience with similarly diagnosed cases, and isolated any unusual features of a particular case, physicians proceed to forecast the probable future of the diagnosed condition.

Such predictive thinking has been a part of medicine since the time of Hippocrates. The Hippocratic Corpus contains a work called "Prognostic," in which the writer connects the importance of careful prognosis with the determination of proper treatment:

> I hold that it is an excellent thing for a physician to practice forecasting. For if he discover and declare unaided by the side of his patients the present, the past and the future . . . he will be the more believed to understand the cases, so that men will confidently entrust themselves to him for treatment. Furthermore, *he will carry out the treatment best if he know beforehand from the present symptoms what will take place later.*[5]

There are, however, inherent problems with this aspect of medical practice. The problems are especially noticeable in neonatal medicine. One problem is that occasionally neonates have multiple anomalies that are complex, difficult to diagnose, and virtually impossible to predict with any certitude as to outcome. A second problem is the overly quick use of prognostic labels (e.g., "nonviable," "hopeless" case, "meaningless" life, "terminally" ill) by some pediatricians who may think on the basis of their own value systems that certain anomalous newborns should die, but who have not done the requisite diagnostic work on which to base such prognostic claims.[6] A third problem is that some newborns (e.g., extremely premature ones) with severe congenital anomalies have not had much of a chance at survival until recent years, and consequently there are insufficient long-term studies of the effects of various treatment options on these children from which to extrapolate to current cases.[7] A fourth problem is that in moving from diagnosis to prognosis, some physicians do not adequately try to specify the prognosis for different neonatal patients having the same general diagnostic condition. A fifth problem occurs when pediatricians employ the prognostic strategy of "hanging crepe": by greatly exaggerating the probability of an anomalous infant's death, the physician appears omniscient when the child dies—or omnipotent (perhaps as in case 2.3) in the event that the child survives with vigorous treatment.[8]

Partially because of these problems, the ethical significance of careful prognosis in neonatal cases can hardly be overemphasized. If physicians overestimate the severity of the long-term consequences of a congenital condition (in terms of a child's ongoing mental deficiency and/or physical handicaps), that prognosis may lead to a decision to allow an infant to die when in fact the child's best interests appear to call for continued life. An example of such unduly pessimistic forecasting of the future can be found in the statements sometimes made by Raymond Duff and Anthony Shaw concerning children with Down's syndrome. In contrast, if physicians underestimate the severity of the long-term consequences of an anomalous condition, that prognosis may result in prolonged, often ineffective treatment of a child whose best interests seem to call for death rather than continued suffering. An example of such unduly optimistic forecasting of the future is found in the statements made by Everett Koop regarding children whose birth defects require dozens of painful surgical procedures. Thus some infants die who should receive treatment and live (according to the principle of beneficence), whereas some other infants live who should be denied treatment and die (according to the principle of nonmaleficence).

The need for careful prognosis is best illustrated by cases of spina bifida cystica. Because of the variability among cases (depending in part on the location and size of the lesion) and the variability of the long-term disabilities caused by the anomaly (depending in part on how quickly the lesion is surgically closed), there is an ongoing debate among pediatric surgeons regarding the correct prognosis for neonates with this condition. Of course treatment is withheld from some infants with spina bifida because their lesions are too large for surgical closure. However, for the majority of newborns with spina bifida, the decision to provide surgery and other forms of treatment largely depends on prognosis—and the availability of clinical means of selection that can reliably distinguish among cases along designated prognostic lines.

To the extent that there is any consensus among pediatric surgeons regarding prognosis and treatment of spina bifida cases, we now seem to be in a fourth phase of medical assessment. In the first phase, prior to the advent of NICUs, newborns with spina bifida were widely regarded as hopeless cases. Consequently they were "treated" with an attitude of benign neglect, and either allowed to die or intentionally killed. Then, beginning in the early 1960s, a second phase of prognosis and treatment came into existence as a result of advances in medical technology. Best illustrated by the policies of John Lorber, R. B. Zachary, and their colleagues in Sheffield, England, this second phase was characterized by surgical attempts to salvage all newborns with spina bifida. Such infants were given vigorous treatment: surgical closure of the spinal defect, shunting of cerebrospinal fluid to other absorptive sites, ileostomies and urinary tract operations, orthopedic operations and prosthetic devices, and so forth. With this vigorous approach to treatment, prognosis often consisted of dividing surviving infants into three groups in terms of their anticipated minimum, moderate, or severe handicaps.

The publication of Lorber's articles on selective nontreatment initiated a third phase of medical assessment of spina bifida in the early 1970s. Concerned about the amount of harm inflicted on spina bifida children with severe physical handicaps, Lorber began to select infants for treatment in terms of their prognosis. Using his "adverse prognostic criteria" (see chap. 3), he decided not to provide treatment for a significant number of newborns (68% of the 37 neonates in his 1973 report) who would subsequently have severe physical handicaps even with vigorous treatment. For him, treatment was—and is—contraindicated in these severe cases because of his prognosis that such children will never be able to have a minimally acceptable quality of life.[9] Some other pediatric physicians agreed with his prognosis in such cases, accepted his proposed clinical criteria, and helped his selective nontreatment policy become officially recognized in British medical circles.[10]

Now the pendulum seems to have swung back to treatment for the majority of newborns with spina bifida. As we observed in chapter 3, John Freeman and R. B. Zachary have disagreed with Lorber's selection policy for years. At least part of their disagreement concerns prognosis, with both of them being less optimistic than Lorber is regarding the outcome of untreated cases (namely, that virtually all untreated children will die within the first year), and more optimistic than he is regarding the kinds of lives ahead for children who receive early and aggressive treatment. This disagreement about prognosis is one of the reasons that Freeman treats approximately 90% of the spina bifida infants he sees in Baltimore, whereas Lorber leaves 60–70% of a much larger number of infants untreated in Sheffield.[11]

Some other pediatric physicians also disagree with Lorber's prognostic criteria and his resulting reasons for nontreatment of numerous spina bifida infants.[12] The most recent clinical study of children with spina bifida suggests that the prognosis for most of these children is much better than indicated by Lorber. In a follow-up study of 100 consecutive spina bifida neonates transferred to Children's Memorial Hospital in Chicago, David McLone points out that all of them were given aggressive treatment initially, 2 died as a consequence of surgery, and another 12 died as a consequence of untreatable hindbrain problems of the Chiari II malformation (displacement and elongation of the medulla). Of the remaining 86 children (from four and one-half to seven years of age), 40 of them are intellectually normal, continent of urine, and community ambulators; 24 are intellectually normal and continent, but do not ambulate in the community; and the remainder have serious physical and mental handicaps.[13] Partially because he discovered that the majority of the infants with severe Chiari II symptoms would have escaped Lorber's selection criteria (because they lacked hydrocephalus at birth, had a low-level lesion, and had functional lower extremities), McLone argues that "it is moral and ethically correct to treat all children born with a myelomeningocele and that no valid criteria exist for the selection of infants for nontreatment."[14]

The importance—and difficulty—of careful prognosis can be illustrated with numerous cases. We will discuss four. The first case concerns prognosis with a premature infant, and the subsequent cases involve infants with spina bifida.

Case 8.2

> Dawn Sobel was moderately premature at birth. She was rushed to the NICU at Stanford immediately after delivery and placed on a ventilator. Later, when her breathing stabilized, she was removed from the machine. Five days later she became unconscious. A spinal tap found blood. Her brain waves grew abnormal, her reflexes erratic. Her parents were informed that there was "possibly serious" brain damage.
>
> Over the next several days the Sobels received mixed messages from the NICU staff: a pessimistic prognosis regarding Dawn's ability to survive and her intellectual ability if she did survive, but aggressive intervention to treat her every time something went wrong. David Sobel remarked: "We didn't know if she would survive and, if she did, if she was so badly off that she wouldn't be any more than a vegetable. If we were going to end up with a severely damaged child, then maybe they shouldn't proceed with treatment so vigorously."
>
> Finally the Sobels believed that the medical staff was going to "let nature take its course." Informed by a nurse the following evening that Dawn would probably not live through the night, the Sobels left the hospital to make funeral arrangements—and to wait for the call informing them of Dawn's death.
>
> The call never came because Philip Sunshine, the head neonatologist, successfully intervened in the case. He discovered a large pneumothorax (an air pocket surrounding the lung) and inserted a chest tube, after which Dawn immediately began improving.[15]

This case demonstrates several things about prognosis with neonates. First, no matter how skilled the medical staff or how sophisticated the NICU, some neonatal cases represent medical mysteries that are difficult to diagnose and to predict as to outcome. Second, there is an integral linkage between accurate diagnosis and careful prognosis. The pessimistic prognosis in this case appears to have been due, in large part, to an inaccurate or at least an incomplete diagnosis of Dawn's medical problems. Third, a pessimistic prognosis can become a self-fulfilling prophecy. If the head neonatologist had not intervened at the last moment in Dawn's case, it is quite clear that she would have died that night in the Stanford Medical Center. As it is, in spite of her parents' initial anger at not being consulted about her treatment, Dawn is now four years old. She has to undergo physical therapy for a stiff left hand and occasionally has shunt failure that requires emergency trips to the hospital, but appears not to have any mental deficiency.

The spina bifida cases have been presented earlier. Case 2.8 involved a male infant whose spina bifida was complicated by hydrocephalus, clubfeet and dislocated hips, and apneic spells. The child's mother was told that even with surgery to close the boy's spine, there would be permanent paralysis and serious brain damage. Given this prognosis, she declined to have the surgery performed. Even though a representative from a spina bifida counseling service tried to convince her otherwise, she continued to think that the prognosis meant that her son would not have a life worth living. Whether her decision was actually in the best interests of her son is impossible to say for sure, but some of the missing elements in the case leave room for doubt. We do not know, for instance, whether the physicians told her about the possibility of shunting the hydrocephalus or having surgical correction of some of the orthopedic problems. Moreover, because we know neither the size nor the location of the lesion, it is impossible to determine whether her son's anomalous condition was actually untreatable, or whether the forecast of "a horrible future" was primarily a quality-of-life judgment indicative of the physicians' views of less-than-normal neonates.

Case 3.5 concerned an 8-year-old boy whose condition of spina bifida was not surgically treated for the first 10 months of his life. Given the high level of his lesion and the prognosis that he would die from the condition, his parents declined to have the spinal opening closed. However, the boy did not develop meningitis and lived to endure the suffering that was clearly exacerbated by the long delay before treatment. The wrong prognosis in this case unfortunately led to a number of medical problems: hydrocephalus, cortical blindness, dislocated hips, numerous fractures, severe hydronephrosis, and severe kyphosis. Some of these problems may have developed even with treatment, but many of them would have been avoided or at least minimized with a more careful prognosis and early treatment.

Case 4.5 was complicated by conflicting medical opinions regarding prognosis for a female infant with spina bifida. The attending physician predicted that the child would have a lifetime of painful surgical procedures, paralysis below the waist, incontinence, and possible mental deficiency due to shunt complications. Other physicians gave a significantly different prognosis: probable paralysis and incontinence, but no mental disability. The girl, having received court-ordered surgery, is still too young for us to ascertain which prognosis was correct. It is possible, however, to suggest that the differing medical views on prognosis were indicative of different perspectives regarding the moral grounds upon which treatment is to be given or denied to spina bifida children. The physician who opposed treatment may have reasoned that the child's future handicaps would not meet a minimally acceptable quality of life, whereas the other physicians appear to have judged that even physically handicapped life was in the child's best interests when compared with the alternative of death.

Select by diagnostic categories

The argument was advanced in the previous chapter that selective non-treatment decisions should be governed primarily by diagnostic categories. If a newborn has an anomalous condition that can be effectively treated, the child should generally be given the recommended treatment. In contrast, if a newborn has a diagnostic condition that cannot be effectively treated, the child should generally be spared from efforts at life prolongation, because such efforts will be futile and/or harmful to the child.

In addition, it was argued that selecting by diagnostic categories is consistent with the principles of nonmaleficence and justice. According to the principle of nonmaleficence, it is justifiable to withhold life-prolonging treatment from all infants who have conditions that "overmaster" them (to use the Hippocratic terminology) and that seem impervious to even the most advanced medical procedures. To persist in trying to treat such infants is to go counter to their best interests and thereby to inflict unwarranted harm on them. According to an egalitarian interpretation of justice, it is morally correct to withhold treatment from all infants born with the same kind of severe anomalous condition—as long as all available means of treating the condition are judged to be counter to those infants' best interests. To take another approach by comparing infants across major diagnostic lines is to engage in unfair quality-of-life assessments, because any less-than-normal infant will lose out in such a comparison.

It is now time to be more specific about which diagnostic conditions call for selective nontreatment. Any serious effort to do this kind of ethical line-drawing must meet three interrelated requirements: indicate as clearly as possible *where* the line is to be drawn between conditions to treat and those not to treat, provide reasons as to *why* the treatment/nontreatment line is drawn where it is, and apply the proposed line-drawing to actual cases.

It is improbable that all persons reading these words will agree with my placement of all the diagnostic conditions to be discussed below, especially since there are differences of opinion in the pediatric medical community regarding some of the conditions. Nevertheless, it seems reasonable that selection by diagnostic categories should be done by placing many of the congenital anomalies in one of three groups: anomalous conditions that should not be treated because efforts to save newborns with these conditions will not succeed; anomalous conditions that should not be treated because of the consensus judgment that life-prolonging treatment is not in the best interests of these infants; and anomalous conditions that should be treated because life-prolonging treatment is in the best interests of these infants. This threefold grouping of congenital anomalies results in the placement of diagnostic conditions as follows:

1. *Withhold efforts at treatment* (desist unsuccessful rescue): anencephaly; other untreatable neurological conditions (e.g., craniorachischisis totalis, myeloschisis, massive subarachnoid hemorrhage, Chiari II malformation); infantile polycystic kidney disease; untreatable types of congenital heart disease (e.g., hypoplastic left ventricle); and multiple severe anomalies requiring repetitious efforts at resuscitation.
2. *Withhold or withdraw treatment* (allow to die): hydranencephaly; trisomy 18; trisomy 13; Lesch-Nyhan syndrome; Tay-Sachs disease; lissencephaly; cri-du-chat syndrome; and metachromatic leukodystrophy.
3. *Treat to prolong and enhance life*: hydrocephalus; most cases of prematurity; esophageal atresia with tracheoesophageal fistula; duodenal atresia; most cases of congenital heart disease; most cases of intraventricular hemorrhage; trisomy 21 (Down's syndrome); hyaline mem-

brane disease; most cases of spina bifida cystica; Apert's syndrome; diaphragmatic hernia; most cases of congenital kidney disease; abnormalities of the abdominal wall; exstrophy of the cloaca; neurofibromatosis; phenylketonuria; maple syrup urine disease; homocystinuria; cystic fibrosis; congenital hypothyroidism; and others too numerous to mention.

The reasons for drawing the treatment/nontreatment line in this manner are fairly straightforward. The congenital anomalies placed in the first nontreatment group seem, on the basis of current medical evidence, to be untreatable. Most of the conditions are rapidly fatal within the first few days of life.[16] At most, aggressive efforts at treatment may salvage these neonates for a short period of time, but for questionable moral reasons. Vigorous attempts at treatment with these generally acknowledged lethal cases appear to be done for the interests (and egos) of the medical personnel involved, not for the interests of the newborns subjected to futile rescue efforts.

When combined with the anomalous conditions in the first nontreatment group, the diagnostic conditions placed in the second nontreatment group represent less than 1% of all neonates. Nevertheless, good reasons are required to deny treatment to the nondying newborns whose conditions place them in this nontreatment group because, in contrast to the newborns in group 1, the nontreatment of infants in group 2 is done by choice. The reasons for nontreatment, in general terms, are that when infants are accurately diagnosed as having one of the anomalous conditions in the second group, a careful prognosis indicates that the lives that can be prolonged for an indeterminate period of time will not be in the best interests of the infants and children who have to endure them. Rather than proving beneficial to these children, life-prolonging treatment will subject them to a fate worse than death.

More specifically, there are several reasons for thinking that death, not severely handicapped life, is in the best interests of infants having any of the anomalous conditions in the second nontreatment group. First, a correct diagnosis of most of these conditions leads to a prognosis of *extremely short life expectancy.* Although some infants with some of these conditions (e.g., Lesch-Nyhan, Tay-Sachs, cri-du-chat) live for a few years after birth, the odds are very high that most newborns in the second nontreatment group will die in their first year of life even if given some forms of treatment. No matter how much sustaining treatment is given, continued life is simply not likely for most of these neonates.

Second, there is *no curative or corrective treatment* for these conditions. Little can be done for these children other than marginal life prolongation, palliative care, and institutionalization in a custodial ward. For the conditions with late onset dates (Lesch-Nyhan, Tay-Sachs, and the late infantile form of metachromatic leukodystrophy), the lack of effective treatment means that infants who appear normal during their first few months of life will experience progressive neurological and physical deterioration that is simply impossible to prevent or minimize.

Third, virtually all of the infants in the second nontreatment group who manage to survive beyond their first year end up with *serious neurological deficiencies.* In most cases the neurological deficiencies are very serious. With rare exceptions, infants with these conditions develop into children with severe (below 50 I.Q.) to profound (below 25 I.Q.) mental retardation.

Fourth, there are a *multiplicity of other serious medical problems* that accompany the neurological deficiencies in these conditions. Most of the infants have some form of congenital heart disease. Most of them also have hypotonia, apnea, seizures, and numerous other clinical features of their particular anomalous conditions.

It may be helpful to focus on some of the conditions in the second group. Newborns who inherit the autosomal recessive condition of Tay-Sachs disease (one form of G_{M2}-gangliosidosis) appear normal for approximately six months, then have an inexorable decline toward a totally vegetative existence followed by death when they are three or four years of age. The progressive loss of contact with parents and the environment is characterized by profound mental retardation, convulsions, paralysis, blindness, inability to feed orally, and severe weight loss.[17]

Male neonates who inherit the X-linked recessive condition of Lesch-Nyhan syndrome also appear normal at birth, then at approximately six months begin a process of neurological and physiological deterioration first evidenced by athetosis (ceaseless, involuntary writhing movements). Along with severe mental deficiency, the most striking neurological feature of this condition is compulsive self-mutilation that requires placing the elbows in splints, wrapping the hands in gauze, and sometimes extracting the teeth. Even then, children with this condition often bang their heads against inanimate objects or take out their aggression on other persons.[18]

Infants (usually girls) with trisomy 18 generally do not survive the first two months of life. The 10% who live past the 12-month point do so with serious abnormalities of the brain, congenital heart disease, problems with apnea and cyanosis, hypertonia, severe gastrointestinal and renal deformities, dislocated hips, and virtually no chance to live to a second birthday.[19]

Metachromatic leukodystrophy is a rare autosomal recessive disease, with the late infantile form being the most common type of the condition. Neonates with the disease appear normal but have a serious disturbance of the white matter in the cerebral hemispheres that results in a diffuse loss of myelin in the central nervous system. Symptoms of the condition appear late in the first year of life, then progress through four clinical stages until, at the age of three or four, children with the condition are decerebrate, bedridden, quadriplegic, blind, without verbal sounds, and in need of tube feeding.[20]

Cri-du-chat syndrome (or 5p− syndrome) is a chromosomal disorder involving a deletion of the short arm of the fifth chromosome. The commonly used name for the condition is a reference to the catlike cry of infants having the disorder. In addition to this unusual cry, the most important aspect of this syndrome is the profound retardation that affects intellectual and motor development. Other symptoms of the condition include severely slowed growth, hypertonia, microcephaly, congenital heart disease, scoliosis, and inability to speak.[21]

The severity of these conditions—and the absence of effective treatment—forces one to conclude that death is preferable to severely handicapped existence for these children. Most reasonable persons—whether parents, physicians, other proxies, or other thoughtful individuals—will agree that the combination of harmful conditions accompanying these birth defects represents a fate worse than death for these afflicted newborns.

By contrast, infants with any of the anomalous conditions listed in the third group should be given treatment to prolong and to enhance their lives. The reasons for drawing the line at this point are several. First, the majority of the conditions *do not involve mental deficiency* at all, thus indicating that these neonates are potential persons in a way that newborns in the first two groups are not. Most of the anomalies in these conditions are physiological ones of one sort or another. Furthermore, for the disorders that do involve the possibility of neurological damage (e.g., hydrocephalus, phenylketonuria, intraventricular hemorrhage) or actual mental deficiency (e.g., trisomy 21), there is either a good chance of effectively treating the condition or at least a reasonable chance that the mental handicap will be rather mild.

Second, there is *curative or corrective treatment* available for most of the mental and physical handicaps associated with these conditions. In some instances (e.g., esophageal or duodenal atresia) the treatment is curative. In other instances (e.g., hydrocephalus, diaphragmatic hernia) the treatment is usually corrective. In other instances (e.g., phenylke-tonuria, maple syrup urine disease, homocystinuria) the treatment involves nothing more sophisticated than a special diet to adjust an underlying error of metabolism. Even for most cases of spina bifida cystica, in which surgery can neither cure nor correct the paralysis below the lesion, there is reasonably effective treatment for most of the physical and mental problems associated with the condition.

Third, most of these conditions *do not require institutionalization* if the affected infants are given appropriate treatment sufficiently early. Of course some parents may choose to institutionalize children with more severe forms of Down's syndrome or spina bifida or some of the other conditions that present ongoing problems, but these disorders do not usually have the degree of severity (as those in the second nontreatment group do) that necessitates placement in a handicapped children's facility. In fact, most children in this third group tend to do better if given care, emotional support, and friendship outside of an institutional setting.

Fourth, as already implied, infants with conditions listed in the third group have significantly *longer life expectancy* than newborns in the second group. A number of the conditions (e.g., congenital heart disease, hyaline membrane disease) cause neonatal fatalities if not effectively treated, but on the whole the availability of effective treatment means that neonates with these conditions will live many years beyond infancy.

Fifth, *very few adolescents or adults* with any of these conditions indicate that they *wish they had never survived infancy*. Even individuals with serious, ongoing handicaps (such as those associated with the more severe cases of spina bifida) rarely indicate to researchers that they would prefer no life to the life they have had. They may covet the normalcy they see in other persons, but they do not want to give up the abnormal lives they have for the alternative of death.

Of the various diagnostic conditions in the treatment group, Down's syndrome and spina bifida stand out because of the frequency of their occurrence and the conflicting points of view regarding the merits of life-prolonging treatment. Down's syndrome is unquestionably a serious congenital anomaly that no one would choose to have, and that no prospective parents would choose as the genetic composition of any of their children. As previously mentioned (in chap. 2), the most serious feature of this disorder is moderately severe to severe mental retardation (typically in the 25–60 I.Q. range). However, the mental deficiency is occasionally milder, with some Down's syndrome children having I.Q. scores in the 60–80 range. In addition, these children have physical abnormalities ranging from relatively minor ones (e.g., shortened fingers, slanting eyes with inner canthal folds) to much more serious ones in some cases such as congenital heart disease (in 40% of the cases), esophageal or duodenal atresia (in 4% of the cases), and increased susceptibility to infections.[22]

Likewise, spina bifida cystica is a serious congenital anomaly that adults would never choose for themselves or their as yet unconceived children. During pregnancy it is possible to screen for spina bifida cases using the combination of ultrasonography, amniocentesis, and alpha-fetoprotein assays. Once born, infants with spina bifida have a number of physical abnormalities that have been previously discussed in chapters 2 and 3. In addition, these children often have hydrocephalus. Whether mental deficiency becomes an acquired feature of spina bifida cases with hydrocephalus depends on the effectiveness of shunting and the medical team's ability to prevent central nervous system infections (ventriculitis and/or meningitis). As a consequence, I.Q. scores in one study of children with spina bifida range from 102 in cases without hydrocephalus, to 95 for shunted hydrocephalus, to 72 for shunted cases with a history of ventriculitis.[23]

The day may come when spina bifida cases will be prevented or drastically reduced in number by having women take multivitamin supplements before and during pregnancy, or by having mandatory screening for spina bifida cases during pregnancy by running laboratory tests on the blood serum of pregnant women. Until that time, the question remains the same for cases of Down's syndrome and cases of spina bifida: is life-prolonging treatment in the best interests of these birth-defective infants? My answer is affirmative in cases of Down's syndrome and in the great majority of spina bifida cases. Children born with either of these anomalous conditions obviously do not have normal lives ahead of them. In this respect, they lack the chance for the quality of life that most normal children enjoy. Children born with either of these conditions also do not have desirable lives—except when these lives are compared with the alternative of death. The argument that these handicapped lives (or others in the treatment group) represent a fate worse than death is neither persuasive nor supported by studies of these children when they reach adolescence and adulthood.[24]

We now turn to cases. If ethical line-drawing is to be persuasive and avoid the charge of arbitrariness, it must stand the test in actual cases. We will turn first to a well-publicized case of Down's syndrome, then discuss several cases presented in earlier chapters.

Case 8.3

Brian West was born on October 16, 1980, as the second son of John and Susan West. The first son was normal. Brian was not, because he was born with Down's syndrome and a severe form of esophageal atresia in which most of the esophagus was absent. The medical recommendation was for surgery to construct a new esophagus out of stomach tissue.

Brian's parents refused to authorize the surgery, arguing that Brian would be better off dead than with a handicapped life of recurring pain. Brian's physicians and some social workers in Orange County, California, disagreed with the parents' decision, arguing that such an operation would typically be done for a normal neonate and that it would be inhumane to let Brian starve to death without the surgery.

An Orange County juvenile court was asked to adjudicate the case. The court took custody of Brian and ordered sufficient medical treatment to keep him alive. That treatment, at various points in Brian's hospitalization, involved the attachment of a permanent abdominal feeding tube, the insertion of a breathing tube in his mouth, the attachment of an intravenous needle to his neck, and regular antibiotic injections. These efforts at life prolongation continued for 26 months, with Brian in a nursing home much of the time.

Late in 1982 the Wests, who had previously avoided publicity, decided to go public with the story of their son's unwanted extension of life. In response to the widespread criticism of the Infant Doe case in Bloomington [case 5.3], the Wests decided to show what could happen to Down's syndrome children who are kept alive in spite of their parents' wishes.

Another reason for the Wests' decision to go public was Brian's health condition in November 1982. The surgery to construct the esophagus was finally performed. Brian, weighing only 15 pounds, responded to the surgery over the next two weeks with respiratory shock, a massive blood infection, and temporary kidney failure. The combination of these medical problems apparently caused brain damage and blindness.

On November 30, 1982, the Wests regained custody of Brian. They indicated that they would support medical procedures to help him eat, talk, and walk, but would oppose any prolonged use of a respirator if that became necessary to help him breathe. Brian died three weeks after his parents regained the legal right to make decisions about his care.[25]

This case has legal, medical, and ethical ramifications. In terms of its legal aspects, the case represents a challenge to prosecutors, other law enforcement officials, and the federal government. The Wests' comments to the press clearly indicate that they believe selective nontreatment decisions are within the province of parental discretion, and that both the public outcry over the Infant Doe case and the HHS notice to hospitals in response to that case were misplaced. As to its medical aspects, the press coverage of the case leaves some unanswered questions. Reports of the case indicate that all the physicians involved in 1980 (and others in 1982) agreed that Down's syndrome is "a mild form of retardation" and that the surgical procedure on the esophagus is the only chance of correcting that disorder. Yet there is no suggestion as to why the surgery was delayed for two years or whether Brian's general health picture was better or worse at two years than during the neonatal period. In terms of ethics, the initial refusal of surgery followed by an inexplicable delay in performing the surgery resulted in the worst possible outcome for a child with Down's syndrome: prolonged suffering, ineffective and delayed treatment, and a possibly preventable death. If the responsible parties in the case had regarded Down's syndrome (with esophageal atresia) as a diagnostic condition calling for life-prolonging and life-enhancing treatment, Brian might have lived longer and under much better conditions.

Other cases also illustrate the importance that selection by diagnostic categories can have in NICUs. Cases 2.2 and 5.3 are the two most highly publicized nontreatment cases, and both of them involved Down's syndrome infants who died after being denied treatment. The publicity surrounding the cases in large part reflected the widespread view that these two infants should not have died in the absence of surgical treatment. The baby boy in the Johns Hopkins case starved to death after his parents refused to authorize surgery to correct duodenal atresia, and Infant Doe died six days after his parents refused to consent to surgical correction of his esophageal atresia with associated tracheoesophageal fistula. Both newborns were thus denied surgery that would be obligatory for neonates without mental deficiency. If the cases had been decided in terms of the treatment/nontreatment diagnostic categories discussed above, the surgery would also have been regarded as obligatory for these infants. The result would be that one or both of them would probably still be alive, although possibly in the custody of other parents.

Case 5.4 involved a newborn with spina bifida cystica. Although some of the details in the case have never been made public, it appears that the infant's parents refused to authorize surgery on the spinal lesion and transferred the child to a hospital in Robinson, Illinois, with the knowledge that the hospital was not equipped to provide the neonatal care the infant required. Following the intervention of state and federal authorities, the child was transferred to Chicago for surgical treatment. If the parents, physicians, and hospital administrators involved in the case from the beginning had regarded spina bifida as a birth defect generally to be treated, the child would have received earlier and more effective treatment. If the case had been handled in this manner, it would neither have received publicity nor played a role in the HHS notice to hospitals.

Case 2.7 involved a baby girl with apparent trisomy 18, apnea, and a heart defect. Given the importance of accurate diagnosis, no treatment should have been withheld from her until chromosomal studies confirmed the presence of the trisomic condition. Once the diagnosis of trisomy 18 was confirmed, however, the rationale presented above for nontreatment of certain diagnostic conditions would apply to this case. With an accurate diagnosis and medical consensus regarding prognosis, the first three questions raised at the end of the case presentation in chapter 2 would be answered in the negative.

Select by withholding optional means of treatment

The secondary method of selection for nontreatment is based on the distinction between obligatory and optional means of prolonging life. As mentioned in chapter 7, this method of selection is occasionally necessary because of the complex realities of neonatal medicine: cases within the same diagnostic category sometimes differ significantly in severity, and some cases simply do not fit established diagnostic categories.

The obligatory/optional distinction can be helpful as proxies attempt to decide on the merits of life prolongation in these complex cases. By calling attention to the necessary balancing of probable benefit and detriment in decisions about medical treatment, the distinction requires that physicians use appropriate clinical tests to determine whether life-prolonging treatment in a particular case is beneficial or harmful on balance. Which clinical tests are performed obviously depends on the anomalous condition(s) in question. If it appears on the basis of these tests that life-prolonging treatment is or will be harmful on balance to the neonate whose life is in jeopardy, that treatment should be judged optional and then be withheld or withdrawn so that the child may die.

The practical import of this distinction in neonatal medicine is twofold. First, it means that life-prolonging treatment in very severe cases of a particular disease may be judged optional, even though most cases of the disease call for treatment. Second, it means that life-prolonging treatment in very severe cases involving multiple anomalies may be judged optional, even though these unusual cases do not belong in either of the diagnostic nontreatment groups discussed earlier. Examples of such cases in which treatment may be regarded as optional (depending on factors in individual cases) include the following:

severely asphyxiated infants,
severe cases of intraventricular hemorrhage (grade 4 cases),[26]
severe cases of spina bifida cystica (when the cystic cavity is at T-12 or above, complicated by progressive hydrocephalus, marked kyphosis, and/or other serious medical problems),
severe cases involving extremely premature infants or SGA infants (those with birthweights under 750 grams),[27]
some cases of conjoined twins,
severe cases of congenital rubella,[28]
severe cases of Niemann-Pick disease (type A cases, the acute neuro-nopathic form),[29]
severe cases of de Lange syndrome,[30]
severe cases of microcephaly (those in which cranial circumference is three standard deviations below the mean),
and other severe cases involving multiple serious anomalies (e.g., case 3.6).

Once again, it may be helpful to discuss cases. How does the obligatory/ optional distinction work as a method of selection for nontreatment in actual cases? We will begin with a highly publicized case, follow it with a case receiving little publicity, and then comment on some of the cases presented earlier.

Case 8.4

Andrew Stinson was born in a community hospital on December 17, 1976. He had a gestational age of 24½ weeks and a birthweight of 800 grams (1 lb., 12 oz.). He was transferred to a regional hospital with an NICU on December 24. At that time his weight had dropped to 600 grams (1 lb., 5 oz.).

Once admitted to the NICU, Andrew was placed on a respirator against his parents' wishes and without their consent. He remained dependent on the respirator until he was finally allowed to die on June 14.

The list of Andrew's afflictions, nearly all of them iatrogenic, is almost endless. He endured bronchopulmonary dysplasia, countless episodes of bradycardia and cyanosis, countless suctionings and blood transfusions, retrolental fibroplasia, numerous infections, demineralized and fractured bones, an iatrogenic cleft palate, pulmonary artery hypertension, and seizures of the brain. The infections alone necessitated several urinary tract operations, the surgical removal of gangrene and necrotic muscle down to the bone of his right leg, and prolonged treatment of recurring pneumonia. In addition, he had a heart defect, a pulmonary hemorrhage, cortical atrophy, enlarged ventricles, microcephaly, and chronic encephalopathy. In his parents' words, Andrew was "'saved' by the respirator to die five long, painful, and expensive months later of the respirator's side effects."

His parents repeatedly stated that they wished the life-prolonging treatment to be discontinued. In response to their questions about turning off the respirator, one physician remarked: "What do you want me to do? Go in and put a pillow over his head?" After months of such emotionally charged exchanges, the medical staff finally decided to "orchestrate" Andrew's death. Rather than withdrawing ventilatory assistance, they opted to allow Andrew to die in a surreptitious manner: wait until he dislodged his breathing tube, watch to see if he (a respirator-dependent patient) might breathe on his own, and then declare him dead after he failed to breathe.

After Andrew's death, his parents had two general observations regarding the ordeal. First, had they known the policies of the NICU before signing the admission forms, they would never have allowed Andrew to be transferred to the unit. Second, had they known that the NICU staff would pursue their own research interests rather than Andrew's best interests, they would never have allowed Andrew to be used to provide the medical residents an educational experience, to give specialists some "interesting consults," or to enrich the hospital with $102,303 from their insurance company.[31]

Case 8.5

Heather Kearney was born in an ambulance in Lubbock, Texas, in April 1982. She had a gestational age of 24 weeks and a birthweight of 770 grams (1 lb., 11 oz.). She was immediately rushed to General Hospital.

With her parents' consent, Heather was placed on a respirator. She remained on the respirator for six months, the only infant in the history of that NICU to require ventilatory assistance for half a year. During that period she had numerous medical problems: patent ductus arteriosus, bronchopulmonary dysplasia, congestive heart failure, apnea, numerous infections, and several operations. She did not, however, have any cerebral hemorrhages, and appeared to have no other brain damage.

Heather's parents decided at the outset of her hospitalization to "give Heather all of us we could while we could." Consequently, her mother quit her job so that she could spend six to eight hours a day with her daughter in the NICU. Her father came to the NICU each night during visiting hours. Separately or together, they spent as much of the first eight months of Heather's life in the NICU as they could.

The NICU staff tried to help. Each month Dr. Thelma Kwan, the neonatologist in charge of Heather, baked a birthday cake for her tiny patient. The NICU nurses posted cards and pictures in an area of the NICU designated for "Heather's stuff."

The emotional strain on the parents was immense. Each time a crisis occurred, they feared for the worst. Often they were told that there was "not much of a chance" of Heather's pulling through. In addition, the financial expense became enormous. By the time

Heather reached the eight-month point, the Kearneys' insurance company had paid approximately $250,000. The remaining costs, including an oxygen machine and a monitor for Heather's care at home, remain to be handled when she is finally released from the hospital.[32]

The obligatory/optional distinction clearly applies to both of these cases. In case 8.4 there appear to have been any number of times in which Andrew's parents judged that his treatment was optional and that he should have been allowed to die. Most reasonable persons on reading the case history have agreed that life-prolonging treatment should have been withheld or withdrawn from Andrew months before he was actually allowed to die.[33] Unfortunately for him, the physicians in charge of his case regarded maximal treatment—no matter how futile, no matter how harmful—to be obligatory. By contrast, the parents and physicians in case 8.5 were in agreement that life-prolonging treatment was in Heather's best interests. Not all parents, physicians, or reflective individuals functioning as Heather's proxies would agree with the decisions actually made in the case, simply because this case is a borderline one in which the obligatory/ optional distinction represents a "close call." For some persons, the extremely low birthweight, prolonged dependence on the respirator, cardiac problems, and mounting financial costs would tip the judgmental scale toward the optional end. For Heather's parents and medical team, the scale was obviously tipped in the other direction, at least partially because of the absence of cerebral complications.

Other cases also illustrate how the obligatory/optional distinction can work as a method of selection in NICUs. Cases 2.4 and 2.5 involved two SGA infants who received life-prolonging treatment in NICUs. In the first case, Mignon was extremely premature and weighed only 482 grams at birth. The treatment given her to keep her alive over the next seven months should clearly have been judged optional because of its detrimental effects on her. Rather than being forced to endure that treatment, she should have been allowed to die. By contrast, the decision to prolong Amanda Solem's life in case 2.5 was undoubtedly correct. Given her birthweight and treatable condition, the treatment administered to her was correctly judged to be obligatory.

Cases 3.6 and 4.4 are additional cases in which life-prolonging treatment appears to have been optional. As previously indicated, case 3.6 is an example of severe cases involving multiple serious anomalies. R. B.

Zachary, the physician in the case, correctly judged in this instance that the whole is sometimes greater than the sum of its parts: the multiplicity of severe medical problems (some of them untreatable) made the prolongation of life a fate worse than death for the child. Consequently, treatment was withheld because of its optional nature, and the child died. Case 4.4 is more of a borderline case, but the initial judgment of optional treatment also seems to have been correct in this case. Involving conjoined twin boys in Danville, Illinois, the medical case quickly became intertwined with legal maneuvers that apparently made all possible treatment seem obligatory. Whether that treatment was beneficial or harmful on balance to the boys remains unknown.

The practice of intentional killing

The clinical application of the last operational criterion is more difficult to discuss, given the illegality of intentionally killing neonatal patients. Cases are especially difficult to come by, because few physicians or parents want publicity for having engaged in nonvoluntary euthanasia with infants. Nevertheless, there are cases, both inside and outside of NICUs, in which birth-defective neonates are intentionally killed.

Case 8.6

A baby was born in Connecticut in 1981. The child experienced asphyxia at birth, had congenital heart disease, was diagnosed as having brain damage, and had numerous other medical problems as well. The parents, who remained anonymous, requested that life-prolonging measures be discontinued.

The physicians responded by saying that nothing they were doing was "extraordinary." They continued ventilatory assistance, antibiotic medications, surgical procedures, and blood transfusions long after the parents believed the situation to be hopeless.

After finally weaning the child from the respirator, the physicians handed the child to the parents to be taken home. The couple was numbed by the NICU experience and the prospect of caring for a brain-damaged child. For weeks they listened to a recurring high-pitched wailing by the child, administered anticonvulsive medicine on a daily basis, hoped in vain for some signs of improvement, fed the child through a stomach tube—and debated the alternatives available to them.

The alternative of continuing medical care at home was rejected, largely because subsequent medical tests showed no signs of improvement. The alternative of institutionalization was rejected, because they could not stand the thought of years later visiting "a 20-year-old vegetable lying on a mat in a rehab center somewhere." The alternative of allowing the child to die from an untreated cold or infection was also rejected, because of the prolonged suffering that kind of dying would cause the child and parents as well.

They finally decided to kill the child by increasing the daily dose of anticonvulsive sedative and by stopping the feedings. When the child was still alive four days later, the parents consulted a physician friend. After reviewing the baby's medical records and examining the child, the physician agreed with the appropriateness of their actions. The child died two days later.

When later asked about intentionally killing their child, the parents responded: "We never doubted that our decision was for the child's best interests. We did it out of love."[34]

In spite of the scarcity of details on this case, it is necessary to address the question whether this act of infanticide was morally justifiable. To do so requires an identification of the parameters according to which such killing can be justifiable. In this regard, it is important to emphasize that the physical location (e.g., a home as opposed to an NICU) of nonvoluntary euthanasia with anomalous neonates has nothing to do with the morality of the killing. Moreover, the morality of this kind of killing does not depend on whether the killing is done solely as an act of mercy to an untreated and suffering infant, or whether the killing is done also as an act of conscientious objection to current laws. Rather, as was argued in the previous chapter, the morality of intentionally killing birth-defective infants hangs on three necessary and jointly sufficient conditions: (1) a decision that life-prolonging treatment is not in the best interests of the child, (2) evidence that the child is experiencing suffering in the absence of treatment, and (3) a quick and painless termination of the child's life. In this particular case, at least the last of these conditions is lacking.

Cases of slow, drawn-out killing also occur in NICUs. We have presented several of these cases in previous chapters: cases 2.2, 3.1, 3.2,

3.4, 3.6, 4.3, and 5.3. Most if not all of these cases would be described by participants as being instances of allowing infants to die. The "allowing to die" category would be chosen to describe these deaths in order to avoid legal complications and because some of the physicians are on record as opposing neonatal euthanasia. However, because life-prolonging treatment appears to have been in the best interests of several of these infants who died, a more accurate description of the deaths in cases 2.2, 3.1, 3.2, and 5.3 would be that of intentional killing. The slowness of the killing was neither humane nor morally justifiable, but it nevertheless appears to have been intentional.

Notes

1. Gordon Avery, statement in the *Washington Post*, March 11, 1974. Quoted in Albert R. Jonsen and Michael J. Garland, eds., *Ethics of Newborn Intensive Care* (Berkeley: University of California, Institute of Government Studies, 1976), p. 4.
2. David G. McLone, "Results of Treatment of Children Born with a Myelomeningocele," *Clinical Neurosurgery* (forthcoming).
3. This case was prepared by Norman Fost and is used by permission. The case is reprinted from his article "Proxy Consent for Seriously Ill Newborns," in David H. Smith and Linda Bernstein, eds., *No Rush to Judgment: Essays on Medical Ethics* (Bloomington, Ind.: The Poynter Center, 1978), p. 1.
4. Ibid., p. 17.
5. Quoted in Stuart F. Spicker and John R. Raye, "The Bearing of Prognosis on the Ethics of Medicine: Congenital Anomalies, the Social Context and the Law," in Stuart Spicker, Joseph Healey, and Tristram Engelhardt, eds., *The Law-Medicine Relation: A Philosophical Exploration* (Dordrecht, Holland: D. Reidel Publishing Co., 1981), p. 190 (emphasis added).
6. Norman Fost, "Ethical Issues in the Treatment of Critically Ill Newborns," *Pediatric Annals* 10 (October 1981): 17.
7. John Michael Hemphill and John M. Freeman, "Medical Aspects and Ethical Dilemmas," in Warren T. Reich, editor-in-chief, *Encyclopedia of Bioethics* (New York: The Free Press, 1978), p. 720.
8. See Mark Siegler, "Pascal's Wager and the Hanging of Crepe," *The New England Journal of Medicine* 293 (October 23, 1975): 853–57.
9. Spicker and Raye, "Bearing of Prognosis on Ethics of Medicine," p. 201.
10. See Gillian Hunt et al., "Predictive Factors in Open Myelomeningocele with Special Reference to Sensory Level," *British Medical Journal* 4 (1973): 197–201; G. Keys Smith and E. Durham Smith, "Selection for Treatment in Spina Bifida Cystica," *British Medical Journal* 4 (1973): 189–97; G. D. Stark and M. Drummond, "Results of Selective Early Operation in Myelomeningocele," *Archives of Disease in Childhood* 48 (1973): 676–83; and Report of

a Working Party, "Ethics of Selective Treatment of Spina Bifida," *The Lancet* 1(1975): 85–88.

11. See John Freeman, "Ethics and the Decision Making Process for Defective Children," in David G. Roy, ed., *Medical Wisdom and Ethics in the Treatment of Severely Defective Newborn and Young Children* (Montreal: Eden Press, 1978), pp. 27–28.

12. Mary D. Ames and Luis Schut, "Results of Treatment of 171 Consecutive Myelomeningoceles, 1963–1968," *Pediatrics* 52 (1972): 466–70; Sherman C. Stein, Luis Schut, and Mary D. Ames, "Selection for Early Treatment in Myelomeningocele: A Retrospective Analysis of Various Selection Procedures," *Pediatrics* 54 (1974): 553–57; and Leonard Diller, Chester A. Swinyard, and Fred J. Epstein, "Cognitive Function in Children with Spina Bifida," in Chester A. Swinyard, ed., *Decision Making and the Defective Newborn* (Springfield, Ill.: Charles C Thomas, 1978), pp. 34–49.

13. McLone, "Children Born with a Myelomeningocele."

14. Ibid.

15. This case is adapted from information in Jack Fincher, "Before Their Time," *Science 82* 3 (July–August 1982): 72–73.

16. See Donald C. Fyler and Peter Lang, "Neonatal Heart Disease," in Gordon B. Avery, ed., *Neonatology: Pathophysiology and Management of the Newborn*, 2nd ed. (Philadelphia: J. B. Lippincott Co., 1981), pp. 438–72; and Joseph J. Volpe and Richard Koenigsberger, "Neurologic Disorders," in Avery, *Neonatology*, pp. 910–63.

17. See Edwin H. Kolodny, "Tay Sachs Disease," in R. M. Goodman and Arno Motulsky, eds., *Genetic Disease among Ashkenazi Jews* (New York: Raven Press, 1979), pp. 217–29; Michael M. Kaback, D. L. Rimoin, and J. S. O'Brien, eds., *Tay-Sachs Disease: Screening and Prevention* (New York: Alan R. Liss, 1977); and Hans Galjaard, *Genetic Metabolic Diseases* (Amsterdam, New York, and Oxford: Elsevier/North-Holland Biomedical Press, 1980), pp. 266–81.

18. See William L. Nyhan, "The Lesch-Nyhan Syndrome," *Annual Review of Medicine* 24 (1973): 41–60; and John B. Stanbury et al., eds., *The Metabolic Basis of Inherited Disease*, 5th ed. (New York: McGraw-Hill, 1983), pp. 1115–38.

19. See M. E. Hodes et al., "Clinical Experience with Trisomies 18 and 13," *Journal of Medical Genetics* 15 (1978): 48–60.

20. See Galjaard, *Genetic Metabolic Diseases*, pp. 215–25; and Stanbury et al., *Metabolic Basis of Inherited Disease*, pp. 881–901.

21. See William L. Nyhan and Nadia O. Sakati, *Genetic and Malformation Syndromes in Clinical Medicine* (Chicago: Year Book Medical Publishers, 1976), pp. 128–31; David W. Smith, *Recognizable Patterns of Human Malformation* (Philadelphia: W. B. Saunders, 1970), pp. 48–49; and E. Neibuhr, "The Cri-du-Chat Syndrome: Epidemiology, Cytogenetics, and Clinical Features," *Human Genetics* (1978), pp. 227–34.

22. David W. Smith and Ann Asper Wilson, *The Child with Down's Syndrome* (Philadelphia: W. B. Saunders Company, 1973), pp. 21–44.

23. David G. McLone et al., "Central Nervous System Infections as a Limiting Factor in the Intelligence of Children with Myelomeningocele," *Pediatrics* 70 (September 1982): 338–42.

24. See Smith and Wilson, *The Child with Down's Syndrome*, pp. 91–105; Kathleen Evans, Veronica Hickman, and C. O. Carter, "Handicap and Social Status of Adults with Spina Bifida Cystica," *British Journal of Preventive and Social Medicine* 28 (1974): 85–92; S. Dorner, "Adolescents with Spina Bifida: How They See Their Situation," *Archives of Disease in Childhood* 51 (June 1976): 439–44; K. M. Laurence and Ann Beresford, "Degree of Physical Handicap, Education, and Occupation of 51 Adults with Spina Bifida," *British Journal of Preventive and Social Medicine* 30 (September 1976): 197–202.

25. This case is adapted from information in the *Washington Post*, December 1 and 23, 1982.

26. See Thomas Milhorat, "Disorders of Neurosurgical Importance," in Avery, *Neonatology*, pp. 970–74; and S. Shinnar et al., "Intraventricular Hemorrhage in the Premature Infant: A Changing Outlook," *The New England Journal of Medicine* 306 (June 17, 1982): 1464–68.

27. See William H. Kirkley, "Fetal Survival—What Price?" *American Journal of Obstetrics and Gynecology* 137 (August 15, 1980): 873–75; Watson A. Bowes, Michael Halgrimson, and Michael Simmons, "Results of the Intensive Perinatal Management of Very-Low-Birth-Weight Infants (501–1,500 grams)," *Journal of Reproductive Medicine* 23 (November 1979): 245–50; and Sylvia Schechner, "For the 1980s: How Small Is Too Small?" *Clinics in Perinatology* 7 (March 1980): 135–43.

28. See Janet B. Hardy, "Clinical and Developmental Aspects of Congenital Rubella," *Archives of Otolaryngology* 98 (October 1973): 230–36.

29. See Stanbury et al., *Metabolic Basis of Inherited Disease*, pp. 831–41.

30. See Nyhan and Sakati, *Genetic and Malformation Syndromes*, pp. 271–74.

31. This case is adapted from Robert and Peggy Stinson, "On the Death of a Baby," *Altantic Monthly* 244 (1979): 64–72.

32. This case is adapted from the *Lubbock Avalanche-Journal*, December 19, 1982.

33. For example, see A. G. M. Campbell and D. J. Cusine, "Commentary 2," *Journal of Medical Ethics* 7 (Summer 1981): 13–18.

34. This case is adapted from the *Hartford Courant*, June 17, 1981.

9

Procedure: Criteria, Options, and Recommendations

> The neonatologist should pursue the course of action which promotes the best interests of the infant *except* when there is sufficient evidence to support the claim that saving the infant's life would place a large burden on the family. In such cases the parents should be given the opportunity to make the decision about whether to go all-out for the infant.
>
> CARSON STRONG, PH.D.[1]

> While we sincerely appreciated the opportunity to be consulted, we wonder whether parents of defective newborns are ever in a position to determine what is best for their child because of their emotional state, lack of knowledge and information, and inherent conflicts of interest. Since the pediatric profession does not approach these infants with any degree of consistency, and has its own conflicts of interest, we regard any decision making by concerned physician and parents behind closed doors of the pediatric unit as a haphazard approach. A more formalized process could be achieved. . . .
>
> PAUL BRIDGE AND MARLYS BRIDGE[2]

Without doubt, decision making is difficult in cases involving birth-defective newborns. In part, this difficulty has to do with the substantive issues discussed in previous chapters. In part, the difficulty has to do with procedural matters: who should decide to treat or to deny treatment to anomalous neonates, and why should these persons be the decision makers?

Several cases previously presented illustrate some of the procedural problems involved in selective nontreatment decisions. In case 2.8 the mother of a spina bifida child was given 24 hours to make a decision about surgical closure of the lesion, virtually isolated as a decision maker when her husband could not cope with the situation, and later pressured by a spina bifida counseling service to change her mind regarding nontreatment. In case 3.1 the parents of a girl with severe bowel obstruction initially complied with a physician's decision to perform several operations, later regretted having agreed to the surgery, and four months after the girl's birth refused permission for further life-sustaining treatment. In case 4.2 the mother of a child with Down's syndrome and other anomalies refused to grant permission for corrective intestinal surgery, had her decision overridden by court order, and believed a year later that the wrong decision maker had made the wrong decision in preserving her handicapped child's life. And in case 5.3 Infant Doe died without treatment on the basis of his parents' decision to withhold treatment, his physician's acceding to that decision, and the failure of efforts in courts of law to override his parents' decision.

Additional cases could be mentioned, but need not because it is obvious that the moral decision-making process in NICUs is complex, especially in cases involving conflicts of interest. This complexity precludes the selection of any particular persons or groups (parents, physicians, hospital committees, or courts) as automatically the best qualified to make all such decisions. Instead, the factors contributing to this complexity jointly establish the context in which one has to decide which of the possible decision makers is the best qualified for certain cases, and why. Simply put, the complicating factors are these: the high stakes involved in the decisions, the uncertainty of making proxy decisions for incompetent patients who have never been competent, serious time constraints, maximum emotional stress on parents, occasional disagreements between parents about the morally correct course of action, conflicts of interest (between parents and child, physicians and child, parents and physicians), the difficulty of accurately predicting neurological impairment and other future handicaps, inadequate communication of information between responsible parties in cases, and the logistical problems in using hospital committees or courts of law.

These complicating factors make it imperative to determine the persons and the procedural guidelines most likely to serve the best interests of anomalous newborns. Consequently, in this chapter we will discuss criteria for selecting proxies, the major options as decision makers, and several recommendations for the process of decision making. In this manner it will be possible not only to call for changes in the currently inconsistent, ad hoc procedures of decision making in NICUs, but to provide suggestions for improving and standardizing these procedures in the nation's hospitals.

Criteria for proxy decision makers

Before addressing the central procedural question ("Who Should Decide?"), it is important to discuss the criteria according to which that question should be answered. Given the ethical context of placing priority on the best interests of handicapped newborns (see chap. 7), one must attempt to determine which of the possible decision makers is most likely to promote the best interests of such infants in particular cases. The first procedural question to be addressed is thus, what are the characteristics or qualities that decision makers in neonatal cases should have in order to make responsible decisions about treatment? Any effort to move directly to select a proxy decision maker without taking up this prerequisite question is comparable to recruiting someone to fill a job for which there is no job description.

If any consensus is to be reached on the best possible decision makers, agreement is needed on the characteristics or qualities sought in the persons entrusted with the responsibility of choosing handicapped life or death for neonatal patients who have never been competent. For birth-defective neonates who live and later become competent, it is also important that they believe the best qualified proxies were the persons who actually made treatment decisions on their behalf. Such proxies should meet as many of the following criteria as possible.

1. Relevant knowledge and information

Persons deciding to provide or to deny life-prolonging treatment in neonatal cases should have three different kinds of knowledge relevant to such cases. First, they should be knowledgeable regarding the medical facts in particular cases. As we have observed in previous chapters, many of the cases in NICUs are medically complex. Accurate diagnosis is often difficult to do, and physicians sometimes disagree about the prognosis in cases where the diagnosis is clear. In order to make life-and-death decisions, proxies therefore either need to be medically trained or to have accurate diagnostic information and consensus prognostic judgments communicated to them in nontechnical language. Second, proxies should be knowledgeable regarding the family setting into which particular anomalous neonates have been born. In very few situations, if any, should family considerations override a birth-defective newborn's interests in life. Nevertheless, a determination of an infant's best interests depends, in part, on a reasonably accurate understanding of the parents' emotional strength and financial capabilities, the physical and emotional well-being of siblings, and the willingness of family members to accept a seriously handicapped child into the family unit. Third, proxies should be knowledgeable regarding possible alternatives to home care by the biological parents. If the decision concerning handicapped life or death hangs on where that handicapped life will be lived, the decision makers need to have current, accurate information on (a) adoptive parents who will take custody of a handicapped child and (b) institutions that are capable of providing long-term care for handicapped children. The availability of such alternatives to the original family unit can mean the difference between life and death for some anomalous neonates.

2. Impartiality

In any proxy decision made on behalf of an incompetent person, one of the fundamental moral requirements is that of impartiality. For proxies of incompetent patients who have previously been competent, the requirement of impartiality means that such decision makers should determine, as objectively as possible, which medical alternative that person would choose if he or she were still able to choose. For proxies of neonatal patients, the requirement of impartiality means that such persons should determine, as objectively as possible, whether life-prolonging treatment would be in the best interests of the individual neonate in question. To maximize the possibility of being objective, the persons making the treatment/nontreatment decision should be disinterested in the particular case at issue and dispassionate in weighing available alternatives. Only in this manner can proxies hope to determine fairly whether life-prolonging treatment will, on balance, be beneficial or harmful to a particular birth-defective newborn.

3. Emotional stability

Too often, decisions about nontreatment are made by persons under severe emotional stress. Parents of an anomalous neonate, having expected a normal child, typically respond with a combination of shock, denial, guilt, anxiety, and helplessness.[3] Physicians in charge of an anomalous neonate are also sometimes under serious emotional pressure as a result of the combination of an overly large caseload, too many diagnostic dilemmas, too little time in which to make critical decisions, too little cooperation from problematic parents, and too much interpersonal conflict with other members of the medical team over how to handle borderline cases. The unfortunate result is that some life-and-death decisions are made by persons who are emotionally ill-equipped to make such decisions. There are, however, several alternatives to this current state of affairs: bring in consultants who are not emotionally involved in the particular case in question, build some additional time into the decision-making process (when the medical condition allows such) to give parents and/or physicians respite from the immediate emotional pressures, or turn the decision making in tough cases over to other proxies who are emotionally stable.

4. Consistency

A common requirement of moral decision making is that of consistency from case to case. In terms of the principle of justice, morally similar cases should be handled in similar ways. For proxies making decisions in neonatal cases, this requirement means that all anomalous newborns having the same kind of treatable diagnostic condition should be given treatment for the condition; all anomalous newborns having severe diagnostic conditions that cannot be effectively treated should generally have life-prolonging treatment withheld from them. In this manner it is possible, all other things being equal, to be consistent in handling cases with the same diagnostic condition. In addition, it is necessary that proxies be consistent in applying the obligatory/optional distinction to cases. Whether dealing with a range of cases within the same diagnostic category or other cases having multiple anomalies, the requirement of consistency means that proxies should determine whether certain treatment options are optional in particular cases by employing the same pattern of reasoning used in other cases having morally relevant, similar features. Having determined, for instance, that life-prolonging treatment was in the best interests of an anomalous newborn in one case, proxies should arrive at the same conclusion in another case having features that are medically and morally similar.

Who should decide?

Unfortunately, no individual involved in neonatal cases is likely to meet all of these criteria. In fact, the applicability of the criteria vary not only from one proxy to another, but also in terms of the particular cases and circumstances that necessitate proxy decision making for neonatal patients. For these reasons it is important to discuss the four major options as decision makers, assess their relative strengths and weaknesses, and put forward the most acceptable alternative for making decisions in neonatal cases.

Parents

As indicated in earlier chapters, several pediatricians and ethicists think that parents are the appropriate decision makers in neonatal cases. Among the physicians discussed in chapter 3, Raymond Duff, Anthony Shaw, and R. B. Zachary clearly believe that selective nontreatment decisions fall within the scope of parental autonomy. For these physicians, parental autonomy is sufficiently important that they usually choose not to override the decisions of parents with whom they disagree. Among the ethicists discussed in chapter 6, John Fletcher, Michael Garland, Terrence Ackerman, and Richard McCormick think that parental discretion is the most important procedural factor in at least some cases involving decisions about life-prolonging treatment. For these ethicists, parents are the best possible proxies in neonatal cases involving the prospect of long-term, emotionally and financially draining treatment of a seriously handicapped child.

Additional support for parents as proxies comes from other sources. According to one national survey, most pediatricians and pediatric surgeons believe that selective nontreatment is appropriately a matter of parental discretion.[4] The Judicial Council of the American Medical Association agrees: "In desperate situations involving newborns, the advice and judgment of the physician should be readily available, but the decision whether to exert maximal efforts to sustain life should be the choice of the parents."[5] The President's Commission for the Study of Ethical Problems in Medicine also recommends parents as the principal decision makers, especially in borderline cases.[6]

Several reasons are usually given for permitting parents to make these life-and-death decisions.[7] First, parental discretion in deciding about treatment in neonatal cases is only an extension of the discretionary decision-making power that society grants parents in other important matters concerning their children. For instance, society gives parents considerable latitude in providing moral education for their children, in deciding whether their children will attend public or private schools, and in most of the decisions that have to be made about their children's medical care. Second, parents, having anticipated the birth of a child and made certain commitments to the child prior to birth, are the most likely persons to be morally committed to the continuing welfare of the child. Even though the particular child in question is not the normal child the parents wanted, they are still likely to have at least a residual commitment to the child and prefer not to have the child die. Third, parents are the persons who will enjoy the greatest benefits if a handicapped child lives, and they are also the ones who will endure the greatest emotional and financial costs whether the child lives or dies. Because of this more intimate involvement with the child—especially if the child lives—parents are the appropriate decision makers regarding life-prolonging treatment.

There are problems, however, with granting parents the right to make selective nontreatment decisions, and some of the problems have to do with the criteria for proxy decision makers discussed above. For one thing, there is no compelling reason to think that all parents of defective newborns are competent to make decisions about life-prolonging treatment. In fact, given the medical and emotional circumstances in which these decisions have to be made, it is sometimes the case that parents are the least qualified persons to make the decisions. They are certainly the most knowledgeable about the family situation into which an anomalous neonate is born, but they are often hampered in their ability to make decisions by several factors: they may be emotionally devastated by the birth of the child, inadequately informed about the medical facts in the case, virtually ignorant of alternatives to their keeping custody and providing long-term care for the child, and/or unable to understand the medical facts in the case even if given that information.

Another problem is that all parents simply do not promote the best interests of the birth-defective children born to them. In fact, it is a false assumption to think that all parents in these circumstances have the capacity to be either altruistic or impartial toward the handicapped newborns in their families. In some instances, it is clear to observers that parents are impartial in making decisions about treatment. In other instances where there is a conflict of interest between the parents and the handicapped child, it is clear to observers that the parental decision about treatment is contrary to the child's best interests. In promoting their own psychological and financial interests, or protecting their chosen life-style and possibly other children at home, some parents simply cannot make impartial judgments about whether a defective newborn should receive treatment or die untreated. As a result, some ethicists who favor parents as the proxy decision makers recognize that parental autonomy must sometimes be checked: "the state should intervene only when the familial judgment so exceeds the limits of reason that the compromise with what is objectively in the incompetent one's interest cannot be tolerated."[8]

In addition, if birth-defective neonates sometimes live or die merely on the basis of parental discretion, the decisions in these cases may adhere to no ethical principles or criteria generally acceptable by other persons. If parents in such situations are believed to have an absolute right—grounded in parental autonomy—to determine whether their anomalous children are given or denied treatment, there exists virtually no possibility for consistency from case to case. Some infants will live or die depending on their parents' determination of whether severely handicapped life or death is in the infants' best interests, however that judgment is made. Other infants will live or die depending on parental inclination, bias, whim, or whatever, with no attempt to determine which course of action is more beneficial or more detrimental to the infants. And still other infants will live or die because their parents, not having any clear ethical criteria on which to base a decision, are easily persuaded simply to go along with the judgments of physicians in charge of various cases.

Physicians

A second possibility as proxy decision makers in neonatal cases are the physicians responsible for the cases. Among the pediatricians discussed in chapter 3, John Lorber, John Freeman, and Everett Koop favor physicians in the role of decision maker. Each of them thinks that a neonatologist should discuss the relevant facts of cases with parents, but believes that the majority of parents will—and should—go along with the recommendations the medical authority makes.

Among ethicists, Carson Strong thinks that physicians are the best proxies in most neonatal cases because they are most likely to promote the best interests of defective newborns. In contrast to many parents, neonatologists function as patient advocates for the incompetent patients under their care. Often making unilateral decisions to treat neonates aggressively, neonatologists should promote the best interests of their patients except when it appears that prolonging a handicapped child's life would cause a great burden for the family.[9]

For these advocates of physicians as proxy decision makers, there are three reasons for having neonatologists make the treatment decisions in most cases. First, physicians possess specialized knowledge regarding congenital diseases and can make informed predictions concerning the long-term effects of these diseases on children and their families. Especially in terms of this medical knowledge, physicians are better qualified than parents to make decisions about treatment. Even if physicians do not make the final decision about treatment in all cases, their specialized knowledge makes them indispensable as consultants for parents, hospital committees, or courts. Second, physicians usually have a level of objectivity about particular cases that parents simply cannot match. Because emotional stress can overwhelm parents, physicians are often more capable than parents in making an objective assessment of a handicapped newborn's best interests and in making rational decisions about treatment. They can thus be patient advocates, even with their own emotional pressures and time constraints, in a way parents often cannot. Third, given their professional involvement with numerous birth-defective newborns, physicians have recurring opportunities to compare children with the same kinds of anomalous conditions, assess the effectiveness of various treatment possibilities, and make comparative judgments about the long-term handicaps associated with certain conditions. In this respect, physicians are capable of being consistent from case to case in a way parents are not because of the more limited contact parents have with other cases.

Nevertheless, physicians present certain problems when they function as the principal decision makers in neonatal cases, and these problems are particularly evident when individual physicians are granted proxy decision-making power in borderline cases. Although neonatologists are clearly the best qualified decision makers in terms of their medical knowledge of congenital anomalies, that knowledge is limited in several important ways. For instance, the possession of specialized knowledge in neonatal medicine does not enable physicians always to make accurate diagnoses, and it certainly does not enable them to make prognoses that are always correct. To observe these limitations of medical knowledge, one has only to compare the kinds of prognostic judgments pediatricians make about children with spina bifida. Moreover, even if medical training in a pediatric specialty brought about greater unanimity in making prognoses that it does, this specialized medical knowledge does not translate into moral expertise. And because treatment/nontreatment decisions are finally moral decisions, once accurate diagnoses and careful prognoses have been made, physicians are no better qualified to make sound moral decisions in these cases than parents or other possible proxies.

A second problem with physicians as proxies has to do with potential conflicts of interest between them and the patients they serve. Although physicians often are able to be more objective than many parents, it is simply not true that physicians are completely impartial in determining the best interests of their patients. Rather, some physicians cast into the principal decision-making role may have their judgments skewed by either of two conflicts of interest. Many, and probably most, pediatric specialists have a serious bias in favor of normal, healthy children. Having cared for numerous handicapped infants and observed the severe problems that confront such infants, pediatricians often tend to view anomalous newborns as living tragedies that should have been terminated prior to birth. To consider prolonging these tragic lives into a seriously handicapped future is a depressing thought, which leads some pediatricians to favor nontreatment in cases in which life appears to be in the infants' best interests.[10] Another bias held by some pediatric specialists is toward research and experimentation. Rather than trying to assess treatment options in terms of the best interests of individual neonatal patients, they tend to view patients—especially those with the most serious, possibly exotic conditions—as relatively rare opportunities to advance the cause of neonatal medicine as a science. Consequently, some seriously defective newborns may be given treatment that will not benefit them but will create research and teaching opportunities for the clinicians in charge of their cases. These two potential conflicts of interest are especially problematic in cases where only one physician (as opposed to a medical team) is allowed to make the final decision regarding life-prolonging treatment.

Furthermore, even though physicians are more capable than parents of being consistent from case to case, they sometimes are not consistent because of the external pressures that influence them. Particularly when treatment decisions are made by individual physicians in charge of cases, those decisions may be substantially swayed by considerations other than the best interests of the child in question or the relationship between two similar cases. The two dominant external pressures on physicians in these situations are the law and assertive parents. For instance, whenever physicians perceive a significant change in legal enforcement patterns (as under the Reagan administration), they sometimes opt for life-prolonging treatment in cases that are medically and morally similar to earlier cases in which they judged such treatment to be optional. Or physicians may simply accede to the demands of assertive parents. The result is that a physician may decide against treatment in a particular case because of parental pressure, even though the same physician in a medically and morally similar case opts for treatment in the absence of such parental pressure.

A hospital committee

For some persons who have addressed the issue of selective nontreatment, a hospital committee is a preferable alternative to parents or physicians functioning by themselves as proxies. Among physicians, Norman Fost is the leading advocate for the use of such committees. Given the complexity of selective nontreatment decisions, he thinks that any individual decision maker needs advice from an informed group representing different professional fields. Among attorneys, John Robertson points to the need for due process in treatment decisions. In his judgment, the requirements of due process can be met in neonatal cases only if there is a committee (or at least a physician outside the case, or a patient advocate) to ensure an impartial representation of a defective newborn's interests. In their article, Robertson and Fost state that "even if after reflection one decides that there is a class of defective newborn infants from whom treatment can be justifiably withheld, it does not follow that parents and physicians should be the sole judge in each case of who shall survive."[11]

Among ethicists, Paul Ramsey is convinced that neither parents nor physicians are the best possible proxies. Instead, he says that any decision about the possible termination of an individual's life should be made by a disinterested party. Paul and Marlys Bridge agree. Having gone through the ordeal of seeing their son die after 78 days in an NICU, and having had numerous difficulties with the pediatrician in the case, they think that "efforts should be made to institute more formal procedures of due process in order to safeguard the best interests of the child rather than of, say, the parents or the hospital."[12]

Cedars-Sinai Medical Center in Los Angeles currently has a committee attempting to safeguard the best interests of defective newborns. Organized in 1981 by Jeffrey Pomerance, M.D., the Life-Support Advisory Committee meets on call approximately a dozen times a year to discuss borderline cases in which parents have expressed the desire to downgrade care for severely defective newborns. In such instances, the attending physician refers the case to the committee for a recommendation. The committee typically consists of the attending physician, one or more other neonatologists (including the head neonatologist), appropriate medical consultants involved in the case, residents connected with the case, a senior NICU nurse, one or more nurses involved in the case, a social service representative, a hospital administrator, and one or more other pediatricians not connected with the case under consideration. Absent from the committee are the parents, attorneys, ethicists, and ministers, although a member of the clergy may attend the meeting if specifically requested by the parents. After discussing the case for approximately an hour, the committee arrives at a consensus recommendation for the physician. Unless the physician opposes the recommended action on moral grounds (in which case the neonate is transferred to another neonatologist), the committee's recommendation is virtually always carried out.[13]

All committees handling difficult neonatal cases do not and need not follow the pattern of the Cedars-Sinai committee. Nevertheless, allowing for variation in committee composition and procedures, there are several reasons for using committees in an advisory role and possibly in the role of proxy decision maker. First, an NICU committee has the possibility of meeting all of the criteria for a proxy decision maker. In contrast to individual physicians and parents, the composite nature of a committee goes a long way toward ensuring emotional stability, impartiality, and consistency on the part of the committee members. Moreover, depending on the expertise of the committee members, a committee is likely to possess the relevant knowledge of the medical facts, family setting, and alternatives to home care that is necessary in making borderline decisions regarding treatment.

Second, an NICU committee can adjudicate conflicts over treatment that sometimes arise between parents and physicians. Without a committee, such conflicts can lead to mutual distrust, power plays, and treatment decisions that may or may not be governed by an objective determination of an infant's best interests. With a committee, especially when parental interests are represented, there is a disinterested party that can discuss the infant's best interests in a context of neutrality between the parents and the attending physician.

Third, such a committee can safeguard an anomalous infant in cases where parents and the attending physician agree on a course of action that is contrary to the infant's best interests. If the committee is called into session by someone other than the attending physician (e.g., by the head neonatologist responding to a report from a nurse or social worker), a selective nontreatment decision by parents and physician can be overruled and the child transferred to another neonatologist's care.

Fourth, depending on the composition of the committee, an NICU committee is likely to be more capable of addressing the ethical aspects of cases than are parents and physicians functioning in relative isolation. Especially if there is a trained ethicist as a regular committee member (not a mere token), this group has the possibility of applying ethical criteria to particular cases and engaging in consistent moral reasoning from case to case.

Of course the use of NICU committees is not without problems. Particularly if the committee moves beyond an advisory role, two or three problems arise. One problem has to do with logistics and timing. Decisions about treatment in neonatal cases are often made rapidly, in response to a crisis situation with a patient. Even decisions about life-prolonging treatment must frequently be made with dispatch, with a delay in deciding about treatment possibly causing deterioration in a patient's medical condition. Consequently, NICU committees necessarily function in a different manner from committees in other institutional settings. Committee meetings are called as cases and circumstances warrant, and committee members must be ready to make life-or-death decisions in a short period of time. In the relatively few hospitals having these committees, such a procedure seems to work rather smoothly, because committee members understand the time constraints involved in the process. However, on occasions when key committee members cannot make meetings, the group decision-making process loses needed expertise and some of its advantages as a proxy decision maker.

A second problem has to do with the mechanics of committee work. Committees are cumbersome ways to make decisions, often frustratingly indecisive, and occasionally simply inept. Assertive, outspoken individuals sometimes dominate committee meetings. Other individuals arrive late or leave meetings early, thus causing needless confusion. Moreover, it is always possible that the compromises brought about by the group process result in a group decision with which no committee member personally and wholeheartedly agrees. For NICU committees, these inherent difficulties of the committee process can mean failure to meet the criteria for a proxy decision maker. Whether an NICU committee succeeds in being well informed, impartial, and consistent largely depends on the committee's chairperson and the belief by committee members that at least in borderline cases the advantages of the group process outweigh its mechanical difficulties.

In addition to these formal problems, another kind of problem is the reason that some physicians and ethicists reject the alternative of an NICU committee. Simply put, no matter how such a committee is composed or how efficiently it works, any committee placed in an advisory or decision-making role necessarily means a reduction of parental autonomy and physician discretion in neonatal cases. Thus, even if an NICU committee is used only in restricted circumstances, it is open to criticism from persons who seriously believe that the only appropriate decision makers are parents and/or physicians involved in the particular cases in question. By its very nature, an NICU committee is relatively remote from the emotional aspects of cases. Consequently, at least some committee members may never have to deal directly with the parents or infant in a case, and most of the committee members are insulated from the consequences of their group decision. A preferable alternative, for critics of hospital committees, is to have the persons most intimately connected with cases make the decisions that affect not only the child but themselves as well.

Courts

The need for a disinterested party as a proxy decision maker has already led to the involvement of the courts in some neonatal cases. As we observed in chapters 4 and 5, several cases of selective nontreatment have been decided in judicial hearings. In all but one of these cases (the Infant Doe case in Bloomington), the court decision has favored treatment over nontreatment.

Few parents or physicians favor turning selective nontreatment decisions over to the courts. For parents, the use of the courts as a proxy means the likelihood of court-mandated treatment contrary to parental desires. For physicians, the prospect of judicial involvement in neonatal cases means unnecessary legal intrusion into medical matters. Of the physicians discussed in chapter 3, only Norman Fost and Everett Koop give any indication of a possibly appropriate role for courts in some neonatal cases. For ethicists also, there is a disinclination to turn to courts to make decisions that can and usually should be made in nonlegal settings.

Among attorneys, of course, there is greater acceptance of courts as proxies. Robert Burt, Dennis Horan, and John Robertson all indicate a willingness to allow courts to protect the best interests of birth-defective newborns and to prosecute parents who jeopardize the lives of their anomalous children by withholding treatment (see chap. 4). Paul Freund agrees. Writing in response to the Johns Hopkins case (case 2.2), he argues that neither parents nor physicians are the most appropriate decision makers. Rather, he says that the only way of protecting a defective newborn's best interests is through a disinterested tribunal: "Resort to a court is indicated, not because lawyers and judges have expertise in mongoloidism, which indeed they do not have, but because there all interests can be caught up and valued, and there a guardian *ad litem* for the child can be appointed as spokesman for the child's needs and claims."[14]

In several respects courts share the same strengths and weaknesses as hospital committees functioning as proxies. At least in theory, courts provide an opportunity for disinterested, dispassionate, and consistent reasoning from case to case. They also have the means to ensure that relevant knowledge, information, and opposing points of view are presented for consideration in a public forum. However, they obviously reduce parental autonomy and medical discretion in making treatment decisions, and sometimes cause formidable problems in terms of logistics and timing.

In addition, courts have strengths and weaknesses as proxies that distinguish them from hospital committees. When judges function as proxy decision makers, they have an unparalleled ability to marshal all of the pertinent facts in a case by summoning witnesses, questioning knowledgeable experts, and investigating the merits of several alternative courses of action. Judges also are able, as Freund points out, to appoint a guardian *ad litem* for the purpose of being an advocate of an incompetent patient's best interests. In these ways at least, courts represent a distinctive —and occasionally necessary—proxy in arriving at treatment decisions that are in the best interests of birth-defective newborns.

Even when considered as a proxy of last resort, however, courts have two weaknesses. The first weakness has to do with place. By not being on the scene in the NICU, and having no personal contact with the case under consideration, judges are more remote than other possible proxies. Of course remoteness may lead to greater objectivity, but it may also lead to less sensitivity for and empathy with the persons directly involved in an emotionally difficult case. The second weakness has to do with judges as individuals. In theory, all judges in all legal jurisdictions provide the same opportunity for an objective hearing of cases. In fact, however, the functioning of judges as proxies in neonatal cases sometimes depends on the personal views of the judges. For instance, in cases involving neonates with Down's syndrome complicated by esophageal or duodenal atresia, some judges in some jurisdictions are reluctant to override parental autonomy—and other judges in other jurisdictions override parental autonomy in such cases simply on the basis of a telephoned request from the attending pediatrician.

A serial ordering of decision makers

Because each of these possible proxies is limited in important ways, it is preferable not to regard any of them as the best proxy for all neonatal cases. Instead, as James Childress observes, a serial or sequential ordering of decision makers is preferable for determining the best interests of neonatal patients.[15] By incorporating each of the possible proxies into a sequential decision-making process, and by restricting the circumstances in which these possible proxies can actually function as decision makers for incompetent patients, the best interests of defective newborns are more adequately served and protected than if any of the alternative decision makers is permitted to make unilateral decisions about life-prolonging treatment in all neonatal cases. The use of a sequential arrangement of decision makers also incorporates the possibilities of (a) appeals to a "higher" proxy and (b) overriding the decision of a "lower" proxy when circumstances merit. Represented as a flowchart, this serial ordering of decision makers can and should work in the following manner:

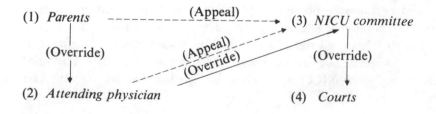

Parents of defective newborns are the primary decision makers in this serial ordering of proxies. Because of the importance of parental autonomy, decisions about medical treatment for anomalous neonates should not arbitrarily be taken away from parents. When parents are adequately informed by the attending physician regarding the diagnosis and prognosis for their child, they are often capable of making informed decisions that the physician can accept as being medically and morally correct. Moreover, in spite of the emotional stress inherent to these situations, at least parents in less difficult cases are often sufficiently stable emotionally to make decisions that are clearly in the infant's best interests.

However, parents have only a defeasible right to make decisions about treatment or nontreatment. There are at least three circumstances in which parents should not have the final word in such decisions: when they simply cannot understand the relevant medical facts of a case, when they are emotionally unstable, and when they appear to put their own interests before those of the defective newborn. Each of these circumstances happens with some regularity in NICUs. In any such situation, physicians involved in the case—and especially the attending physician—should override parental autonomy to protect the best interests of the child. No birth-defective newborn should be left to die untreated merely because of the desires or discretion of parents, especially when there appears to be a conflict of interest between the parents and the child.

As previously noted, physicians are sometimes better qualified to be proxies than parents are. Because of their technical knowledge, greater objectivity, and professional involvement with numerous birth-defective newborns, physicians are often capable of determining when parental decisions are contrary to the best interests of anomalous neonates. For instance, when parents refuse to consent to recommended treatment that the neonatologist believes will restore an infant to consciousness, or correct an anomalous condition the infant has, or extend and enhance the infant's life for a significant period of time, there is sufficient reason to think that these particular parents are ill-suited to be proxy decision makers. Given their role as patient advocates, neonatologists in such situations have two appropriate courses of action. They may, in reasonably clear-cut cases, simply override the parents' wishes and provide the necessary treatment. Or in borderline cases, they may choose to override the parents' wishes by referring the cases to the collective wisdom represented by an NICU committee.

There are limits, however, to an attending physician's right to override parental discretion and assume the responsibilities of proxy decision maker. The physician's right to decide, like that of parents, is defeasible. If it appears (to the parents, other physicians, nurses, or social workers) that an attending physician in a case is pursuing interests other than those of the neonatal patient, either the physician should be removed from the case by the head neonatologist, or the major decisions regarding treatment in the case should be turned over to an NICU committee. No birth-defective newborn should be harmed through overtreatment or under-treatment merely because of misplaced respect for medical discretion, especially when there is the possibility of a conflict between the newborn's interests and the physician's research interests.

The NICU committee is the focal point of a serial ordering of decision makers, because it more nearly meets the criteria for proxies in neonatal cases. In hospitals having these specialized committees for neonatal cases (as opposed to hospital ethics committees handling cases from numerous clinical areas), it is possible to arrive at a group consensus regarding the appropriate course of action in at least four different kinds of situations: (1) when there is serious disagreement between parents and the attending physician regarding treatment options; (2) when a newborn has one or more congenital anomalies that place the infant in a treatable diagnostic category, but parents and attending physician have agreed not to provide the necessary treatment; (3) when the major treatment decision in a borderline case hangs on the obligatory/optional distinction, and the attending physician is uncertain on how to make the close call; and (4) in the unlikely event that the attending physician in a particular case thinks that an untreatable, suffering infant should be intentionally killed.

Depending on which of these kinds of situations arises, an NICU committee performs three functions. In situations involving conflict between parents and the attending physician, the committee functions as an in-house appeals board. As such, it may act on an appeal coming from either the parents or the attending physician. In situations in which parents and the physician have agreed on action contrary to an infant's best interests, the committee functions as an institutional check on such abusive practices. Obviously not responding to an appeal from either parents or physician, the committee may carry out this second function on the basis of a report from a concerned nurse or social worker. In the third and fourth kinds of situations, the committee functions primarily as an advisory board for a physician trying to make a tough decision. In addition, however, the committee may represent a procedural safeguard in these situations against the possibly abusive practices of individual physicians.

Courts represent a last-resort proxy that is needed infrequently. In the majority of cases, the responsibilities of proxy decision making are adequately handled by parents or physicians or NICU committees. Even cases requiring adjudication can usually—and preferably—be handled on the hospital scene by NICU committees. However, in rare instances a judge must override the decision of another proxy when he or she is convinced by the evidence that a particular infant's interests are not being served. Acting on the basis of a report by a concerned nurse or social worker, a judge in such instances may need to have a custody hearing or possibly consider criminal proceedings against parents and/or physicians who are acting contrary to the law. A well-balanced, effectively working NICU committee usually makes such criminal proceedings unnecessary, because few physicians (because of peer pressure and administrative pressure) go counter to the recommendations of such committees.

Procedural recommendations

Several procedural aspects of selective nontreatment remain to be addressed. There are limits, of course, in how far a layperson in medical matters should go in suggesting how NICUs should be managed. With these limits in mind, an appropriate way of concluding this analysis of selective nontreatment seems to be that of making several recommendations regarding policy and procedure. Presumably, the recommendations will be used, revised, or rejected depending on their merits.

First, more hospitals need to use NICU committees as an important part of the decision-making process. Compared with other possible proxies for neonatal cases, committees are much more likely to be medically informed, impartial, emotionally stable, and consistent. In addition to having more NICU committees, there needs to be a balancing of the composition of some committees already in existence. Although the membership of these committees should be weighted toward appropriate physicians and nurses, important roles can and should be played in committee deliberations by the following persons: a patient advocate (perhaps a nurse), a parent advocate, a professionally trained ethicist, a social worker, and possibly an attorney. With more widespread and standardized use of NICU committees, the need for federal and state legal intervention in nontreatment cases will be substantially lessened if not eliminated.

A second recommendation is not only that nontreatment decisions generally adhere to diagnostic categories, but that guidelines based on diagnostic categories be made public by hospitals. An example of how this approach could work is found in the report published by the clinical care committee of Massachusetts General Hospital. In that report the committee stated that critically ill patients in the hospital are classified according to four therapeutic options ranging from maximal therapeutic effort (for class A patients) to the discontinuation of therapeutic efforts (for class D patients).[16] Although the report was not addressed to the clinical context of NICUs, similar guidelines could be drawn up by neonatologists and used as public information. The guidelines could provide information regarding diagnostic conditions not generally given aggressive treatment in a hospital's NICU. By having such guidelines made public by a hospital, parents having children born in the hospital would be able to know earlier and more clearly the general perspective held by neonatologists in the hospital regarding aggressive treatment for serious congenital anomalies. Unfortunately, the current uncertainties of the law make the public use of such guidelines highly unlikely.

Another recommendation concerns procedural safeguards for infants who may be denied life-prolonging treatment. Although selective non-treatment is justifiable in some cases, it is in the best interests of all neonatal patients in NICUs that caution surround the withholding of treatment in any given case. For that reason, there are three safeguards that should accompany any decision in favor of nontreatment: adequate consultation, a sufficient lapse of time, and a written record of the reasons for withholding treatment. More specifically, the proxies in a case should consult with appropriate medical specialists and other professionals before making a decision to deny treatment. The decision should not be carried out for a set period of time (perhaps a week) to allow for greater emotional stability by the parents and the possibility of a custody hearing, should that be warranted. And the attending physician should provide written reasons concerning why the diagnostic condition was not treated, or why treatment in this case was judged to be optional. Although physicians may be reluctant to provide written reasons, the practice of having them do so is preferable to the practice of unaccountable medical discretion.

Additional procedural safeguards are needed in the extremely rare instances in which the principle of nonmaleficence seems to call for the intentional killing of an untreated, suffering infant. In the event that such a course of action is seriously considered by an attending physician, two safeguards are needed to supplement the ones just discussed: a consensus of the NICU committee supporting the action, and group participation in the act of intentional killing. The first safeguard is intended to minimize the possibility of abuse by parents and/or physicians acting apart from the informed consent of other professionals in the NICU. The second safeguard is intended to bring about shared legal liability as well as to minimize abuses. An anonymous neonatologist at a conference on selective nontreatment once remarked that neonatal euthanasia would be justifiable in some cases "if the parents administered the syringe of KCl prepared by the judge, and all the lawyers, priests, economists, psychologists, and journalists within a 50-mile radius were witnesses, and no physicians, nurses, or medical or nursing students were allowed to be present."[17] The point of the statement is well made, even though the particulars are off base. If a particular case seems to justify intentional killing under the conditions set forth in chapter 7, other persons involved in the case should be witnesses in order to provide emotional support for and share the legal liability of the physician who does the killing.

Finally, there is the need for greater attention to be given to the emotional needs and religious concerns of parents who have infants die in NICUs. In focusing our attention on the medical possibilities of prolonging and enhancing the lives of defective newborns, and in addressing the circumstances in which nontreatment is sometimes medically and morally justifiable, we often neglect the very real needs of bereaved parents to hold their dying or dead babies. One hospital doing significant work with a neonatal hospice program is Children's Hospital in Denver. In that hospital's NICU there is a separate room called the "family room." Furnished with a sofa, soft chairs, and soft lighting, the room provides the opportunity for parents to spend time privately with their newborns who cannot or should not have their lives prolonged because of serious congenital anomalies.[18] More NICUs should have such rooms, and possibly a separate room for nurses and physicians who also on occasion get caught up emotionally in a particularly difficult case. Having made or had some part in a selective nontreatment decision, bereaved persons need a private place to cry, to think, possibly to pray—and to hold the body of a child too seriously handicapped to continue living.

Notes

1. Carson Strong, "Decision Making in the NICU: The Neonatologist as Patient Advocate, *Hastings Center Report* (forthcoming).
2. Paul Bridge and Maryls Bridge, "The Brief Life and Death of Christopher Bridge," *Hastings Center Report* 11 (December 1981): 19.
3. Peter Rothstein, "Psychological Stress in Families of Children in a Pediatric Intensive Care Unit," *Pediatric Clinics of North America* 27 (1980): 613–20.
4. Anthony Shaw, Judson G. Randolph, and Barbara Manard, "Ethical Issues in Pediatric Surgery: A National Survey of Pediatricians and Pediatric Surgeons," *Pediatrics* 60 (October 1977): 588.
5. The Judicial Council, *Current Opinions of the Judicial Council of the American Medical Association* (Chicago: American Medical Association, 1982), p. 9.
6. President's Commission for the Study of Ethical Problems in Medicine and Biomedical and Behavioral Research, *Deciding to Forgo Life-Sustaining Treatment* (Washington, D.C.: U.S. Government Printing Office, 1983), pp. 6–8, 197–229.
7. In addition to several of the items cited in chapter 6, see Richard A. McCormick, S.J., and Robert Veatch, "The Prolongation of Life and Self-Determination," *Theological Studies* 41 (1980): 390–96; and Warren T. Reich and David E. Ost, "Public Policy and Procedural Questions," in Warren T. Reich, editor-in-chief, *Encyclopedia of Bioethics* (New York: The Free Press, 1978), pp. 735–40.
8. McCormick and Veatch, "Prolongation of Life," p. 396.
9. Strong, "Decision Making in the NICU."
10. See Rosalyn Benjamin Darling, "Parents, Physicians, and Spina Bifida," *Hastings Center Report* 7 (August 1977): 10–14.
11. John A. Robertson and Norman Fost, "Passive Euthanasia of Defective Newborn Infants: Legal Considerations," *Journal of Pediatrics* 88 (1976): 887.
12. Bridge and Bridge, "Brief Life and Death," p. 19.
13. Telephone interview with Jeffrey Pomerance, M.D., March 7, 1983.
14. Paul A. Freund, "Mongoloids and 'Mercy Killing,'" in Stanley Joel Reiser, Arthur J. Dyck, and William J. Curran, eds., *Ethics in Medicine* (Cambridge, Mass.: The MIT Press, 1977), p. 538.
15. James F. Childress, *Who Should Decide?* (New York and Oxford: Oxford University Press, 1982), pp. 172–74.
16. "Optimum Care for Hopelessly Ill Patients: A Report of the Clinical Care Committee of the Massachusetts General Hospital," *The New England Journal of Medicine* 295 (August 12, 1976): 362–64.

17. Albert R. Jonsen and Michael J. Garland, eds., *Ethics of Newborn Intensive Care* (Berkeley: University of California, Institute of Government Studies, 1976), pp. 174–75.
18. *New York Times*, March 18, 1983.

Cases

*Boldface numbers indicate the page on which a case is fully described.

Additional legal cases

Glossary

Agyria—also known as **lissencephaly**, a malformation in which the con-
volutions of the cerebral cortex are not normally developed and the
brain is abnormally small.

Anencephaly—a condition of arrested development of the brain; at least
the cerebral hemispheres are absent, and sometimes the brain is
totally absent.

Apert's syndrome—a condition involving the premature fusion of the
cranial sutures, mental retardation, and symmetrical **syndactyly** of
the hands and feet.

Apgar score—a simple numerical method of clinically evaluating the
medical conditions of neonates at one and five minutes after birth.

Apnea—episodic arrest of breathing.

Best interests test—along with the **substituted judgment test**, one of the
legal standards used to determine the validity of proxy consent; this
test involves an appeal to what most reasonable persons would
choose in a situation of moral choice.

Bilirubin—a yellow pigment produced by the breakdown of red blood
cells in the liver; jaundice is caused by elevated levels of the pigment.

Bradycardia—slowness of heart beat, as evidenced by a pulse rate below
60 beats per minute.

Bronchopulmonary dysplasia (BPD)—a progressive, chronic lung disorder caused by protracted periods of mechanical ventilation with
high concentrations of oxygen.

Changeling—according to a traditional theory used to explain congenital anomalies, a supernatural substitute in the form of a physically deformed child who has taken the place of a "real" child.

Chiari II malformation—a severe, untreatable hindbrain condition involving the displacement and elongation of the medulla.

Congenital rubella syndrome—a serious condition involving mental deficiency, congenital heart disease, **microcephaly**, and problems with eyesight and hearing.

Craniorachischisis totalis—rarely found in a living neonate, this abnormal development of neural tissue results in the fissure of the skull and spinal column.

Cri-du-chat syndrome—a chromosomal disorder caused by the deletion of the short arm of the fifth chromosome; the condition is characterized by a catlike cry, profound mental deficiency, microcephaly, and congenital heart disease.

Custody/care distinction—decisions regarding short-term medical treatment do not necessarily entail long-term responsibilities of custody, in that it is legally possible for parents to give up custody to another party.

Cyanosis—a bluish discoloration caused by reduced hemoglobin in the blood.

De Lange syndrome—with an unknown cause, this condition consists of severe mental deficiency, congenital heart disease, excessive facial and body hair, microcephaly, and limb reduction.

Deontological theories—ethical theories that deemphasize or deny the importance of consequences of actions by stressing other right-making features of actions, such as doing one's duty or keeping one's promises.

Diaphragmatic hernia—a protrusion of the abdominal organs into the thoracic cavity through an abnormal opening in a neonate's diaphragm; the condition has a high mortality rate and requires immediate surgery to relocate the organs and correct the underlying diaphragmatic defect.

Down's syndrome—also known as **trisomy 21**, this most common major congenital malformation is caused by faulty chromosome distribution; the condition is characterized by mental deficiency, physical abnormalities, and a higher than normal susceptibility to infection.

Duodenal atresia—often associated with Down's syndrome, this condition involves either the absence or the obstruction of a portion of the upper part of the small intestine.

Edema—excessive accumulation of fluid in intercellular tissues.

Electrolytes—mineral content of the blood.

Esophageal atresia—usually associated with **tracheoesophageal fistula,** this condition exists when the upper esophagus ends in a blind pouch rather than connecting with the stomach.

Exstrophy of the cloaca—in neonates having no cloacal membrane, the common passage for fecal, urinary, and reproductive discharge is turned inside out.

Gastroschisis—an abnormality of the abdominal wall consisting of edematous, matted intestinal loops hanging outside an opening at the base of the umbilical stalk.

Guardian *ad litem*—a guardian appointed by a court to represent the interests of a minor or an incompetent person.

Hyaline membrane disease (HMD)—also known as **respiratory distress syndrome,** HMD is a developmental disorder in which premature lungs have difficulty coping with a gaseous environment and undergo stress attempting to do so.

Hydranencephaly—the complete or almost complete absence of the cerebral hemispheres.

Hydrocephalus—caused by a pathological obstruction along the pathway of cerebrospinal fluid circulation, this condition is a progressive enlargement of the head from increased amounts of cerebrospinal fluid in the ventricles of the brain.

Hydronephrosis—a condition in which one or both kidneys are enlarged because of ureteral obstruction.

Hyperalimentation—also known as **parenteral nutrition,** the intravenous administration of a greater than normal amount of nutrients.

Hypoplasia—incomplete development of an organ; some newborns have hypoplastic kidneys or a hypoplastic pulmonary artery or a hypoplastic left ventricle in the heart.

Hypoxia—often caused by perinatal asphyxia, this common condition among newborns consists of a diminished amount of oxygen in the blood supply.

Infantile polycystic kidney disease—a fatal genetic condition involving grapelike clusters of cysts throughout the kidneys.

Intentional killing—in a medical context, an act of euthanasia whereby a physician or someone else causes a patient to die.

Killing/allowing to die distinction—killing patients can usually be distinguished from allowing them to die in terms of causation and the intention of the moral agent, as well as from the fact that some patients do not die when treatment is withheld from them.

Kyphosis—sometimes referred to as hunchback, this condition consists of an abnormally increased convexity in the curvature of the thoracic portion of the spine.

Lesch-Nyhan syndrome—an X-linked recessive condition that involves a process of neurological and physiological deterioration from approximately the sixth month of life; the most striking feature of the syndrome is compulsive self-mutilation.

Leukodystrophies—disturbances of the white matter of the brain; metachromatic leukodystrophy is the most common of these neurological disorders, especially in its late infantile form, which severely affects the central nervous system.

Lissencephaly—see **agyria**.

Meconium ileus—intestinal obstruction due to gelatinous secretions of the intestinal glands; the incompletely digested meconium is usually in the distal portion of the small intestine.

Meningitis—bacterial infection of the meninges, with high morbidity and mortality; the condition is difficult to diagnose in newborns, because the classical symptoms have a late onset and the early symptoms can be confused with those of congenital **hydrocephalus**.

Meningomyelocele—synonymous with **myelomeningocele**, this form of spina bifida cystica has neural elements in the cystic cavity; the term generally refers to any cystic lesion of the spinal column with evidence of neurological dysfunction.

Microcephaly—abnormal smallness of the head; with the head size more than two standard deviations below the normal size, serious mental retardation is usually involved.

Myelomeningocele—see **meningomyelocele**.

Myeloschisis—a cleft spinal cord, due to the failure of the neural plate to form a complete tube; newborns with the condition do not usually survive the first week of life.

Neonate—a newborn in its first four weeks of life.

Neurofibromatosis—an abnormal development of the nervous system, muscles, bone, and skin; soft tumors are distributed over the entire body.

Niemann-Pick disease—also known as **sphingomyelin lipidosis**, the condition is characterized by accumulation of sphingomyelin in the organs and tissues; the three types of the disease are autosomal recessive in inheritance, with type A developing in infancy and causing severe central nervous system damage.

Nonvoluntary euthanasia—in contrast to voluntary and involuntary euthanasia, this type of killing patients for reasons of mercy is done without the expression of patient preferences regarding the continuation or termination of their lives.

Omphalocele—a herniation of the abdominal organs at the point where the umbilical cord connects with the abdomen.

Ordinary/extraordinary means distinction—a moral and legal distinction between medical procedures that are obligatory in prolonging a patient's life because they provide a reasonable hope of benefit, and medical procedures that are optional because they are futile, non-beneficial, and/or harmful on balance to the patient.

Parenteral nutrition—see **hyperalimentation.**

Patent ductus arteriosus (PDA)—a cardiovascular channel that connects the pulmonary artery to the descending aorta in a fetus; it normally closes shortly after a full-term birth, but in premature infants sometimes remains open and pours too much blood back through the lungs.

Perinatology—a subspeciality of pediatrics that concentrates on medical care of the fetus during the last two months of pregnancy and the newborn during the first month of life.

Polydactyly—a developmental anomaly characterized by a greater than normal number of fingers and/or toes.

Potentiality principle—the potential for a nonperson to become a person in the normal course of his or her development.

Primum non nocere—the oldest ethical principle in medicine; originally used in the Hippocratic literature, it requires that physicians, above all else in the practice of medicine, avoid harming their patients.

Principle of beneficence—an ethical principle requiring that moral agents further the important interests of other persons whenever their proximity and efficient alternatives allow them to do so with only minimal risk to themselves.

Principle of nonmaleficence—an ethical principle requiring that moral agents avoid intentionally or negligently harming other persons; see **primum non nocere.**

Prune-belly syndrome—**hypoplasia** of the abdominal musculature in some newborns; given its wrinkled and flabby shape, the abdomen has an appearance somewhat like a prune.

Respiratory distress syndrome (RDS)—see **hyaline membrane disease.**

Retrolental fibroplasia—formation of fibrous tissue behind the lens; caused by excessively high concentrations of oxygen in the treatment of premature infants, the condition involves detachment of the retina, an arrest of growth of the eye, and occasionally blindness.

Scoliosis—a lateral deviation from the normally vertical line of the spine.

Sepsis—generalized infection due to pathogenic microorganisms spread throughout the bloodstream.

Sphingomyelin lipidosis—see **Niemann-Pick disease.**

Spina bifida cystica—in contrast to **spina bifida occulta**, this condition is a major neural tube defect consisting of a cystic lesion on the back;

the lesion may or may not include neural elements and results in paralysis below the lesion.

Spina bifida occulta—a relatively minor neural tube defect along the spinal axis; there is no visible exposure of meninges or neural tissue.

Substituted judgment test—along with the **best interests test**, one of the legal standards used to determine the validity of proxy consent; this test involves an attempt to determine what an incompetent person would choose in a given situation of choice.

Syndactyly—the most common congenital anomaly of the hand, characterized by a webbed attachment of adjacent fingers; feet sometimes display the same kind of webbing of digits.

Tay-Sachs disease—an autosomal recessive condition that occurs with higher than normal frequency among Ashkenazic Jews; symptoms of the condition appear approximately six months after birth and signal an inexorable decline of mental and physical ability until death occurs at the age of three or four.

Teleological theories—in contrast to **deontological theories**, these ethical theories emphasize the consequences of actions; thus the rightness or wrongness of an action depends on whether it produces, or is intended to produce, a greater balance of good over evil than any available alternative.

Teratogen—an agent or factor that causes malformations in an embryo or fetus.

Tort—a wrongful act other than breach of contract that can be settled through a civil action.

Tracheoesophageal fistula—an abnormal passage connecting the distal part of the trachea with the lower part of the esophagus, thereby causing an abnormal connection between the trachea and the stomach; usually associated with **esophageal atresia.**

Trisomy 13—also known as Patau syndrome and D_1 syndrome, this condition consists of an extra chromosome from any one of the D group of chromosomes; the condition results in the incomplete development of the forebrain, severe mental deficiency, major eye abnormalities, and congenital heart disease.

Trisomy 18—also known as Edwards syndrome, this condition is caused by an extra chromosome 18; newborns with the syndrome have severe mental deficiency, difficulty in breathing, low birthweight, rocker-bottom feet, and severe gastrointestinal and renal deformities.

Trisomy 21—see **Down's syndrome.**

Utilitarianism—an ethical theory according to which the sole standard of rightness or wrongness is the principle of utility; this principle, which states that one should always promote the greatest possible balance of good over evil, may be developed into rules (rule-utilitarianism) or appealed to directly (act-utilitarianism).

Vertebrae—the spinal column consists of 33 bones, classified as the 7 cervical, 12 thoracic, 5 lumbar, 5 sacral, and 4 coccygeal vertebrae; individual vertebrae are designated by letters and numbers, with T-12 referring to the twelfth thoracic vertebra just above the first lumbar vertebra (L-1).

Wrongful birth—a **tort** suit brought by the parents of a handicapped child born as the result of the defendant's negligence.

Wrongful life—a tort suit brought by a severely handicapped child, with the aid of a **guardian ad litem,** in which he or she claims that birth resulted from the defendant's negligence.

Index